3—

AF884286

Fifty and Beyond

Compliments of the

JEWISH COMMUNITY FOUNDATION OF SOUTHERN ARIZONA

3822 East River Road, Suite 300
Tucson, Arizona 85718

Tel. (520) 577-0388
Fax (520) 577-0681
promise@uswest.net
www.jcf-tucson.org

THE FUTURE IS BUILT ON A STRONG FOUNDATION

Fifty and Beyond

The Law You and Your Parents Need to Know

Kenney F. Hegland
Professor of Law

Allan D. Bogutz
Nationally Recognized Elder Law Attorney

Carolina Academic Press
Durham, North Carolina

Copyright © 1999
Kenney F. Hegland and Allan D. Bogutz
All Rights Reserved

Library of Congress Cataloging-in-Publication Data

Hegland, Kenney F.
Fifty and beyond : the law you and your parents need to know / Kenney F. Hegland, Allan D. Bogutz.
p. cm.
ISBN 0-89089-784-0
1. Aged—Legal status, laws, etc.—United States Popular works. 2. Retirees—Legal status, laws, etc.—United States—Popular works. 3. Retirement—United States—Planning. I. Bogutz, Allan D., 1946- . II. Title.
KF390.A4H44 1999
646.7'9—dc21 99-22887
CIP

Carolina Academic Press
700 Kent Street
Durham, North Carolina 27701
Telephone (919) 489-7486
Fax (919) 493-5668
E-mail: cap@cap-press.com
www.cap-press.com

Printed in the United States of America

Dedication

Dedicated to the moment when, years from now, pausing before the bathroom mirror and despairing the age in our eyes, we suddenly realize:

> "Hey, it's fine. I enjoy life; I don't take myself too seriously, and I have important things to do... my friends, family and community still need me."

We'll smile, turn away and get busy.

Kenney Hegland
Allan Bogutz

Contents

What You Don't Know....

"Baby isn't talking. I'm worried. Worried sick! It's been months. Not a single word. Not even 'Mama.' Something must be wrong! I'm calling Dr. Scott."

"But Dear, it's two in the morning"

When our children were small, we turned to Dr. Spock. With *Baby and Child Care* on the night stand, we slept better. It got us through the tough times. Here, we looked into the future—"The First 12 Weeks," "Teething," "The Terrible Twos"—and took comfort knowing that others had gone before. We learned when to phone the doctor, and when to go back to sleep.

Growing up, there are predictable problems; so too with growing older. We offer a glimpse into the future. What dangers will you or your parents face? Things do go bump in the night. But if you wake up in a cold sweat, we'll be on the night stand.

You'll have almost 60 years of legal experience on your side.

For nearly three decades, at the University of Arizona, U.C.L.A., and Harvard, Professor Hegland has taught law students how to use the law to solve life's problems. For as many years practicing elder law attorney Allan Bogutz has met with his clients and their families, advising them, helping them, encouraging them.

You need to hear what we have to say.

- A recent study of terminally ill patients reported that 38% died in a coma, hooked to machines for *ten or more days* before their death; 31% spent all or most of their family's savings on their last illness. There are better ways for you and for your family.
- Newspaper ads tout the wonders of *Living Trusts*, inviting readers to *free* seminars (where they will be *sold* kits for

$1,200–$1,500). We'll tell you whether you need a living trust and, if so, how to get one for a lot less.

- You may be caring for an elderly person in your home. How can you get help?
- You may be *house rich, cash poor*. How can you get your money out?
- We'll tell you if you need to *avoid probate* (you probably don't), and how to avoid it if you need to (and we'll even tell you what probate is).
- We'll tell you what you need to know about *Social Security* and *Medicare*, and retirement finances.
- We'll discuss *housing options*, from staying put to moving to a retirement community; we'll spend time discussing how to select a nursing home and how to pay for it.
- We'll warn you about common scams, offer tips about dealing with bill collectors, and discuss the tragic topic of elder abuse. There are solutions.
- We'll tell you how to fight employment and housing discrimination.
- We'll describe the wonderful institution of *hospice care*, and introduce you to the comforting notion of "dying well."
- We'll walk you through the legal aspects of divorce and marriage in the Golden Years.
- And finally, and perhaps most importantly, we'll be there when disability or death strikes your family.

We will cover a lot of material. Don't be overwhelmed. You don't have to *learn* it!

You didn't have to learn Spock. Thumbing through his book, you would get a general idea of things, such as "All babies don't learn to talk at the same time." Later, if your baby seemed late talking, you could go back and reread the details. Conversely, if your baby was talking, but *not to you,* you could skip "Talking, Late," and turn to "Rejection, Early."

Our most difficult problem is alerting you to problems you do not know you have. In the section that immediately follows, we have a *Summary to be Skimmed*. Read it to get a good sense of the book and of the dangers that might lie ahead. (Count yourself as extremely unlucky if you confront every crisis we describe.)

Aging sneaks up.

Speaking to a high school class, an elderly woman is asked: "How does it feel to be old?"

"I don't feel old," she replies. "I feel like I did when I was your age. How does it feel to be a teenager?"

Busy with the hurly-burly of our daily lives, we slip slowly into the future.

There are things you must do now, even if they seem wildly premature. Without putting too fine a point on it, once you're dead, it's too late to write a will, and once you're lying comatose in the hospital, it's too late to decide on the kind of treatment you want.

There is another priority: *talking with your family*. For a whole tangle of reasons, adult children fear talking about difficult topics with their aging parents; aging parents fear talking to their adult children. Sons and daughters, mothers and fathers, should have a conversation that matters. It will be richly rewarding, and it will make your relationships deeper. Most important, it will continue.

We'll tell you how to start that conversation. Sometimes it's hard. But once it starts, expect high humor, deep emotion, and comforting closeness.

* * *

This is *not* a Self-Help Book, replete with Important Forms, Blanks-to-be-Filled-In, and Boxes-to-be-Checked. Your legal health and your family's well-being are too important for that.

Form books have inherent, insurmountable, and fatal problems which, because we didn't write one, we are happy to share:

- *State laws differ.* What works famously in California may violate an Oklahoma statute or a Vermont Supreme Court case. (Actually, anything that works famously in California is suspect.)
- *Law changes.* Today's wise choice may be rendered foolish by an act of Congress, by your state legislature, or by a judicial opinion. Ready-made forms smack of yesterday's newspaper and of Sis's hand-me-downs.
- *You deserve better.* The decisions you will be asked to make are of the utmost importance to you and your family. Sim-

> ply put, sometimes (but not always) you need to sit with a professional to flesh out all of the implications. Reducing life's complexities to a check list is folly.

As was Spock's, our goal is to educate you on problems you might face. As did he, we will tell you when you can handle them yourself, and when you need professional help. *Sometimes it is imperative to call the doctor, even at 2 a.m.*

* * *

Finally, a few words about style.

We refuse to write down to our readers. Editors, mostly in their thirties, have advised us to: "Kill the jokes, the poetry, the background stuff. Just tell them how to stretch their Social Security Check."

These editors think that at age fifty we shuffle over to the couch, sit blankly before a static TV, and drool oatmeal.

Fiddlesticks!

We have not lost our humor, our curiosity, and our intellectual excitement. Neither have you. Together we'll discuss many interesting things, things that may have troubled you for a long time. Do courts make up the law as they go along? How can you prove discrimination in the face of an employer's denial? Do lawyers have ethics? Do they have families?

We don't *write* like lawyers. Years ago, a Yale Law Professor wrote:

> *There are two things wrong with almost all legal writing. One is style. The other is content. That, I think, covers the ground.*
>
> *Readers like a dash of pepper or a dash of salt along with their information. They won't get any seasoning if lawyers can help it. Lawyers would rather be dignified and ignored.*

We will *not* be ignored! We *believe* in this book. We will to help you have a better life by helping you through hard times.

It's that simple.

Pass the salt.

A Summary for Serious Skimming

This summary will give you a good feel for what's in the book. There may be chapters you want to read now, others that you can come back to when the need arises.

Part One Retirement's Big Three—Money, Medical Care and Housing

Chapter 1 An Overview of Retirement

Common questions and fears about retirement; how to prepare for retirement and how to enjoy it. Part-time work, starting your own business, and, of course, the tax consequences!

Chapter 2 Social Security

Here, briefly, the history of Social Security, how it works, and why it may be going broke. This will enable you to be a more effective participant in the current debate about its future. Then we turn to brass tacks: *eligibility, benefits, early and late retirement,* the effect on your check if you *work*, and *who else*, besides you, can get your benefits, (sometimes even your grandchildren).We also include a brief discussion of Veterans' Benefits.

There are *safety nets* for folks who can't make ends meet on Social Security. We will describe them.

Chapter 3 Private Pension Plans

Common pension plans, retirement accounts, and your options at the time of retirement. What kind of annuity should you take? Consider using retirement benefits as an estate planning tool.

Chapter 4 Investing and Budgeting

You'll have less income and some new expenses, mostly in the area of medical care and insurance. Should you keep your life insurance? What about withdrawals from IRAs, and the exciting new possibility of converting your IRAs into Roth IRAs? We'll discuss investment options as well.

Chapter 5 House Rich, Cash Poor

How can you get cash out of your house without selling it? There are several methods, including *reverse mortgages* where the *bank pays you* a monthly payment. We'll also look at renting or selling your house. We have some great news in terms of capital gain taxes.

Chapter 6 Retirement Housing

Should you join us in the Southwest? The issue may be getting help in your own home or moving to an *assisted-living* facility. We look at the options and consider pros and cons. Nursing homes are discussed in Chapter 27.

Chapter 7 Medicare and Health Insurance

What are your insurance needs before the magical year of Medicare Eligibly (65)?

After 65, there is *Medicare*. What does it cover? More importantly, from a planning perspective, what doesn't it cover? Should you get additional insurance or join a Medicare+Choice Program?

We close with some tips on buying insurance.

Chapter 8 The Problem of Long-Term Care

Long-term custodial care can trigger major financial problems. Insurance is available. We will also look at the federal *Medicaid* Program—which does pay for long-term care—and how you might make yourself eligible without first bankrupting your family. This is known as *Medicaid Planning*.

Chapter 9 Tax Breaks, Taxes on Pensions, and Mark McGwire's Home Run Ball

You (and your children) may be missing some. (Discover just one and you have more than paid for this book.) We also look at the tax implications of being the "lucky fan" who caught the record home run ball. We will discover deep jurisprudential issues and relive one of the best moments of our century.

Part Two Family Concerns

Chapter 10 On the Limits of Law

A cautionary tale, praising mediation and counseling.

Chapter 11 Grandchildren

Grandchildren living with you for the summer? There are documents you should prepare, just in case. What are your legal rights concerning *visitation*? What should you do if you think your grandchildren are *abused* or *neglected*? What if you are raising your grandchildren? Is financial help available? Should you consider adoption?

Chapter 12 Family Financial Dealings

Are you liable for your spouse's bills? For your child's? Must your spouse or your children pay for your medical care? Bottom line – before you loan your children money or pay their bills, read this chapter!

Chapter 13 Divorce and Remarriage

Divorce is quite disruptive in the golden years. We'll tell you why, and advise you on alternatives.

As to *remarriage*, congratulations. Being naturally cautious, we advise prenuptial agreements. Also be aware of the legal ramifications for estate planning and pensions. A particular problem arises if both partners have children from prior marriages.

Chapter 14 Abuse and Neglect

Why don't relatives recognize abuse? Why don't victims complain? How can you protect your relatives (or yourself) from physical, mental, or financial abuse? What agencies help? And what can you do if *you* are becoming an abuser?

Part Three The Bad Guys

Chapter 15 Bigots

Most forms of age and disability discrimination are illegal. If you think you may have been a victim, what are your rights and remedies? How do you go about proving it?

Chapter 16 Con Artists

Beware—not only is the AARP headed your way, so, too con, artists —with "Great Opportunities" and "Heart-Wrenching Stories." A quick read of this chapter could save you thousands.

Chapter 17 Bill Collectors

Falling behind on your payments? Which bills should you pay first? What can bill collectors do to you? Their bark, you will learn, is worse than their bite. What about Bankruptcy?

Part Four Putting Your Own House in Order

Sure, it ain't over until the Fat Lady sings – but, alas, she's a tad erratic.

Chapter 18 Keeping Control of Your Medical Decisions

We fear dying hooked to a machine in a hospital. There are legal documents you can sign to maintain control over what happens to you in the hospital, even if you become senile.

Chapter 19 Keeping Control of Your Finances

If you become mentally incapable, to help you manage your money and property, your family may have to go to court. You can avoid this mess by setting up *joint accounts, Durable Financial Powers of Attorney* and *Living Trusts.* We compare your choices.

Chapter 20 Wills and Estate Planning

Wills can do more than divide your treasures; you can appoint guardians for your minor children, and you can set up creative trusts to accomplish wondrous things. We start with estate planning goals, and then compare alternative ways of reaching them.

Chapter 21 Avoiding Probate and Estate Planning Alternatives

Avoiding probate isn't always a great idea. But, if you need to avoid it, we'll tell you how. We will describe the basic techniques – life insurance, joint ownership, making gifts. We describe the other main option, creating a Living Trust, in Chapter 23.

These options should be considered even if you are leaving most of your estate under a Will.

Chapter 22 Trusts for Special Needs

This should be read by anyone who wishes to give money or property to individuals not able to manage it, such as minor children or mentally disabled relatives. Trusts, created during your lifetime or at your death, give you great flexibility in the timing and management of your gifts.

Outright gifts to disabled relatives may make them ineligible for public assistance until the money is spent. Trusts can avoid this result.

Chapter 23 Living Trusts

Living Trusts can provide for financial management if you or your spouse becomes mentally incapable *and* they can be used as a Will substitute, as a way of passing your property without going through Probate. They are very popular and are advertised extensively. But before you lay down your $1500 for the *free seminar,* read the chapter. We'll save your money yet again! (This time, spend it on yourself!)

Chapter 24 Estate and Gift Taxes

Death may be certain but estate taxes *aren't*. Only large estates are taxed (those exceeding $650,000 in 1999, $675,000 in 2000 and $1,000,000 by 2006. Your lawyer can set up a simple husband/wife trust that will shield $1.30 million (increasing to $2 million in 2006), from dear Uncle Sam.

Part Five Bad Times

Chapter 25 On Training for Ill, Pumping Iron, and Sending Dylan Thomas to Bed

This chapter discusses how you might avoid physical and mental disability by staying active. It also discusses the need to confront death in order to fully live.

Chapter 26 Disability in the Family

If a loved one is disoriented, look for correctable causes—perhaps there is a problem with medications, alcohol, or depression. We discuss the problems of *memory loss, driving, hearing loss*, and *caring for* elderly relatives in your *home*. We have special advice for families of relatives with Alzheimer's.

Chapter 27 Nursing homes

Selection. And patient rights.

Chapter 28 The Legal Aspects of Mental Disability

Guardianships or *Conservatorships* may be needed to access the funds of and to make medical decisions for mentally disabled relatives. The law also allows for forced hospitalization of individuals *who present a danger to themselves or others*. We'll tell you what steps to take.

Chapter 29 Deciding for Others

If you are a guardian or simply deciding an important issue for another person, what does the law say about how you should go about it? Will you fall to temptation? Many have.

Chapter 30 Terminal Illness

The doctor tells you that your spouse has pancreatic cancer and has only a short time to live. Do you tell?

We begin with that heart-breaking question. We also discuss how to collect on life insurance *early*, the wonderful program of *hospice care*, and the agonizing decision to *terminate* medical care. We close with a discussion of euthanasia.

Chapter 31 Death in the Family

We'll walk you through these trying times—from burial decisions to paying the last expenses. We begin, however, with a discussion of the myths surrounding mourning. Mourning isn't the same for everyone, and it isn't something to "get over" in order to get on with the rest of your life.

Chapter 32 Probate

What is probate? When will it be needed? What happens? And are you a disgruntled heir?

Part Six Getting (and Giving) Help

Chapter 33 Getting Professional Help

Here we help you find an able and responsible professional, whether a lawyer, an accountant, or a financial planner. We'll help you reach an agreement on services and fees. And what if things go bump?

Chapter 34 A Family Conversation

Many families live in emotional isolation. Adult children don't want to bring up touchy subjects, and aging parents stand mute in fear of burdening their children. Instead, everyone talks about the weather.

We strongly encourage family conversation on the issues of aging. It can bring a family together, and will help it through the hard times that will surely come. We tell you how to get one started, and some of the things you might want to talk about.

Simply put, this is our most important chapter – but you won't get much out of it if you skip the rest of the book.

But, then again, it's your book!

Fifty and Beyond

Part One

Retirement's Big Three — Money, Medical Care, and Housing

Chapter 1

An Overview of Retirement

When we first get THE LETTER from the American Association of Retired Persons which cheerfully advises us that we are now eligible, do we smile in satisfied contentment and congratulate ourselves "Overall, Good Job!"?

No. We go into a deep funk. And kick the dog.

"What is this? Some kind of cruel joke? I'm only fifty! I won't be eligible for the AARP for, what, another 30 years!"

Having lived at least fifty years in a society that celebrates youth and denies age, we just *know* that once we retire we are on that quick slippery slope to walkers, senility, and bedpans.

We're wrong. People are living longer and living better than at any other time in history. Yet the facts seem unable to break the stereotype. The horrible thing about the stereotype is that we buy into it. One of the most difficult aspects of aging is overcoming our own negative view of the elderly.

"Well, at least I'm not as old and wrinkled as that guy over there."

This loathing is not inherent in the nature of things. It is born of thousands of billboards, all with smiling, happy models under 25; it is born of countless jokes, jokes we have all told, jokes we have all laughed at, jokes at the expense of the elderly.

Elsewhere in the world, the "Elder" is respected. Elsewhere, societies recognize and celebrate our wisdom and knowledge.

The trick is to move beyond denial (beyond Grecian Formula and face lifts) into acceptance and enthusiasm: "Hey, I never thought I would make it this far. Many haven't. I've been blessed. How can I make the most of it?"

In the marvelous book *tuesdays with Morrie*, Mitch Albom writes of his weekly meetings with his old professor, Morrie, a man dying of Lou Gehrig's Disease. One day they talked about aging. "Do you envy the young?"

> *"Mitch, it is impossible for the old not to envy the young. But the issue is to accept who you are and revel in that. This is your time to be in your thirties. I had my time to be in the thirties, and now is my time to be seventy-eight."*

Enough preaching.

a. Common Retirement Questions

1. When can I retire?

You can begin drawing Social Security at 62, and under many pension plans, you can retire well before then. On the other hand, if you go on working after 62, every year you work (until age 70) will increase your Social Security benefits and your benefits under most pension plans. *Mandatory retirement is illegal* in most cases. See Chapter 15-f.

2. How much income will I need?

To maintain your pre-retirement lifestyle, as a rule of thumb, you'll need pretax retirement income equaling about 70 to 80% of your pretax working income.

Expenses go down: no more saving, no more college tuition, and no more work expenses (work clothes, business lunches, Mylanta). One expense that will go *up* is medical insurance.

We'll spend a lot of time in chapters that follow discussing the financial side of retirement: Social Security, pension plans, getting money out of your house, and financial planning and budgeting.

3. How about medical insurance?

Medicare is a marvelous program providing hospital care. However you will not be eligible for Medicare until you are 65, and thus medical insurance may be a major expense if you retire before then. As we will discuss, you will probably be able to keep up your employer's insurance until you turn 65, but only by paying a premium – possibly a hefty one.

Medicare, the basic Medicare known as Part A, does not cover many routine medical expenses such as doctors' visits and prescriptions. You'll have to buy additional insurance or enroll in one of the many options now offered by Medicare+Choice. We describe them in Chapter 7.

4. What about housing?

When they retire, many people move to more forgiving climates—here or abroad—and many buy into Retirement Communities. There are legal and emotional ramifications, as well as substantial risks. We discuss them in Chapter 6-e.

As we get older, health and medical concerns must be considered in relation to housing. We'll look at making your own house safer or moving into a Continuing Care Retirement Community.

5. The unasked question.

"When I retire, how will I fill my days? My life?"

We have literary airs and call this the *existential angst* question. Let's first address the fears of a more routine nature.

b. Common Retirement Fears

Death is on the doorstep.

Most people will spend *15 to 19 years in retirement.* That's a lot of time. Consider all you did in your first 15 to 19 years. You learned to walk, got acne, and maybe even went on a date.

I will get sick.

A recent study: 37% of retirees showed no change in their health; 40% *got better.*

Current Life Expectancies

Age	*Men*	*Women*
50	26.0 more years	31.0 more years
55	21.9	26.7
60	18.2	22.5
65	14.8	18.7

And you haven't been reading the daily newspaper if you are unaware of the numerous studies showing the remarkable benefits of physical exercise programs. These programs can be started anytime—except tomorrow.

I will get senile.

Senility is not a disease. It is a symptom of different medical conditions, many of which are *treatable*.

Retirement may create a void. Working keeps us on our mental toes. Science shows that our *minds*, as well as our biceps, *need exercise*.

Take classes at community colleges. Learn a new language. Work crosswords.

Good news, bad news for *couch potatoes:* the bad news is that you'll get fat; the good news is that you won't realize it!

Gail Sheehy, in *New Passages*, calls the years between 45 and 85 a "Second Adulthood." She details our exciting opportunities, now that the responsibilities and worries of our "First Adulthood" are gone. Many have done their best work after the age 60, including Winston Churchill, Earl Warren, and Ronald Reagan.

But don't expect contentment to drop in your lap! Retirement is hard work.

We cannot stress enough the need to confront and overcome your fears about aging. Many just give up. Fears become self-fulfilling prophecies, and alcoholism and depression become common (and often confused by relatives as senility).

c. Existential Angst

Science is meaningless. It does not answer our only question— "How should I live?"

Leo Tolstoy

Well *law* doesn't answer that question either—but it can help. Existential angst aside, there are *always* tax consequences.

Working at the office or raising our children, we are blessed; we don't have time for existential angst. It is always painfully clear what we have to do. But what happens when the alarm clock falls silent?

Butcher, Baker, Candlestick Maker. Work defines us, gives us our daily bread, *and* our daily gossip. Retirement will be a jolt.

- How will you spend your days?
- Where will you get your sense of self-worth?
- How will your retirement affect your family, friends, co-workers and all those who depend upon the fruits of your labors—customers, students, clients, and patients.
- And what of your spouse? He or she promised to keep you till death do you part. But for *24 hours a day*?

As lawyers, we are absolutely convinced of the value of writing things out. People read and think quickly. And superficially.

Reading "How will you spend your days?" you probably thought: "Now that's a good question. I'll probably go for a few walks. Now, what's the next question?" If you sat down and began to write your answer, you would find your mind slowing. You would find yourself coming up with possibilities you never imagined before.

For professional athletes, retirement comes very early. It may be hard to think of a 350 pound defensive lineman with existential angst, but there you have it. A sports agent friend urges his clients to keep a diary during their playing years, noting what they like to do in their spare time. Not a bad idea for the rest of us.

Learning to relax, learning how to enjoy our well-earned rest, may be a major chore.

Bookstores are full of books urging us to "take time to smell the flowers." A friend once remarked, "Well and good, but the people who write those books aren't out smelling the flowers; they are inside, pounding out another book!"

But know this: Many plan for years what they will do during their retirement. They may find, however, that they have run through their *entire* list in the *first six months*. So much for camping on the shores of beautiful Lake Woebegon. Now what? Go back to Go?

Books in the library are brimming with good ideas for successful retirement written, no doubt, by driven and compulsive folks, folks who have *never* been to Lake Woebegon.

Many retirees take part-time jobs, go into business, or volunteer.

d. Part-Time Work and Opening a Bookstore

One of our favorite quotes comes from George Bernard Shaw:

> *I am of the opinion that my life belongs to the whole community and as long as I live, it is my privilege to do for it what I can. I want to be thoroughly used up when I die, for the harder I work, the more I will live. I rejoice in life for its own sake. Life is no brief candle for me. It is sort of a splendid torch which I have got hold of for a moment and I want to make it burn as brightly as possible before handing it on to future generations.*

Helping others, being of service, is deeply human. No wonder work offers more than income:

- Studies show that folks who continue to work part-time are healthier than those who don't.
- Mental abilities tend to remain strong if used. Continuing to learn new things, improves memory. (True/false: We have said this before.)
- Retirement jobs can be *more fun* because they are less stressful (who cares if you don't get promoted?).

If you decide to continue working, *dare to eat a peach*! No need to do the same old stuff. Raise chickens. Teach children. Rob trains.

Getting a job.

Small companies are best. They are more flexible in terms of working conditions and in recognizing and using your talents and experiences. However, some large companies, such as McDonald's, go out of their way to hire seniors. There are surely others. Call around.

Some jobs take *advance planning*. Learn the computer. Many consider "going into teaching," but remember that teaching certificates are usually required for public school teaching. On the other hand, community colleges, elder hostels and other community education programs want your skills and will not demand much paperwork. Teach a class on contract bridge; teach kids to weld. If you are considering this route, find out what is required in terms of further schooling.

Starting your own business.

"They see the bookstore, but not the inventory."

Joe Tolstoy, Leo's Great Grandson

While this is not a book of literary criticism, we think that young Tolstoy's deep meaning is that running a bookstore is a whole lot more complicated than simply talking with teary customers about your favorite romance novel.

Look before you leap. Opening a business is *risky*. You can lose your life's savings. And everyone thinks they can open a restaurant.

- Check with the Small Business Administration for advice.
- Try the type of work on for size. Before opening a bookstore, work in one.
- Be leery of retirement work *scams*. Folks selling *Franchises* and *Home Work Opportunities* make their money selling to *you*. Sharks circle, offering exciting, *can't miss*, big-buck opportunities. Ask for references—people who have already invested.

Of course, it always *costs* money to get into a business, either to buy supplies or to show "commitment," but be very suspicious of any *opportunity* that costs you to get in.

Never, ever cash in your retirement or your savings to invest in a business, unless you are very, very sure. Always run opportunities past your most cynical friends. (We can loan ours.)

Get disinterested advice. The person offering you the opportunity is *never* disinterested. That person is a salesman. Consider contacting SCORE, the Service Corps of Retired Executives. It can put you in touch with people who have "been there" and "done that."

e. Social Security Implications of Working

The first $9,600 or $15,500 you earn (depending on whether you retired at 62 or 65) will have *no effect* on your Social Security check. Thereafter, you pay a rather stiff tax for working: a reduction in your Social Security check of $1 for every $2 or $3 you earn (again depending on when you retired). After age 70, there is no such tax.We'll go through the painful details in the next chapter.

f. Volunteering

Volunteering is richly rewarding. Many tell us that their volunteer work is the most rewarding of their lifetime. And it needn't be full time!

You have a lifetime of experience. Many in your community could use it. Most locales have *Volunteer Clearing Houses*. In addition there is the RSVP (Retired Senior Volunteer Program) in nearly every community. You can make an important difference in the lives of children, seniors, shut-ins, and in all sorts of good programs in your area.

The best place to start is at your local *Area Agency on Aging,* discussed in the next section.

If you are on the Net, try www.cns.gov/senior/index.html to get in touch with the National Senior Service Corps.

g. Area Agencies on Aging

Area Agencies on Aging, created by the federal Older Americans Act, address the needs of folks aged sixty and over by providing such services as meals on wheels, senior centers, transportation, home care, respite and adult day care. They are simply a marvelous source of information and help, and we will refer you to them often. To find the office in your area call Eldercare Locator 1-800-677-1116. On the Web:

http://www.aoa.gov (Administration on Aging)

However, as much as you can get good advice from others, never overlook yourself as a marvelous source of ideas. Get busy writing out *your* thoughts.

What can I do during my retirement?

Chapter 2

Social Security

a. A Quick Summary

- Social Security provides retirement benefits.

Retired individual workers average around $9,400 per year—couples, both receiving benefits, $15,700. Benefits vary depending on how long you worked and how much you earned. Benefits are adjusted to keep pace with inflation.

If you or your parents' only income is from Social Security, check with your Social Security Office about *Supplemental Security Income (SSI)*. It is a program which pays additional benefits to people with very limited income and property. See Section (l) in this Chapter. Also consider *Veterans' Benefits,* Section (k).

- Social Security allows for early retirement (age 62), but you pay a price.

- Often it makes good sense not to start taking cash benefits until age 70.

- When you are about to retire, apply two or three months before your retirement date.

- It is very important to get yourself eligible for Social Security in order to be eligible for Medicare.

To be eligible for Social Security, you generally need to have paid into the system for 40 quarters or 10 years. If you are close but not yet there, take a job to make yourself eligible; your monthly retirement benefit might be small but you will be *eligible for Medicare*. You can get in the Medicare Program without 40 quarters but you must pay a stiff premium.

- Social Security provides life insurance for your family.

If you die and leave *minor children,* they can receive benefits until they marry or turn 18 (if they are full time students, until 19). If they are disabled, the benefit can continue after 19. The average widowed mother with two children receives around $18,600.

Your spouse can collect Survivors' Benefits when he or she turns 60 (50 if disabled, and earlier if they are caring for your minor child). Elderly widow or widower, living alone, receives around $9,000. In some cases, *dependent parents* can also receive Survivors' Benefits.

- Social Security provides disability insurance.

If you become disabled before you retire, you and your family may receive disability payments. Your disability must, however, prevent you from almost any form of gainful employment, not just your last job, and must be of a more or less permanent nature, not, for example, a broken leg. Disability benefits do not begin until after six months of disability. An individual disabled worker receives around $8,800 per year while a disabled worker with spouse and children receives around $14,600.

- If you are not eligible for Social Security based on your own work record, you may be based on your spouse's, even if you are divorced.

Homemakers, who stayed home doing the hard work of raising the family, are not eligible for Social Security (they haven't paid in). They can, however, get benefits as the spouse of an insured worker.

A divorced spouse (married at least 10 years) of a covered member is entitled to a benefit equal to one-half of the insured member, at age 62 or earlier if caring for a dependent child.

- If you or your parents are unable to manage finances, consider a "Representative Payee" arrangement.

Social Security benefits can be paid into a representative payee account, thus allowing a friend, a relative, or even a volunteer at a local agency, to pay the bills.

- Creditors cannot attach Social Security checks. Once the checks are deposited in a bank account they may be attached.

b. A Brief History: Social Security and Its Discontents

Before the nitty-gritty (*who's covered, early and late retirement, computation of benefits*), a brief aside on the history of Social Security and its current woes. You won't hurt our feelings if you skip it.

Social Security is the child of the Great Depression, the time of folks selling apples, losing farms, and fearing tomorrow. Franklin Roosevelt, elected President, assured the nation that "*The only thing we have to fear is Fear itself.*" One of his New Deal Programs was Social Security. It has prospered.

In 1935, prior to Social Security, 70% of persons over 65 were living below the poverty line.

- The poverty rate among folks over 65 is no longer 70%. It is 12% (about the same rate for people under 65).
- 90% of retired folks draw benefits. If one were to buy a private policy that provides the same benefits as Social Security and Medicare, for a typical couple the cost would be close to half a million dollars.
- Of those drawing benefits, 60% receive more than half of their income from Social Security.
- Social Security, in addition to retirement benefits, provides life and disability insurance.
- Administrative costs are about 1% (compared to around 15% for private pension plans).

Benefits are adjusted yearly for inflation.

The *Consumer Price Index* (CPI) is used to find the rate of inflation. Benefits are then adjusted to keep up with inflation. Social Security uses the term COLA (Cost of Living Adjustment).

The Bureau of Labor Statistics compiles the CPI by tracking the prices of roughly 80,000 goods and services, and compares those prices to those charged in 1982-1984. Let's make up an example:

	1982–84	1996
Hamburger	$ 0.80	$ 1.20
Ford auto	$10,000.00	$14,500.00

In 1996, the CPI stood at 158.6 (meaning that it then cost $1.58 to buy what $1.00 could in 1982-84).

Inflation for 1996 was set at 3.3%; Social Security Benefits were automatically increased by that percentage.

It has been argued that the CPI overstates the rate of inflation. First, it fails to account for *substitution of goods* (when hamburger goes to $1.20, people might switch to chicken). Second, it fails to account for the *improvement of goods* (today's Ford is a better car - you are getting more car for your money and thus the price increase should not totally be attributed to inflation).

If the CPI overstates inflation, then Social Security benefits are going up faster than they should. We note, however, that many experts disagree with the notion that the CPI overstates inflation.

The Bad News — Monthly benefits are low.

Social Security was *never intended* to be a full retirement plan. In fact, at the time it was passed, life expectancy wasn't much beyond 65.

Today, benefits are calculated so that lower income workers receive a higher percent return than do higher end workers.

A worker who has earned only half the national average will receive about 56% of his average salary. A worker who has earned the national average will receive about 42%, while folks with high incomes will top out at 28%.

Most financial experts estimate that, once you retire, you will need about 70% or 80% of your pre-retirement income. Look at the figures above again. Social Security doesn't even come close. It is a *serious mistake* to think that Social Security will maintain your standard of living.

And we've all heard that Social Security is *going broke.*

Well, it isn't. Not for a long time at least.

- Financed by a payroll tax of 15.3% on the first $72,600 of earnings (split between worker and employer), Social Security *today* is *actually making money*. That is, more money is collected from today's workers than is paid to yesterday's. It is estimated that, by 2019, the Social Security Trust Fund will have a surplus of $3.3 trillion. If that money is actually there in 2019, Social Security would remain solvent for another decade or so. (We will see why the money might not be there in a moment.)
- *2019 is a key year*. Then Social Security will begin to *lose* money —it will pay out more than it collects. Why? The number of workers, compared to the number of retired, is falling. In 1960, it was 6 to 1; in 2019, it will be to 3 to 1. This is because folks are living longer *and* because the birthrate is falling.

With fewer workers paying into Social Security for each retired person drawing on it, something has to give. It should be noted, however, that dependent/worker ratio is not as stark as it might otherwise appear. While it is true there are more dependent retired individuals, there are fewer dependent children. For illustration, in the 1950's typically a working husband would support his wife and three or more children; today both the husband and wife work to support one or two children.

In any event, there is a coming crisis in Social Security. Today there are about 43 million recipients; in 2030 there will be 85 million. Possible solutions to the crisis are the stuff of daily newspapers and Presidential Commissions.

- Raise employment Social Security taxes, by raising the rate of tax, or raising the limit on the income that is taxed.
- Reduce benefits and/or increase taxes on benefits.
- Raise the retirement age. It is already going up over time to 67. Better than something mandatory, encourage people not to retire by making employment more meaningful.
- Allow for *privatization*, either by allowing individuals to invest some of their Social Security dollars in the stock market *or* by allowing the Social Security Trust Fund to play the market.

The Social Security Trust Fund is not a huge pile of dollars sitting in a vault somewhere, just as our excess money is not under the pillow. You and I put our money into the bank or buy stock; neither the bank nor the corporation put our money in a room; rather they put it to good use. By law, Social Security can only use its excess money to buy U.S. Government Treasury Bills. The federal government then uses this money to help pay the cost of government.

The idea behind privitization is that the stock market generally has a higher return than the interest paid on Treasury Bills. Of course, the market is more risky and there is the danger, if large amounts of the Social Security Trust Fund is invested in the market, that politics, rather than financial judgments, will dictate investment decisions.

Some have expressed the fear that the federal government will be unable to pay back Social Security when it needs the funds to pay beneficiaries. When the federal government was generating huge deficits, this fear was real. Now that that problem has been somewhat corrected, default is much less likely. Further, the federal government has never yet defaulted on its obligations.

There is currently a general political attack on "entitlements" such as Social Security. Those who would drastically limit or abolish Social Security attempt to create generational hostility by convincing younger workers that they are working hard so that retirees can play. Many young folks have been convinced that Social Security will not be there for them. It will be. A few quick further rejoinders:

- If Social Security is abolished, the cost of caring for the nation's elderly will not go away; it will simply fall on working sons and daughters.
- Social Security is *not* just for old people. Of the 43 million who are currently drawing benefits, only 65% are elderly. The rest are the families of workers who have died or have become disabled. It has been estimated that the death benefit of Social Security is comparable to a $320,000 life insurance policy and the disability benefit is comparable to a $200,000 disability policy. Hence current workers are benefitted by Social Security as well as their parents.

For a very interesting look at the political attack on "entitlements," see Theodore Roszak, *America the Wise.*

c. Eligibility and Computation of Benefits

Eligibility

You must have paid into the system for *40 quarters* (a ten-year work history). These quarters need not be all at one time. That is, quarters earned as a teenager can count along with those earned later in life. Some government work is not covered by Social Security nor are some forms of private capitalistic endeavor, such as drug dealing (reason enough to go straight).

How to check your account and what to do if there is a mistake.

Call Social Security (*1-800-772-1213*) for *Form SSA-7004* (Request for Earnings and Benefit Estimate Statement). Or you can request one on the Internet: http://www.ssa.gov. The statement will estimate your retirement benefits. It will show how much you have contributed and what benefits your relatives may receive.

Use form SSA-7004 every few years to check that your wages have been reported correctly. This is important as benefits are calculated on your earnings. Generally you have *three years* to have corrections made–but if you find that an employer simply didn't report any income, you can have this corrected at any time.

Computation of Benefits

A train leaves New York going 60 mph. Two hours and 13 minutes later, another train leaves Los Angeles going 62 mph.

What is the capital of Nova Scotia?

That's the formula Social Security uses to calculate your benefits.

First, Social Security figures your *average monthly salary.* Then it gives you a percentage of that figure. It is assumed that you worked 35 years: your total earning will be spread out over this period, even if you actually worked less time. Even though you will be eligible for Social Security after 40 quarters, the longer you work and the more you earn, the greater will be your benefit.

The key figure is *Primary Insurance Amount (PIA)*, the monthly amount you will receive at *full* retirement. If you retire early, you'll get less. If you retire late, you'll do better. Let's see how this works out.

d. Early, Late, and Full Retirement

At "full retirement age," you will receive your full PIA. What is your full retirement age? Like the rest of us, it's getting older.

Year of Birth	*Full Retirement Age*
Before 1938	65 yrs
1938	65 yrs and two months
1939	65 yrs and four months
1940 (Year of the Dragon)	65 yrs and six months
1941	65 yrs and eight months
1942	65 yrs and ten months
1943-1954	66 yrs

After 1954, it goes up two months every year until 1959 when it becomes 67 years.

Early Retirement

You can retire at 62 and get a monthly check. *But there are prices to be paid.*

You still won't be eligible for Medicare.

You have to wait until 65, so health insurance will still be a concern. Under a program called *COBRA,* you will be able to continue your employer's health insurance, but *you* (not your employer) pay the premium. (See Chapter 7-a for more details.)

Your monthly check will be a little lighter.

Because you will be drawing benefits longer, they are reduced if you retire early. If you retire three years before full retirement (62 is the earliest age you can begin receiving benefits), there will be a *permanent* reduction of *20%* in your monthly benefits. Currently the reduction is 5/9 of 1% for each month you retire before your full retirement age.

If you retire early, your earnings from outside work will incur a greater penalty.

If you retire at *full* retirement age, you can earn, as of this writing, about *$15,500* a year *without* affecting your social security check. After that, a $1 reduction will be made for each $3 earned in excess of the threshold. (Once you reach the age of 70, there is no reduction for any outside earnings... have a ball!)

If you take early retirement, the amount you can earn without affecting your check *falls* to about $9,600 and the *rate of reduction increases* to $1 for each $2 earned, a 50% tax rate (not counting any other taxes you will pay on your earnings).

Before taking early retirement from Social Security, check its impact on your private pension plan.

Some private pension plans have what is known as an *integration of benefits clause* which operates to *reduce your pension payments* in light of what you receive from Social Security. Depending on the rate of reduction, it might be best to delay taking Social Security as long as possible.

On the other hand, there may be *financial incentives to retire early.*

- If you have a *child under 18* or *a spouse over 62*, when you retire *they can begin* drawing benefits from your Social Security. This may increase your family's total benefit to 150% to 180% of your monthly benefit. More on this in Section (f) of this chapter.

Late Retirement

You don't have to begin drawing cash benefits at age 65. If you don't, you are *still* eligible for Medicare at age 65. By not drawing cash benefits at age 65, you will increase your monthly checks when you begin taking them. In theory, you will get fewer checks. Fair's fair. If you wait until 70, your checks may be between 25% and 35% higher. After the age of 70, there is *no* further increase in benefits.

If you go on working after 65, maybe it is a good idea not to begin drawing your cash benefits. Before age 70, there is substantial *tax* on what you earn. This tax is in the form of reduction of benefits, in the amount of 33% to 50% of those earnings. At age 70, there is no longer any such tax on earnings.

Similarly, if you are receiving enough from your private pension plan, consider late retirement.

Bottom line, there is no reason not to take your cash benefits at age 70, but there are reasons to wait until that age.

e. Income Taxes and Your Benefits

We have already seen that *earned* income can reduce your Social Security check (until you reach the age of 70). These reductions do not apply to income from investments, interest or, thankfully, royalties. However, the tax man is not done with you. A portion of your social security payments may be taxed as regular income. Generally about 50% will be, depending on your other income.

f. Family Benefits

The basic notion is, when you retire, your income will go down. If you have a family to support, you will need more money.

The following people can begin drawing benefits *at the time* you do:

Spouses

Your spouse, if 62 (or younger, if caring for one of your children under 16), can draw benefits up to half the amount of your monthly check.

Of course, many spouses age 62 will qualify for social security *in their own right*. Social Security will automatically pay the higher benefit.

Kids and Grandkids

Your unmarried and dependent children (including adopted and out-of-wedlock), under 18 (or 19 if still in high school) are entitled to draw up to one-half of your monthly benefit. So, too, are older *disabled* children, if they were disabled before they turned 22. *Grandchildren*, if they are "dependent" upon you, may also draw benefits.

Payments to these folks *will not* reduce your check. There is, however, a *family maximum*: the *combined* payments will *not be allowed to exceed 150% to 180% of your monthly payment.*

Finally, if you defer your retirement beyond 65, these folks *cannot* receive benefits until you do.

g. A Note to Divorcees

At the time of divorce, the family's assets are divided. Pensions create problems. How do you divide something that has yet to mature? (We aren't talking about your ex-spouse, we're talking about pension plans.) Divorce lawyers get rich figuring this one out. See Chapter 13-a.

Social Security has an automatic solution. As an ex-spouse, if you were married *at least ten years,* you are entitled to a benefit equal to one-half of his or her full retirement amount. You must be 62, or younger if you are providing care for a dependent minor.

Unfortunately, your take *doesn't* reduce their check—Social Security ain't perfect!

h. Appeals

When you file a claim, a Social Security worker will be assigned to your case. Keep track of your communications with that person. If a claim is denied either totally or in part, you will receive a letter stating the reasons. (Get a written denial: oral ones can't be appealed.) If denied, you have *60 days* to ask for a Reconsideration. Your case will be reviewed by another case worker. If your claim is turned down again, you can ask for a hearing. You can call witnesses and testify yourself.

Should you get a lawyer? Yes, in *disability cases* because the evidence is often quite technical. Lawyers who work in this field usually work on a *contingency* basis, which means that if you don't win, you don't pay. (You may have to pay certain costs, however.) The lawyer's fee is limited, by statute, to 25% of any back benefits you receive.

For other Social Security appeals, a lawyer, knowledgeable in the field, can rather quickly and inexpensively evaluate the strengths of your case. A call to your local *Legal Aid Office* or *Lawyer Referral Office* is the way to start.

If you lose your administrative hearing, the next step is Federal District Court. There you need a lawyer.

i. Overpayments

Who among us will ever forget the little Monopoly Man falling over backwards: "Bank Error in your favor." Sometimes it actually happens.

If Social Security thinks it has overpaid you, they will write you a letter telling you that they will reduce further payments until the overpayment is corrected. If you think they are wrong about the overpayment, file a *request for reconsideration.*

Even if there has been an overpayment, if it will work a real hardship for you to pay the money back, ask for a *waiver.* If you do so within 30 days, they will not reduce your check until the matter is resolved. They will ask you to fill out a questionnaire.

j. For Further Information

Social Security Administration 1-800-772-1213

It also has information on *Railroad Retirement Benefits.*

The Social Security Handbook (SSA Publication No. 65-008) can be obtained at your Social Security office or downloaded from the SSA Homepage

http://www.ssa.gov

k. Note on Veterans' Benefits

In recognition of their service to our country, the Federal Government has an extensive program of veteran benefits, including: monthly compensation; pensions; medical and nursing home care; and support services in the home.

Most benefits are available only if you have seen active service and were not dishonorably discharged. Benefits are available if you have a service connected disability, or, if you qualify as low-income, with a non-service-related disability. Spouses, dependent children, and survivors may also draw benefits.

The Department of Veteran Affairs publishes a yearly edition of *Federal Benefits for Veterans and Dependents*. Local offices have copies.

I. Safety Nets for Low-Income Folks: SSI, Medicaid, and Help with Medicare Premiums

SSI stands for Supplemental Security Income, a program run by Social Security. It pays monthly checks to the poor, age 65 or older. (It also provides benefits to younger people who are blind or disabled.)

If you are entitled to SSI, you can usually get food stamps and Medicaid. Medicaid is a federal program which helps low-income individuals pay hospital and doctor bills.

As of this writing, the monthly SSI payments are: $500 per month for one person and $750 for a couple. These amounts are higher in some states, and will be lower if you have other income.

What are the property and income limits?

Property. Generally, the value of your home, your car, and most personal items are not counted. Cash, bank accounts, stocks, and bonds are counted. For a single person, they cannot add up to over $2,000; for a couple $3,000.

Income. Basically everything coming in is counted: Social Security, pensions, earnings and even the value of food, clothing and shelter that you receive. The amount of income you can have and still be eligible depends on the state in which you live. If you think you might be eligible, call the number listed below to get specific information.

However, as a general matter:

If you don't work, your monthly income must be less than

$490 for one person
$725 for a couple

If you are working, your monthly income should be less than

$1,025 for one person
$1,495 for a couple

If you believe you are eligible (or close enough to check it out) call Social Security at 1-800-772-1213 (Hearing impaired: 1-800-325-0778).

Ask about *Medicaid*, a federal health program for the poor. Ask also about programs which help pay premiums for additional *Medicare* coverage. For more on *Medicaid*, see Chapter 8-b, and for more on *Medicare* see Chapter 7.

Chapter 3

Private Pension Plans

Fans of the 10th Amendment—which seems to limit the scope of Federal Power—might find it curious that most pension plans are governed by Federal Law. What do they have to do with conducting foreign affairs and providing for the common defense?

What the federal government cannot do directly, it can do by way of Big Carrots and the Internal Revenue Code. If a business wants to deduct its contributions to pension plans, those plans must conform to Federal requirements. If the plans do, employee contributions are deductible from current income.

A rule of thumb about retirement accounts: *"Deduct now, pay later."* If money going into your pension fund was deductible from your income tax, when you draw it out, it is taxed. This usually works well. When you are working, your income (and tax rate) is higher. "Deduct now, pay later" tends to even things out.

Compare this tax treatment to money you set aside in a savings account. As these were *post tax* dollars, when you take them out, they do *not* constitute income. Visualize yourself as an apple; the IRS cannot take two bites.

a. Kinds of Pension Plans

Pension plans vary a great deal. In general:

1. They favor, unlike Social Security, higher paid employees.
2. They favor long-term workers; the longer you work, the more you will get.
3. The normal retirement age is 65.
4. Your employer is obligated to give you a yearly statement of where you stand.

There are two kinds of basic pension plans.

Defined Benefit Plans

Under these plans, your retirement payments are based on a percentage of your earnings (usually the average of your last three to five years of work). The percentage goes up the longer you have worked, say 2% per year. If you have worked 30 years, you will get 60% of your average earnings over the last few years.

Defined Contribution Plans

Under these plans, retirement contributions are put in a retirement account. This amount is invested. If the investments do well, your retirement benefits will be high; if the investments do badly, you are in trouble.

In a defined *contribution* plan, the employee takes the risk of market variations; in a defined *benefit* plan, the employer takes the risk. It is also worth noting that contribution plans are not insured while benefit plans usually are.

401(k) Plans

These plans are like defined contribution plans, but give the employee somewhat more flexibility as there are no fixed contributions. The employer may match an employee's contributions up to a certain amount. 401(k) Plans can be risky. First, they depend on how well the investments do, and, second, they are not insured. On the other hand, depending on the market, they can do much better than defined benefit plans.

What type of plan should you have? You generally don't have much of a choice in the matter; you take the kind of plan your employer offers.

Assuming you are locked into your pension plan, what do you need to know?

1. *Before you retire*, you need to know if you are *vested.*
2. *When you retire*, you need to know your options on taking your money.
3. If there is *trouble,* you need to know where to look for help.

b. Getting Your Contributions Back: Vesting

If you have made contributions to your retirement account, you are entitled to get them back, no matter what, whether you were laid off, quit, or fired. However, you will not be entitled to your *employer's* contribution until your rights *vest.* Most plans vest after *five* years, but this varies widely: some vest in a month, some in seven years (the maximum length allowed under federal tax law).

Before you quit a job (or retire), make sure your rights have vested. Check your *Individual Benefit Statement* (a document your employer will give you). If you only have a year or so to go before vesting, stay. For older employees, rights vest at the normal retirement age, even if they haven't put in the traditional number of years. Get a job at 62. If the normal retirement age is 65, you can retire at 65, and be entitled to your pension even though it usually takes longer for it to vest. (But the pension won't pay very much.)

c. Cashing Out

Some plans (such as *401(k) Plans*) allow you to *cash out* when you retire. That is, you can take all of the money in your account. This can be *very dangerous.* Unless you do it right, you will have to treat the entire amount as current income and your tax bill will be *staggering.* However, if you do it correctly, it might be a good idea to roll the money over into a traditional IRA or a new Roth IRA. See Chapter 4–c. Consult your fund manager or an accountant.

Most people don't opt to cash out. Rather, they take an annuity. There are choices here as well.

d. Annuities (and using your annuity as an estate planning device)

An annuity is simply an agreement by a bank or other financial institution to pay you a certain monthly amount for a certain number of years. There are several forms:

Fixed Term Annuities

These pay monthly payments over a fixed period of years. The risk is that you will outlive the fixed period and then you will be in a fine kettle of fish. However, if you have assets to cover this possibility, a fixed term annuity may be the way to go; monthly payments will be higher than with a *life annuity*.

Life Annuities

Payments continue until death.

Joint and Survivor's Annuities

Here monthly payments are made to you and, after you die, to your designated survivor, usually, but not always, a spouse. Because the annuity is now betting against two lives (so to speak), the monthly payments will be less. Another alternative is the *joint and 50% survivor's annuity,* which pays half the monthly amount to the designated survivor.

Under federal law, *if you are married*, you must elect a joint and survivor's annuity, with the survivor getting at least 50%. A single life annuity (one paying only you, leaving nothing for your spouse at your death), is possible *only* if your spouse agrees in writing.

When does a single life annuity make sense?

A *single life annuity*, which will pay the highest monthly payments, may make sense *if* your spouse has adequate retirement income *or* is in such bad health that it is unlikely he or she will outlive you.

If you are in the fortunate position *of not needing all of your pension*, consider making your *children* the surviving beneficiaries. This will probably take a big bite out of your monthly check, but it will provide your children with monthly payments long after you have gone. Who knows? They might actually thank you.

e. Pension Troubles

Your plan goes broke.

Defined benefits are usually insured by the Pension Benefit Guarantee Corporation (800- 400-PBGC). *Defined contribution plans* are not. Even in those plans which are covered, some of the plan's benefits may not be, such as disability and early retirement.

Your employer changes the plan.

If your employer changes the plan to your detriment, first make sure that the plan allowed him to do so. Get a copy of the plan. This is a tricky, fact-specific area. If changes in benefits are substantial, consult a lawyer who specializes in employment or pension law.

Your individual claim for benefits is turned down.

Plans will tell you how to appeal. Again, some lawyers specialize in pension law.

You get divorced.

You will probably have to divide the worth of the pension – and this gets complicated. See Chapter 13-a.

You forget where you worked.

Remember after the War? You spent four or five years with that little company outside of town. What was its name? Did it have a pension plan that you just forgot? Old tax forms will give the employer's tax number and perhaps the number of the retirement plan. If you haven't kept old tax forms, for a fee the IRS will provide a copy. Once you have these numbers, perhaps the Pension Benefit Guaranty Corporation can help you (800–400–PBGC). www.pbgc.gov

You may be looking at another Bank Error in Your Favor!

Chapter 4

Budgeting and Managing Finances

College Bars have "Free Ladies Nights." Elder Bars have "Free Gentlemen Nights."

The good news is that the game's the same; the better news, as least for some of us, is that the odds, at long last, have improved.

In three out of four marriages, the husband dies first. In many marriages, he's been the one paying the bills and making the investments (leaving the trivial decisions to his wife, such as where to live, where the kids should go to school, where to go on vacation and who to have over for dinner).

Women, get involved with finances! Push the issue! But be subtle. Avoid: "Dear, you're not looking good today. Tell me about our savings."

The AARP has a special program: Women's Financial Information Program.

This chapter, on budgeting and finances, is for husbands, too (although, of course, they *already* know it all—as well as that little-known shortcut to McCallsburg—and there is *absolutely* no need to *ask* for directions!).

a. Rethinking Money

Retirement requires a *major* shift in thinking about money. Working, you could count on periodic raises. With a relatively high income, you could ride out new roofs, old cars, and braces. The daily mail brought applications for credit cards from obscure banks, and bank loan officers greeted you with toothy grins and sweaty palms.

No more. Income is fixed and credit falls on hard times. If you have never budgeted before, the time is now. We'll look at new expenses you'll have, and one you might want to drop: life insurance. Then we look at IRAs and the new Roth IRA. We will look at investment alternatives. In our next chapter, we will tell you how to get cash out of your house.

b. Budgeting: Life Insurance, Big Items, and Medical Insurance

There are scores of budget books. All have long, depressing lists of expenses we don't even realize we have. Thanks. Here we flag some special items to consider at retirement.

Life Insurance

Consider canceling life insurance. Your children are now adults and, in some cases, have actually moved out.

> *A cartoon shows an elderly couple in their kitchen. Their son, unshaven and in a T shirt, leans against the counter, sipping a beer. The father says, "Son, we think it's time for you to move. Your mom and I would like a little time, by ourselves, before we die."*

If you get your money out of life insurance, you can move it to income-producing investments or into a kind of insurance you might need: *long-term care insurance.* (See Chapter 8-a.) On the other hand, life insurance is a good way to pass on money to loved ones. (See Chapter 21-c.)

This is complicated and you need to consider such issues as the tax benefit of keeping the policy, the option of borrowing against it, or even making it a gift. You should talk to your lawyer, accountant, or financial adviser.

Big Ticket Items

During your working years, when you needed to replace the car, you would get a car loan and repay it out of current income. Once you retire, however, you will find it more difficult to borrow money, even though you have good security. Lenders look not only at security, but also at income stream. Does the borrower have enough income to repay the loan without selling other assets? In this regard, *age discrimination* in lending money or extending credit is unlawful. (See Chapter 15-b.)

During retirement, budget for big item purchases *before* you buy. Think you will need a new car in three years? How much will you have to spend? Put something aside each month.

Health Insurance and Costs

In Chapters 7 and 8 we discuss the problem of medical insurance. For now, realize that medical costs will be a *major* new hit on your budget.

Briefly:

> If you retire *before* age 65, you will need to *purchase health insurance* to cover what you lost when you retired. This can be quite expensive.
>
> At age 65, you will have Medicare. Medicare is a great program, but it covers basically just hospital stays. Most everyone buys additional coverage by purchasing Medicare Part B insurance (which will reduce your monthly Social Security check by $43.80). But neither basic Medicare or Medicare Part B covers routine tests, dental work, prescriptions, eyeglasses, or hearing aids (ranging from $500 to $2000). You will probably want to purchase insurance to fill Medicare's gaps, or perhaps join a Medicare HMO. See Chapter 7 for a description of Medicare.
>
> Even if you have extensive insurance, you can count on increased expenses in the medical area which will not be covered, such as over-the-counter medications and vitamins.

Finally, you may want to purchase long-term care insurance. See Chapter 8.

c. IRAs and Roth IRAs

Individual Retirement Accounts (*IRAs*), were created to allow individuals to put a little extra aside for their retirement. The federal tax code offers two carrots: tax deduction at time of contribution and tax deferral on the interest earned on contributions.

1. Contributions to an IRA account are *deductible* from federal taxes.

A $2,000 contribution (the maximum yearly contribution) will reduce your income by $2,000. If you are paying taxes at a 30% rate, then the $2,000 deduction will result in a $600 tax savings (30% of $2,000). In effect you get a $2,000 saving account for only $1,400.

2. Interest earned on money in your account is *tax deferred.*

This means your savings grow much faster than they do in regular savings accounts. Rather than paying taxes on the yearly interest earned (as you do in a regular savings account), the total amount you would have paid in taxes stays in your IRA account and earns interest itself.

To illustrate: You put $10,000 in a regular savings account which pays 5%. The first year, you will earn $500 in interest and pay, at a 30% tax rate, $150 in taxes. Thus you would have, at the end of Year One, $10,350 in your account ($10,000 plus $500 interest minus $150 taxes). If the money was in an IRA, because taxes are *deferred,* at the end of Year One, you have a balance of $10,500. Now in Year Two, you will earn *$517* interest in a regular savings account ($10,350 times 5%), but *$525* in an IRA ($10,500 times 5%). Over time, small increases add up. Recall the Rockies.

Tax deferral is not the same as *tax exemption.* When you take money out of your IRA, you pay income taxes on it. In 1997 Congress created the *Roth IRA*. It is different from traditional IRAs in three fundamental ways:

1. Contributions to a Roth IRA, unlike traditional IRAs, are *not tax deductible.*

In this regard, traditional IRAs are better. Your $2,000 contribution to a Roth IRA actually costs you the full $2,000 (while it costs you only $1,400 in the traditional IRA, as explained above).

2. Unlike traditional IRAs, timely *withdrawals* from Roth IRAs are *tax-exempt*!

This feature makes them very attractive, both in terms of retirement income (tax free), and in terms of an estate planning device, as your beneficiaries will be able to make tax free withdrawals as well. Withdrawals from traditional IRAs are subject to tax.

3. Unlike traditional IRAs, which *require you* to begin making withdrawals at the age of 70, you need not make any mandatory withdrawals.

This feature also makes Roth IRAs very attractive as an estate planning tool. You can continue to accumulate money in the account until the time of your death. At the time of your death, your beneficiaries must begin making withdrawals, but again, they will be tax free.

So what is one to make of all of that engaging prose? When all is said and done, what is one supposed *to do*?

1. *Make your IRAs your last cookie jar.*

Use up your regular saving accounts first. The interest you are earning in your regular saving accounts is taxed. The interest you earn in your IRAs is either *tax deferred* or, in the case of Roth IRAs, *tax exempt.*

2. *Consider using your IRAs as estate planning devices.*

Just like retirement annuities, IRAs are often overlooked as estate planning devices. We discuss this in Chapter 21-e.

3. *Consider converting your traditional IRA's into Roth IRAs.*

If you convert, you will have to pay taxes on the deferred earning in your traditional IRAs. However, given the features we just described, conversion may still make sense. Obviously this will be a matter of careful consideration for you and your accountant or tax adviser.

Finally, no discussion of IRAs would be complete without a discussion of:

Substantial Penalty for Early Withdrawals

You can *begin drawing* from your IRA (traditional or Roth) in the *year you reach 59.* Of course, you can take the money out before, but you will pay a penalty.

The "substantial penalty"on early withdrawals is an excise tax on the amount withdrawn, now 10%. It is imposed in addition to regular income taxes. However, the Rule of Eight suggests that, if the money had been in the account for eight years, the tax-free earnings on those funds will offset the penalty. You will get more benefit from compounding interest than you will lose in paying the tax.

In the case of Roth IRA's, you can take out the money you put in at any time without penalty or tax. This is because you did not get a tax deduction when you put it in. However, money you earned in the account cannot be withdrawn without complying with the withdrawal limits.

Finally, you may be able to make withdrawals from your IRA before 59 and without penalty for educational expenses, first-time home purchases, and if you have very large medical bills (exceeding 7% of your adjusted gross income). Talk to the fund manager or your accountant.

d. The Danger of Invading Capital

Assume that you have $100,000 in investments. In addition to your Social Security and pension earnings, you figure you need an additional $11,000 in income per year. You invest the $100,000 in CDs paying 6% or $6,000 per year. The first year, you withdraw $5,000 of principal to add to your $6,000 of interest to get to your $11,000.

Well and good. But note what happens.

Next year you will have only $95,000 in CDs and thus they will pay only $5,700. You will have to *invade principal a tad more* next year. Not only that, you will *need more* money next year, thanks to inflation. As inflation has been running at slightly more than 3%, you will need $11,330 the next year (3%x $11,000 = $330). Thus, in year two, you will have to invade principle to the tune of a $5,630. (Remember, in year one, you only needed $5,000.)

In year three, your CD balance will be $89,370 (producing, at 6%, $5,362.20) and forcing you to now withdraw, given inflation, $6,307.70.

You get our drift—downward.

Because your principal is going down and your expenses are going up, soon your principal will be gone! Finished! Kaput! It is quite possible you will outlive it!

If you have $600,000 invested at 5.5% and must invade $17,000 a year, what with the dwindling principal and inflation fueling increased needs, you will go through the $600,000 in 14 years.

Because of this phenomenon and because people are living longer, many advise that you continue a somewhat *aggressive* investment plan, putting at least some of your money into stocks. Mutual funds can give both income and growth. Real estate, too, has proved a good hedge against inflation.

e. The Danger of Going for Broke: Stock Frauds

Some folks, realizing that they don't have much of a nest egg, put most of their savings into risky investments, hoping to make a killing. Don't. Because you no longer have an income stream, you may not be able to ride out bad turns in the market. Losses now may be permanent.

As Lincoln said (or maybe it was Yogi), it is better to spend down your principal over 14 years than it is to lose it in one.

Guard against stock fraud. You will get a call from a "broker," who will be a tad vague about how he got your name. He will tell you of a very hot stock out there, one which will greatly out-perform the market. Usually the stock is in a small company—which allows for price manipulation. Some of these people are very persistent and some are very friendly and understanding. Just don't do it! They are crooks!

f. Investment Options

Getting Investment Advice

Consider professional help in planning your finances, especially if you have investments of $100,000 or more. *Professional financial planners* are preferred: they work on a *set* or *hourly fee,* and not on a commission. Commissions tend to skew advice. Insurance agents, stock brokers, and bank advisors will naturally like their own products best. Dispassionate advice is better.

Overview of Options

Investment strategy turns on the issues of *growth (and risk)* versus *income (and safety)*. Here are some options.

a. Annuities

Annuities are essentially agreements by a financial institution to pay you a certain monthly amount over a certain number of years, or until you die. We have already met them in our discussion of private pension plans. See Chapter 3-d.

You can also buy annuities. If you have money in the bank and don't want the hassle of investing it, you can give it to a financial institution in return for its guarantee to pay you a yearly income as long as you live. (It is considered bad form for these institution to send you cigarettes at Christmas or Sky Diving Brochures on your birthday.) There are fixed-term annuities as well, those which pay you, not for life, but over a certain number of years. If you don't make it that long, your beneficiary will get the payments for the remainder of the term.

Annuities are a good, steady source of income. But they are only as secure as the company that issues them. Ask around. One problem with annuities is that you cannot get your money out to cover emergencies. Another is that fixed annuities eventually exhaust the principal.

b. CDs

Don't confuse these with those round, silver things teens buy to play their terrible music.

(Remember when it was we who played the terrible music?)

CDs (Certificates of Deposit) are essentially long-term savings accounts. However, unlike regular savings accounts, with a CD you are locked in for a certain period. Because of this, the bank knows it will have use of your money for a longer period, and will hence pay you more interest than it would on a regular savings account. CDs pay less than Annuities, however, as they do not consume the principal.

c. Stocks and Bonds

When a corporation needs money, it can either borrow it by issuing *bonds* or raise it by selling *stock*, an ownership interest in the corporation. From an investor's point of view, bonds are generally safer (a corporation must pay them before issuing dividends to stockholders). On the other hand, bonds generally pay less than stocks. The return on bonds is fixed at a certain percent, say 6%; stocks are ownership interests and, if the corporation does well, there will be healthy dividends and the value of the stock will go up. But then again, if the corporation does badly (or if the stock market crashes), the value of the stock falls. Stocks are risky.

The problem, however, with CDs and safe market investments is that while they guard the principal investment, they do not account for inflation. After a period of time, the purchasing power of the original investment will be less than it was originally.

Alas, investments that protect against inflation, such as stocks, are risky. You can lose most of your principal in a week or so.

We cannot leave the topic of finances without recounting one of our favorite stories.

The 1980s were the heyday of the junk bonds. "Junk bonds" are bonds issued by shaky corporations. Because they are riskier, they pay more interest. It was discovered, by some very clever people, that junk bonds paid more interest than their risk justified. That is to say, these corporations paid 2% higher interest than "Grade A" corporations, but their default rate was only 1% greater. In essence, investors buying junk bonds were getting more money on their investments than the risk they were taking justified.

The market was fierce and bond traders were making millions. One made over $400 million in one year. Two of his colleagues were discussing his success.

"The guy's nuts," one said. "If it were me, after I made ten million, I would retire."

"That's why it will never be you."

Chapter 5

House Rich, Cash Poor

Quite likely your house is worth a lot more today than when you bought it. Unless you bought in our neighborhood. But we digress.

It is likely that you own your home, mortgage free. Three out of four elderly households are owned; 82% of those are mortgage free.

How can you get money out of your house and into your pocket? There are three ways:

1. Sell it

Under recent federal law, you won't have too much worry about taxes on the gains you make selling your home. But by selling it, you lose the security of ownership and turn an exempt asset (one your general creditors and Medicaid can't touch) into a non-exempt one.

2. Rent or lease it

Talk to your insurance agent and make sure you have the right kind of insurance for renters. As to taxes, what you receive in rent is reportable income, but you will have deductions that will help. Be aware, however, that if you rent your house for a long period of time, you might lose favorable capital gain treatment if you then sell it.

3. Borrow against it

Here we meet the *Reverse Mortgage*. The Bank *pays you* a monthly amount. The balance of the loan (what the bank paid you plus interest) falls due at your death. At that time, the bank sells the house, gets its money, and gives the rest to your heirs.

There are other forms of borrowing against your house that have an obvious advantage: You get money out of your house and *you don't have to move*. But there are also substantial problems going this route.

This chapter will flesh out these points. In the next, we discuss general retirement housing concerns, from seeking warmer climes to moving to smaller digs. Before all of that, however, a few reminders.

a. Quick Reminders for Home Owners

- Check with local and state tax offices to see if *property tax breaks* are given to seniors. Often they are. (See Chapter 9.)
- Home owners are the frequent targets of scam artists. Protect yourself from *home repair fraud.* (See Chapter 16 on protecting yourself from common frauds.)
- *Never, ever,* sign any paper giving someone a security interest in your home unless it is for a loan from a bank, has affordable monthly payments and relates to home expenses, such as a new roof. Don't put your house at risk by borrowing money to go on a cruise.

b. The Pros and Cons of Selling Your Home

In the past a major problem in selling your home was that if you made a profit, capital gains taxes took a big bite. There is now great news! Since 1998, you can sell your home and there are no federal taxes on the first $250,000 of profit ($500,000 for married couples). However, you must have lived in the home for two of the last five years.

Even though taxes are no longer a major concern, there are still other legal issues associated with selling your house.

- Your home is generally an *exempt* asset; the money you receive from it isn't.

In most states, a *homestead,* a legal document, can be filed with the Office that deals with property title in order to protect your home from creditors (i.e. they cannot seize it and sell it). But once you sell your house and put the money into bank accounts or stocks, creditors can get it by obtaining appropriate court orders. (The folks who hold the *mortgage* on your house can go after it, even if it is homesteaded.)

- Most welfare programs, such as Medicaid, allow you to *keep* your home.

If Medicaid is a possibility, don't sell your house. You will be turning an exempt asset into one that can be taken.

c. Renting or Leasing Your Home

If you have ever been a landlord, this won't strike you as a happy choice. However, there are management companies that will do the hard work—collecting, making repairs, etc.

Rental income is taxable income. However, there are deductions. The costs of getting the place ready to rent, advertising, management fees, costs of repairs, and insurance are deductible. These, however, leave you at square one in terms of income. Yes, you can deduct these amounts, but you actually paid out this money.

The deduction that can leave you ahead is the *depreciation allowance.* Now that your house is income-producing, you can take a depreciation allowance which will offset some of the rent you receive. A depreciation allowance is given to income-producing property in the recognition that in 20 or 30 years it will wear out and must be replaced. In essence, the replacement cost is spread out over the life of the asset.

Assume the cost of a new store was $2 million. If the depreciation period is 20 years, then the owner can make a yearly deduction of $100,000 from current income ($100,000 x 20 years = $2 million).

Note that the store owner does not actually pay out the $100,000 each year, even though she can deduct it from other income. In this sense, taking depreciation allows you to come out ahead by taking deductions for money you have not actually paid out that year.

The downside to depreciation allowance is that the amount taken *lessens* the owner's *basis,* and thus, when it is sold, there will be a greater gain and hence higher capital gain taxes. Say that after twenty years, our store owner sells the store for $1 million. All of that would be a capital gain because the owner's basis is now zero.

But worrying about what will happen in twenty years isn't something that keeps most of us tossing and turning. If you are renting or leasing your home, talk to an accountant, or phone the IRS (1-800-829-1040) to learn more about taking depreciation. It gets a tad complicated but it is worth it.

Another downside to renting your house is that, to avoid capital gain taxes if you sell it, you must have lived in it at least two of the last five years.

d. Traditional and Reverse Mortgages

If you are having difficulty making ends meet, *don't* mortgage your home, at least without first seeing if you are eligible for *SSI*–Chapter 2-l, *Medicaid*–Chapter 8-b, or other income assistance programs. Mortgages should be your last alternative. They put your home at risk—fail to pay on time and you may lose it.

With *traditional mortgages* and the newer *Home Equity Accounts* (essentially a line of credit secured by a mortgage on your home), the bank advances you money and you pay it back. Such mortgages are harder to arrange once you have retired. Steely-eyed loan officers usually look to income flow.

One advantage of such loans, however, is that the amount you pay in interest is tax deductible. The amounts you pay in interest on credit cards, car loans, and other consumer purchases are not deductible. (You cannot deduct interest payments on home equity loans over $100,000, unless the money was for home improvement.)

Reverse mortgages are relatively new. They allow you to get money out of the house while you go on living there. The lender pays you a monthly amount or gives you a lump sum. This loan, together with interest, is not to be repaid until you move or die. Then the loan will be repaid out of the proceeds from the sale of the house. Any money left over will go as you direct.

At first blush, reverse mortgages are quite attractive. You stay in your home, get income, and don't have to pay it back for a long time. Go slowly! Reverse mortgages can be expensive. You may pay over $4,000 in loan fees. And the issues surrounding reverse mortgages are complicated. Must you pay taxes on the amounts you receive? How does the arrangement impact on eligibility for SSI and Medicaid? What happens if the amount of the loan is larger than the amount the house sells for?

Rather than try to answer these questions for you, we advise that you talk to a specialist in the area. To find one, contact your Area Agency on Aging or send $1 plus a self-addressed stamped business envelope to:

Preferred Reverse Mortgage Lender & Counselor List
NCHEC Preferred
7373 147th St Room 115
Apple Valley, MN 55124

Imaginative lenders, lawyers, and crooks have come up with other creative ways for you (and them) to get cash out of your house, such as *sale-lease backs* and *sale of the remainder interest in the house.* These are very complicated and have weird tax considerations. Talk to an accountant.

Be extremely cautious with "loan companies." Many are offering loans that you cannot afford, and they end up owning your home. If an offer sounds too good to be true—it is.

* * *

"Never talk with strangers" got us through childhood. From here on out, it's: "Okay, talk to them, but never give them a security interest in your house!"

Chapter 6

Retirement Housing

On a hill overlooking San Diego's beautiful Mission Bay, one house stands out. Rather than a lawn, there is a cement slab. Smack in the middle, sits a lawnmower, similarly cemented.

Retirement is a good time to rethink your housing situation. House too big? February too cold? Bathroom too dangerous? Lawn too thick?

In the early days of retirement, when everyone is healthy, there is the urge to move to warmer climates or even exotic lands. Most of us, however, stay put. Down the road our thoughts and plans must turn to matters of health:

- Getting help in the home or apartment
- Moving into an *assisted-living facility*

Note: the tax consequences of selling your house are discussed in the last chapter.

a. Moving to Warmer Climes

Golf, sunshine, and bridge. Not a bad combination, that. *Go slowly*. Many buy a new house in a retirement community only to find:

- that the retirement development is on shaky financial ground and that many of the promised benefits are in jeopardy;
- that they miss their friends and family and even the shrieks and laughter of the neighbor's kids; and
- that their slice is incurable and (as they always suspected) that their spouse compulsively overbids.

Trying to resell their new house, they find the bottom has fallen out. *Rent* in the new location before you buy. If you do, you will probably want to rent out your own house back home. In the previous chapter, we discussed some issues surrounding renting your house. Check with your insurance company to see if your home is covered for renters.

So, where to go?

Margaritaville has always appealed to us, but, alas, hangovers get worse.

David Savageau's *Retirement Places Rated* can provide you good information about different locales. Many move to such places as Mexico, Costa Rica, Canada, and Ireland where the cost of living is less. Check the quality of medical care, whether your insurance will pay (Medicare won't), and consider the cost of air fare back to the States.

b. Buying a New Home

Even if you are extremely active now, you may not be later. If looking for a new home, make sure it will accommodate possible disabilities. Are the hallways wide enough for a wheelchair? Is the house located near shopping? Medical facilities?

c. Staying Put (with a little help from our friends)

Most of us *stay put*. Make sure the house is *safe*. Consider grab bars in bathrooms, various alert systems, and turning down the thermostat on the water heater. Check with your Area Agency on Aging for community help in making repairs and improvements.

Medically required improvements: If you rent, federal law prohibits landlords from refusing to allow you to make medical improvements, as long as you agree to assume the cost of removing them when you leave. The cost of improvements which are *medically* required may be deductible. See Chapter 9.

As we age, it will become more difficult to manage things, but with just a little help, we will be able to get along just fine:

- *"Meals on Wheels"* and other forms of home services, such as minor repairs and upkeep, are provided by community and non-profit groups under the federal Older Americans Act of 1965. Check with your Area Agency on Aging.
- *Hospital beds* and other kinds of *medical equipment* can

be rented or purchased. Check with Medicare to see what they will pay for.

- *Home nursing* services are available. In a few circumstances, Medicare will pay. Otherwise you will have to look to your long-term care policy; many cover home care. Finally, if you must pay out of your own pocket, you may be entitled to deduct the expenses from your income taxes. See Chapter 9.

Sometimes children or other relatives move in to help out. There may be an understanding that, when you die, they will get the house. This might make a great deal of sense.

But *don't put the title in their names now!* If the house is in their names, their creditors might be able to reach it. And there are tax consequences. It is generally a *bad* idea to make a life-time gift of your home to your children (they will *not* get a stepped-up basis, and you may incur a gift tax). It is better to give it to them at the time of your death under your Will. See Chapter 20-f.

Rather than giving them the house now, you can make a formal contract. In return for described services, you promise to give them the property by your Will. To be enforceable, the contract must be in writing and signed by all parties. Best to see a lawyer.

Some folks, in return for occasional help, rent out part of their homes. Be careful in selecting the right tenant/helper: abuse and theft are always possible.

At some point you may decide that maintaining your own home is too much work. You might want to move to a facility where you don't have to do all the cooking and cleaning, and where there are new people to meet and new opportunities to explore.

d. Assisted-Living Facilities

The housing options for older persons are quite numerous, not only in size and location, but also in the level of support they offer. The questions, however, are the same.

What are the costs?
What are the conditions?
What programs and services are offered?
How much independence will you have?

Shop around, visit at least two, visit at different times of day, and talk to residents as well as officials. Your options run from essentially *boarding homes* and *assisted-living facilities* (apartments with various levels of support services), through the newer *continuing care retirement communities (CCRCs)*. CCRCs claim to provide extensive care, support, and nursing facilities on site. Many purport to guarantee care for life, first in an independent unit, then, if necessary, in the nursing or intermediate wing.

e. Continuing Care Retirement Communities (CCRCs)

Most assisted-living facilities charge by the month; others insist on a *buy-in*. Be careful buying in.

- Some have bought in with their life savings ($300,000 to $500,000), only to have the facility go broke.
- Others have bought in and died in the first year, with the facility keeping all of their money.
- Others have bought in while healthy and vital only to find, when they need it, that kinds of care they need are not covered in the contract.
- Others have found after ten or so years, that they want to move, but all of their money is tied up.

There are about 1,200 CCRCs nationally and there are *no* federal regulations. Some states regulate them. To get into such a facility, one must be in relatively good health, and often pay a hefty up front payment (from $300,000 to over $500,000 per person). There are set monthly fees and perhaps additional charges for nursing care.

Some points to consider:

- Treat the move as you would a major investment. Ask for an audited financial statement. Have your accountant review it. A guarantee of life-care is only good as long as the facility does not go bankrupt and as long as it maintains adequate beds in various levels of care.
- Once you buy in, it may be difficult to get your money back

if you don't like it. Before buying in, *hang out.* Ask other residents about the facility.

- Are the medical facilities and services up to what is advertised?
- Are there enough physicians? Are there long waits? Are specialists covered or must you pay for them yourself?
- What is the policy about moving residents into the nursing wing? There have been complaints that some facilities do so quickly, so that they can then sell the individual's apartment to someone else. Along these lines, what are the policies about the institution seeking guardianship over residents?
- If a spouse dies, must the survivor move into a separate single's unit? A forced move at this time can be traumatic.
- Will the facility take Medicare payments? Some will not.
- What is the refund policy? If you die relatively soon, do your heirs get any of the money back?

f. Section 8 Housing for Low-Income Individuals

If you are age 62 or older and have an income below the median in the area, you may be entitled to *"Section 8" rent subsidy* for certain independent facilities. Under it, you will pay only a certain percentage of your income as rent with the federal government picking up the difference.

g. For Further Information

The American Bar Association *Guide for Older Americans* has a nice checklist of questions concerning assisted living and continuing care facilities. It is published by Time Books, a division of Random House.

The American Association of Homes and Services for the Aging publishes *The Consumer's Directory of Continuing Care Retirement Communities.* 800-508-9442

http://www.aahsa.org.

The *AARP* has several publications:

Staying at Home
Selecting Retirement Housing
Housing Options for Older Americans
800-424-3410
http://www.aarp.org

And your local Area Agency on Aging can help too.

They might even know someone who will help you cement your lawnmower.

Chapter 7

Medicare and Health Insurance

Two prisoners sit on their bunks, lamenting life's vagaries. One sighs, "Well, I had a sneaky lawyer. But not sneaky enough."

What does this have to do with health insurance? In the heat of a trial, a lawyer will fire a question which is wildly besides the point—only to draw an angry objection:

"Objection, your Honor, Irrelevant!"
"I'll tie it up later, your Honor."

Not likely. But the promise usually satisfies the judge.

"Overruled."

As to our prisoner joke, we'll tie it up later.

Promise.

This chapter deals with health insurance. We begin by discussing insurance needs before you turn 65: disability insurance and COBRA insurance (if you retire early). Then we discuss insurance needs after you turn 65. You will be eligible for Medicare and, while it is a terrific program, it won't cover all of your needs. There are two parts to Medicare, Part A and Part B. Part B is optional. Most people keep it. Even if you do, you will need additional insurance. Maybe you will decide to buy a Medigap policy or join an HMO.

Don't buy dread disease insurance. We'll offer some other general tips on shopping for health insurance.

Long-term custodial care presents special problems. It is quite expensive, and few of the costs are covered by Medicare or traditional insurance. Our next chapter will focus on this problem.

This chapter is important, yet information-intensive (that is, boring). Candidly, we have already gone with our best joke (and it was irrelevant).

Before reaching 65, consider:

- Disability Insurance
- "COBRA" if you lose your employer's health coverage

After 65, consider three questions:

1. Should I keep Medicare Part B?
2. Should I join a senior HMO?
3. Should I purchase Medigap insurance?

Finally, whatever your age, consider long-term care insurance. (Chapter 8.)

a. Insurance Needs Before Age 65

Disability Insurance

A bad back at age 58 can prevent you from reaching retirement in good financial shape.

Don't rely on Disability under Social Security. Under Social Security, your disability must be severe and the payments will be small. Social Security pays only if you are unable to perform any gainful employment —such as cashier at a self-service gas station.

COBRA

"COBRA," like life itself, is full of sound and fury, signifying nothing. (Actually it signifies "Comprehensive Omnibus Budget Reconciliation Act"—which, in turn, signifies nothing.)

COBRA is the federal law that allows most folks (those working for employers with 20 or more covered workers) to continue their employer's health plan if they lose coverage because of early retirement or layoff. They can continue the policy for up to 18 months, but they must pay the premium (usually the same rate charged the employer plus a 2% administrative charge). This is known as Continuation Coverage.

If the first 18 months doesn't get you to the magical year of Medicare (65), you have a right to convert the policy but at a higher premium and with more restrictions. This is known as Conversion Coverage.

Professional organizations, service clubs, and the AARP offer group policies that will likely save you money.

If you had to retire because of disability, it may be possible to obtain COBRA coverage for longer than 18 months.

A related program protects you if you change jobs. The Health Insurance Portability and Accountability Act of 1996 (HIPAA) allows you to take your health insurance eligibility with you if you change employers. That means you cannot be denied coverage under your new employer's health plan. However, your coverage may not be with the same insurer.

b. Medicare: Eligibility and What Parts A and B Cover — and Don't Cover

Medicare is a marvelous program. The basic plan, Part A, covers most hospital costs. It has kept countless families from bankruptcy and has given millions more peace of mind: "If I get sick, at least I will not bankrupt my family."

With daily hospital charges ranging from $500 to $1,000 per day, this was a very real possibility.

To be eligible for Medicare, you must be 65 (or disabled or blind). In addition to being 65:

- You must be eligible for Social Security or, if you aren't,
- You are the spouse, widow, or widower of an eligible member. Ex-spouses, if married for more than ten years and not remarried, can also qualify. (See Chapter 2-f.)

If you don't fit into one of these categories, and are 65 or older, you can still purchase coverage. The current premium is $309 per month. This figure gives you some idea of how much insurance coverage Medicare provides.

While there may be reasons to put off taking your cash benefits from Social Security at age 65 (See Chapter 2-d), and while there may be reasons to delay signing up for Medicare Part B (see below), there is absolutely no reason not to sign up for Medicare Part A when you turn 65.

You should apply for Medicare through your Social Security Office three months before you turn 65.

Part A Coverage

Medicare Part A basically covers most hospital costs, many skilled nursing facility care costs, some home care costs, and hospice.

All of this gets quite technical and you will receive a booklet explaining the ins and outs—*Medicare and You*. But, for now, you don't need to know the details of what Part A covers; what you need to know is what it doesn't cover.

Medicare Part B Coverage

Medicare Part B covers some of the major gaps left by Part A, most notably doctor fees. It also helps with outpatient hospital services (including emergency room visits), ambulances, diagnostic tests, laboratory services, some preventive care such as mammography and Pap smear, outpatient therapy services, durable medical equipment and supplies, and a variety of other services. It also picks up some home health care services.

You pay a $100 deductible per year and 20% of the other charges. You may have to pay more if your doctor does not agree to accept Medicare approved limits on charges.

c. Should You Keep Medicare Part B?

When you sign up for Medicare, you will be automatically enrolled in Part B. You will pay a monthly premium, at this writing, $43.80 per month. It will be taken from your Social Security check. You can opt out of Part B coverage and save the premium. Should you?

First, realize that it is a great value. It has been estimated that this premium covers only about 25% of what you get in terms of benefits. It is, as they say, a very wise investment.

The only people who should consider opting out are folks who are covered by an employee health insurance policy, either their own or their spouse's. Ask the employer's benefits office how the health plan fits with Medicare Part B—if it duplicates Part B coverage, then decline Part B.

One reason to decline coverage, if you are covered by an employment plan, is that you save the monthly premium. Another is a tad more obscure. Once you start Part B coverage, you have six months to sign up for a Medigap policy. We will discuss these policies momentarily. For now, know that if you don't sign up in the first six months, you may end up with a policy that covers less and costs more. By opting out of Part B, you do not have to sign up for a Medigap policy until you lose your employment coverage. Hence you save those premiums as well.

However, don't try to outsmart Medicare by waiting to sign up for Part B until you get sick. You might be tempted to save money and pick up Part B only when you need it. This is known as adverse selection, like putting down your bet after the horses have crossed the finish line. Bureaucrats, whatever else you may think of them, weren't born yesterday. For every 12 months you delay in taking Part B coverage (unless it is because you are covered by an employee plan), you will pay a permanent premium increase of 10%.

Without being enrolled in Medicare Part B, you cannot join a senior HMO or participate in any of the new Medicare+Choice Programs.

Note: If you are low income, there may be state programs that will help you pay your Part B premium and some of Medicare's co-pays and deductibles. See section (f) of this chapter.

However, even with both Part A and Part B coverage, there are substantial medical costs that are not covered. We will first review those gaps and then point to your two options in filling some of them, buying a Medigap policy or joining a Senior HMO.

Services Medicare Does Not Cover

Neither Part A nor Part B covers long-term care, which can be a major expense (see Chapter 8). Unless you have Medicare Part B, doctors' fees will not be covered (and even with Part B, some routine care will not be covered). Prescriptions are likely to be a costly item and the news isn't good. Part A covers drugs while you are in the hospital but, after that, you are mostly on your own. Medicare Part B does not cover most prescription drugs. Neither Parts A nor B covers services not related to treatment of illness or injury, such as dental care or dentures, cosmetic surgery, routine foot care, hearing aids, eye exams or glasses.

Medigap policies, which we will discuss momentarily, can be purchased to cover some of the above items.

Except for certain limited cases in Canada and Mexico, Medicare does not pay for treatment outside of the United States.

The "Reasonable and Necessary" Exclusion

Even if a particular treatment or procedure is covered, Medicare can deny you coverage if it determines that, in your case, it is not "reasonable or necessary." While these denials can be appealed, keep this possibility in mind when you consider opting out of the traditional Medicare system and going with an HMO or Medicare+Choice program. We describe this choice in a moment. For now, keep the question in mind:

"Who is more likely to deny coverage on the basis that it is not 'reasonable or necessary'? The traditional program, an HMO, or Medicare+Choice program?"

There is no one answer to this question. You will have to get information on local conditions.

d. Should You Obtain Medigap Insurance?

As we have seen, there are many gaps in medical coverage, even if you have Part B. If you join a Medicare HMO, you will not need Medigap coverage. If you don't join an HMO, give thought to a "Medigap" or "Supplemental" policy.

Medigap policies are offered by private insurance companies. Under federal rules, the policies they offer must cover the same items. There are ten standard policies. Depending on the policy, they help pay Medicare deductibles and co-pays and other out-of-pocket medical costs.

Two factors may make these policies less of a bargain than they seem. First, many of the Medicare "gaps" that they cover are unlikely to occur. For example, under Part A, many of the co-pays kick in only after 60 days in the hospital and very few patients stay that long. Second, in general, they only cover what Medicare covers. That is, Medicare does not cover most nursing home costs; neither do Medigap policies. However, some Medigap policies offer coverage of prescription drugs, a major omission form Medicare coverage.

In shopping for Medigap policies, be clear as to what "gaps" are covered and whether it is likely you will ever need that coverage.

If you are going the Medigap route, however, sign up during the open enrollment for Part B (when you turn 65 or after 65 when you are no longer covered by an employer's health plan). The open enrollment is during the six months after you sign up for Part B. During it you can purchase any Medigap policy you wish. After that enrollment period, you may be stuck with the policy the insurance company is willing to sell you. The policy may make you wait six months for coverage of pre-existing conditions and may be more expensive.

There has been a lot of fraud associated with the selling of Medigap policies. The federal government does not "recommend" any particular policy or any particular company. If an agent tells you differently, he is lying. If you believe that you have been a victim of Medigap fraud, call the Medicare Hotline at 1-800-638-6833 or, for hearing impaired, 1-800-820-1202.

For more information, read *Guide to Health Insurance for People With Medicare*. You can get a free copy by calling 1-800-638-6833.

e. Should You Join a Medicare HMO? A Medicare + Choice Program?

If you stay with the traditional Medicare Program, Parts A and B, you will receive an insurance card and then go about arranging for your own doctors and treatments. Most doctors accept Medicare patients. You simply present your card and they will bill the private insurance organizations (Medicare carriers) which actually administer Medicare. You will be billed any co-pay.

Many Health Maintenance Organizations (HMOs) offer various programs for seniors. You receive basic coverage by assigning to them your Medicare Part A and Medicare Part B rights. When they provide you with a covered service, they bill Medicare.

In return, you receive all of the benefits you are entitled to under Parts A and B or Medicare. In addition, to get your business, most HMOs throw in some extras, perhaps some breaks on prescriptions, dental care, hearing aids, or eye glasses. They may charge small supplemental fees, say $5 a visit or prescription.

Be sure to read the small print concerning HMO extras as there may be substantial limitations. Some HMOs, for example, cover prescriptions but only up to $300.

Most HMO's will offer you additional coverage, but they will charge an additional premium. In this respect, they are like a Medigap policy, allowing you to purchase more coverage. Unlike a Medigap policy, however, HMOs restrict you to certain doctors and facilities.

The advantages of HMOs are:

1. *Expense*. An HMO program will probably be less expensive than purchasing comparable coverage from Medigap companies. This is because they are competing for your Part A and Part B coverage, and also because they will restrict you to certain providers. (With a Medigap policy you can go to any provider that accepts it. Again, if you are in an HMO, you will not need a Medigap policy.)
2. Coverage. HMOs can offer more complete coverage; with Medigap policies, there may be some procedures, such as routine checkups, that might fall through the cracks.
3. *Convenience*. Some HMOs maintain "full service" facilities. Relying on traditional Medicare supplemented with Part B and a Medigap policy, you have to make your own arrangements and may have to drive all over town. However, some HMOs have their providers scattered all around town, so convenience would not be a factor with them.

The disadvantages are those usually associated with HMOs:

In the comic movie *mafia*!, the Godfather has been shot 47 times. His son and the son's girlfriend come to visit. The Godfather is alone in his room, sleeping. The girl is shocked."Your father is dying. Where are his doctors? Where are the nurses?"

"He's in an HMO."

In an HMO you lose your right to select your own doctor and to consult a specialist without a referral. There are repeated allegations that HMO doctors must put costs before care.

Press this issue when discussing your options with any HMO provider.

Anecdotal evidence suggests that HMOs treat their senior members better than others because Medicare oversees the treatment of Medicare patients. It sets out precise guidelines concerning treatment and appeals.

If you feel you are not getting the care you should be getting, appeal.

Often decisions are reversed. Your HMO will have a set of written procedures for you to follow. Friends at your Area Agency on Aging can help.

You can only enroll in an HMO during a yearly enrollment period and, until December of 2001, you have the right to switch at any time to another HMO or go back to the traditional program. (Special rules apply for those with Medigap or employer-provided insurance.) In December 2001, there will be new restrictions on your ability to switch plans.

> In *mafia*! the Godfather survived (until coming to an even worse end). We never learned whether he stayed with the same HMO, one of the many serious flaws in the movie.

Medicare + Choice Plans

In 1997, Congress created additional health plan options, known as Medicare+Choice. They include:

HMOs with Point of Service Option. These will allow you to selectively go out of the HMO network to receive services, with higher out-of-pocket payments.

Preferred Provider Organizations. These are like an HMO. There will be a network of providers but you would be allowed to go outside it, and the plan will pay a percentage of the costs, with your picking up the remainder.

Provider-Sponsored Organizations. These are relatively new and work much like an HMO, except that they are formed by a group of hospitals and doctors who directly take on the financial risk of providing comprehensive health care benefits for Medicare beneficiaries.

Private Fee-For-Service Plans. These would allow you to elect a private indemnity-type plan, with Medicare paying the premium to cover traditional Medicare benefits. You would pay the additional premiums for the additional coverage you obtained. The idea here seems to be to provide for a "luxury" Medicare program for those willing and able to pay more.

Medical Savings Accounts. Up to 390,000 Medicare beneficiaries can participate in the demonstration project. You would choose a Medicare Plan with a high deductible; Medicare pays the premium with the "savings" deposited into your Medical Savings Account which you can use to pay the deductibles or to purchase services not covered under the policy.

These are the various plans that providers, if they wish, can offer. The early going indicates, however, that very few providers are creating these new programs and thus it is doubtful that all, or any, will be offered in your area in the near future.

How can you sort through your options? Should you stick with the traditional program (Parts A and B and maybe a Medigap policy), a traditional HMO, or should you join, if available, a new Medicare+Choice Plan? Some points to consider:

1. *Costs.* How much will you have to pay in premiums, deductibles and co-pays?
2. *Coverage.* Prescription drugs and hearing aids can be quite costly. Usually the more extensive the coverage, the higher the premium. However, as with all insurance, you don't want to pay for coverage that you will most likely never need. Often a good case can be made for self-insurance. For example, if you have enough money for a good hearing aid ($500 to $2,000—see Chapter 26-d), you might not want to buy insurance that will buy it for you if the yearly premium is high and you think your chances of needing a hearing aid are low. Don't simply buy the highest price policy because "it's there."
3. *Choice.* Usually the more choice a plan provides in terms of doctors and hospitals, the more you will pay. How important is it to you to have the right to select your own doctor and your own specialists?
4. *Compassion.* If you need an expensive operation, which program is most likely to approve it? This will be hard to know in advance, but push any program you are considering to respond to this concern. They have heard it before.
5. *Second thoughts.* In December 2001 it will become more difficult to switch from one plan to another. Be sure to factor this into your decision.

For what it is worth, it has been our experience that if you are healthy, HMOs offer good care at a smaller cost. However, if you are sick or are likely to be sick, then the traditional program has the advantage because you have greater choice as to specialists and because Medicare carriers (the people who approve traditional Medicare charges) are often more generous than HMO administrators.

Things may be different in your area or with the new Medicare+Choice options. Talk to as many people as you can. For more Medicare Information:

www.Medicare.gov
Social Security 1-800-772-1213
Your State Health Insurance Counseling Program
Your Area Agency on Aging

Note: if you have medical expenses which are not covered by insurance, they may be deductible from your taxes. See Chapter 9.

f. Help for Low-Income Folks

If you are of low income and limited resources, your state may have a program which pays some of your Medicare costs, including premiums, deductibles, and co-insurance.

- You income must be at or below poverty guidelines.
- You cannot have resources such as bank accounts or stocks worth more than $4,000 (for one person) or $6,000 (for a couple). Your home and car don't count.

Even if your income is slightly above the poverty guideline, you may get help paying your Part B premium. Contact your local welfare office or Medicaid agency. The names of the programs are "Qualified Medicare Beneficiary," "Medicare Buy-In Program," "Specified Low-Income Medicare Beneficiary," and the "Qualifying Individual Program."

If you have young children in your care, ask about your State's Child Health Program to help pay for their medical care.

g. Dread Disease Insurance

One of the basic rules in buying insurance is not to buy double coverage. That is a very real possibility with "Dread disease" insurance, policies covering such things as cancer. Be *very cautious* here. With Medicare, Parts A and B, you may very well have all the insurance you need. For example, people with cancer seldom spend more than sixty days in the hospital, an amount of time covered by Medicare.

Before purchasing any such policy, ask the agent:

1. What expenses does it cover that are not covered by Parts A and B of Medicare?
2. What percentage of people with the disease actually incur those otherwise uncovered costs?
3. Typically, what is the dollar amount of the otherwise uncovered costs?

If you have any questions as to the company, call your State Insurance Commissioner.

h. Some Tips on Buying Insurance

In 1991 *Consumer Reports* sent an investigative reporter to fourteen insurance sales agents. The reporter posed as a relative of an older person seeking a long-term care policy. The results were sobering: lies, ignorance, and violations of ethical standards and state laws. Every agent misrepresented some aspect of their policy, and no agent explained all the benefits and restrictions correctly.

Of course, in 1991, long-term care insurance was relatively new, which might explain some of these shocking and quite disappointing findings. Nonetheless, do not automatically believe what an insurance agent tells you, either about his policy or that of a competitor. Be aggressive. If the agent tells you something about the policy, have the agent point to the language in the policy itself.

1. Contact at least two companies and compare coverage and premiums.

2. Check limitations on *pre-existing conditions* (usually defined as those that required a doctor's visit within the last six months).
3. Avoid buying double coverage. (Anyone who sells you a policy in violation of various anti-duplication laws may be criminally and civilly liable. Call 1-800-638-6833 the Medicare Hotline to report suspected violations.)
4. Compare policies in terms of maximum benefits (dollar amounts per treatment or number of days of care).
5. Know whom you are dealing with. Check with your state insurance department to make sure the company is licensed. Ask to see the agent's license as well—a business card is not a license.
6. Don't lie on the application or "conveniently forget things," even if the agent tells you it is fine to do so. If you lie, the company can cancel your policy rather than pay on it.
7. Don't pay cash. Write a check payable to the insurance company, *not* to the agent. Get a receipt with the company's name, address, and telephone number.
8. Take your time. Legitimate sellers will not pressure you to decide today.

Finally, don't fall victim to consumer scams in this area. A common one is to represent that a policy is endorsed or recommended by the government. Another is to send out letters that look like they come from government agencies. If you think you have been a victim, call the Medicare Hotline (1-800-638-6833).

So that is that. In the next chapter we discuss the problem of long-term custodial care.

Before we leave the general topic of health care, be aware that there are a lot of consumer fraud in the marketing of "alternative medicines." We discuss this in Chapter 16-b.

As to the prisoner joke, like all good trial lawyers we are counting on you forgetting our promise to tie it up later. Maybe later. Much later.

Chapter 8

Long-Term Custodial Care

Long-term nursing home care can bankrupt. The average cost ranges from $40,000 to $80,000 per year. Stays of five years or longer are possible. Be forewarned: Medicare, even supplemented by Medigap policies, covers only a small portion of nursing home costs. This is a particular problem for women. Men are more often cared for at home, and women live longer.

Long-term care insurance is available. And once a family has exhausted its own resources, Medicaid is available. We'll discuss both.

Note: If your family is currently paying large nursing home bills, they may be deductible from Federal Income Tax. See Chapter 9-b-3.

a. Long-Term Care Insurance

This insurance is tricky. Help is available. All states regulate long-term care insurance, and all have free or low-cost insurance counseling programs. Contact your Area Agency on Aging or call

Eldercare Locator (1-800-677-1116).

There is also *A Shopper's Guide to Long-Term Care Insurance*, put out by the National Association of Insurance Commissions. It even has a worksheet. Check with your library or Area Agency on Aging.

Long-term insurance may not be for you. Like all forms of insurance, it's a gamble. Maybe you will never go into a nursing home—most people don't. Estimates vary. According to a 1991 article in the *New England Journal of Medicine*, if you are 65 now, the changes of your being in a nursing home are:

Length of Stay	*Men*	*Women*
Never	67%	48%
Less than a year	19%	21%

1 to 5 years	10%	18%
More than 5 years	4%	13%

You may be rich enough to be self-insured. Or poor enough not to care. The latter sounds a bit cruel, but the truth is that insurance protects your estate from being devoured by nursing home costs before you turn to *Medicaid*. If you don't have a lot to be devoured, then you don't need insurance. As we shall see, you won't lose everything.

Assuming you are in the market for insurance, the earlier you start, the lower the premium and the better the coverage. Also, if you wait until your 60s or 70s, a medical condition may lead the company to deny you. A problem with "early shopping," though, is that policies will be canceled for non-payment of premium. If you are buying now, be sure you can afford the premiums over the long haul. And, of course, the earlier you begin paying, the longer you will pay.

To give you some idea of costs, a policy today at age 55 is around $1,500 per year.

Make sure the policy is guaranteed, and that the premiums will not increase. Other desirable features in such policies include:

- Protection against inflation.
- Coverage of all levels of nursing care (skilled, intermediate, custodial).
- Home and assisted care coverage.
- Low deductibles and not-too-difficult prerequisites—such as hospitalization.
- At least one year maximum benefit period, preferably at least three years.
- Coverage of Alzheimer's disease and other dementia.
- A forgiving pre-existing conditions limit—no longer than six months.

You might also want to glance at our list of points concerning buying insurance. See Chapter 7-h.

b. Safety Net of Medicaid: Medicaid Planning

Our worst nightmare: waking up sick and alone, in a dirty back alley. Medicaid protects you. You will not be left on the streets.

In 1965, Congress passed Medicaid. This program is designed to be a health-care safety net for the poor. It provides a full range of benefits, from doctors' bills to hospitalization. It *will* pay for custodial (nursing home) care.

Medicaid is for the poor, for those who cannot afford to pay for their own care. Live long enough, however, and you may become poor, especially if you are paying $3,000 to $6,000 a month for your nursing home care. Some members of the middle-class, in order to make themselves eligible for Medicaid, take steps so that they become legally "poor."

Books have been written. Lawyers specialize. Critics fume! "Medicaid was designed to help poor people, not subsidize the middle class."

Fortunately, this is not a book of legal ethics.

Realize, if you are considering this route, being a Medicaid patient in a nursing home probably means low-end service with few services. Your nursing home and physician will be selected for you. Generally it is better to pay your own way if you can, with savings or insurance. However, given that there are case managers who overlook Medicaid patients, some believe that they get better care than paying patients.

To be eligible for Medicaid support, you can't have too much income, or too many assets. If you do, you must "spend down." Does this mean you lose everything? No.

- There are exempt assets (usually your home, your car, and personal items).
- Your spouse is obligated to pay for some of your care, but he or she will not be left destitute. There are property and income exemptions.
- Your children are *not* obligated to repay Medicaid. As to your children's obligation to support you, see Chapter 12-d.

How can you make yourself eligible while preserving your estate?

Convert nonexempt assets into exempt assets.

All that fancy language means is "Turn in your Saving Bonds and buy a fancy house."

Put your assets in trust.

This method is risky and will only work if you make the trust irrevocable, and put in the assets more than five years before you need to go on Medicaid. Otherwise the state will penalize you by delaying your eligibility. The delay can be substantial.

Give your assets to your kids.

This will work only if the gifts are made more than *three* years before you need to go on Medicaid. Gifts within the three-year period will cause a delay in your eligibility.

There is a quirk in the law. If you apply for Medicaid within 36 months of making a gift, you will not be eligible to receive benefits for a period of time, and the more the gift, the greater the length of time of non-eligibility. This eligibility period can easily extend *beyond* the 36 month period. However, if you don't apply for Medicaid until 36 months *after* giving the gift, there is no delay on your eligibility.

Put excess income in trust to be paid to Medicaid.

At least 22 states have income limits on Medicaid. Say the income limit for a couple is $3,000 per month. A couple has income of $3,200 a month. The husband must be put in a nursing home. It charges $2,800 monthly. Ineligible for Medicaid (because their income exceeds the limit), the wife must now live on $400!

Medicaid law will now allow this couple to put $200 per month in trust to be paid to Medicaid and thus bring down their income to make them eligible. Once eligible, the wife will be allowed to retain a substantial portion of the $3,000 monthly income for her own use.

Planning concerning Medicaid is a tricky business, and often turns on specific state laws. Mistakes can be quite costly. Do not to attempt it on your own. Seek legal advice.

For a referral, contact the National Academy of Elder Law Attorneys, 1604 N. Country Club Road, Tucson, Arizona 85716 (520-881-4005). www.NAELA.org.

Chapter 9

Tax Breaks, Taxes on Pensions and Mark McGwire's Home-Run Ball

Taxes are certain...and *complicated.* Here we flag some tax benefits you may be overlooking. For specific questions:

- Call the IRS. 1-800-829-1040 (Ed. note: Cute, "1040," very cute!) http://www.irs.ustreas.gov
- See an accountant. Fees paid for tax advice and help are deductible.

a. If Your Children Are Supporting You

If your children are supplying more than one-half of your support, they may be entitled to significant tax breaks. They may be able to claim you as a dependent (and thus get an additional *dependency exemption),* and may also be able to claim head of household status (and thus increase their *standard deduction* as well as taking advantage of the *head- of-household* tax rate). Finally, if you have substantial medical expenses, they might be able to deduct some of them.

b. Federal Tax Benefits

Let's define some terms and show their impact on your tax bill. *Deductions* reduce your taxable income. They reduce your tax bill, but not by the full amount, only by the amount that would have been taxed had the amount been included. Assume you are paying taxes at the 28% level: a $700 deduction will translate into a tax savings of $196 (28% of $700).

Exemptions work the same way. If some of your income is exempt, it need not be reported and hence will not be taxed.

Tax credits are better (and rarer). They reduce taxes dollar for dollar: a tax credit of $500 would reduce your tax bill by $500.

What federal tax rules might be of most interest?

1. Standard Deduction

Turning 65 entitles you to an additional amount if you are taking a standard deduction and *not itemizing* deductions. Additional amounts can be taken if the taxpayer is blind.

2. Personal Exemptions

Regardless of age, every taxpayer is entitled to a personal exemption. In 1998, it was $2,700. This exemption is not increased at 65 nor for blindness. You can take this exemption whether you itemize or not.

3. Medical Expense Deduction

If you have *significant* medical expenses for yourself, your spouse, or a dependent, some may be deductible. *You must itemize to take them.* Medical expenses not compensated by insurance are deductible *in excess of* 7.5% of adjusted gross income. This is the major limitation; most people never get up that high.

And what counts toward that 7.5%?

- the costs of medical care including "diagnosis, care, mitigation, treatment, or prevention of diseases . . . affecting any structure or function of the body." This includes medicine, prescription drugs, medical transport, glasses, seeing-eye dogs, artificial teeth, and artificial limbs.
- the costs of *medically required home improvements,* prescribed by a physician to the extent their cost exceeds the increased value they give the house. For example, if a $1,500 elevator or therapy pool increases the value of the home $600, then $900 would be counted as a medical expense. (The $600 would be added to the basis of your house and thus, when it is sold, would not represent a capital gain.)

- the costs of nursing homes can be included, but only if the primary reason was medical care, as opposed to custodial care. This is generally not a difficult deduction to make since medical care is arguably a major component of any nursing home stay.
- a portion of long-term care insurance premiums.

4. Tax Credits Concerning Disability

A tax credit is available to folks 65 and older or those under 65 who are retired on permanent and total disability. The amount is 15% of the taxpayer's "section 22 amount" and its calculation defies easy description. Just be aware of it, discuss it with your accountant, or look for it on your 1040.

5. Interest Deductions

Interest you pay on your home mortgage (and home equity loan) is deductible. Other kinds of interest payments, such as on credit cards or store accounts, are generally not deductible.

6. Home Taxes

Many states give taxpayers over 65 a break on property taxes. In terms of federal taxes, if you are still paying for your house, that portion of your payment that represents interest payments continues to be deductible. The cost of home improvements is not deductible unless they were medically required (see the discussion of "medical expense deduction" above). However, keep records as to home improvements as their cost can be added to the amount you paid for your house to figure its basis. What this means is that if you sell your house for more than you paid for it, you can deduct from your gain the cost of home improvements. This is less important than it used to be in light of the next point.

Capital Gain Taxes from the Sale of Your Residence

Since 1998, you can sell your home and pay no federal taxes on the first $250,000 of profit ($500,000 for married couples). This exemption requires that you have lived in the home for at least two of the prior five years.

Reverse Mortgage Payments

In Chapter 5-d, we discussed how you might get cash out of your home's equity without selling it. The most popular way is the reverse mortgage. The monthly payments are not taxable as they are really loans to you.

7. Exempt Income

Money you receive from certain sources or for certain reasons need not be included in your gross income. Here we list some of the most common:

Inheritance and gifts. (If you start earning interest on them, the interest is taxable.)

Compensation for physical injury or illness through insurance, judgments, or Worker's Compensation.

Public assistance benefits.

Interest on some government bonds.

Veteran's benefits.

Social Security. Generally about 50% of your Social Security payments are taxed. The exact percentage will turn on the amount of other income you have.

Earnings on criminal activity are not exempt from income taxes. Al Capone learned this the hard way. This puts criminals in something of a bind. Report your income, the IRS turns you in and you get arrested. Don't report your income, the government need not show that you committed any specific crime, only that you had a lot of income and didn't report it. The IRS allows individuals to file numbered returns. If they then get caught with large amounts of cash, they can point out that they were at least paying taxes on it.

c. State and Local Taxes

Almost all states offer older citizens tax breaks in one or more areas: sales tax, income tax, or property tax. Because of the wide range of these plans, we advise you to contact your accountant or the agency in your state that is responsible for collecting taxes.

d. Taxes on Pensions, Annuities, and IRAs

"Dollars will be taxed just once, But once for sure!"

If the money you put into your retirement plan was tax deductible at the time of contribution, your retirement benefits will be treated as regular income when you receive it. Money going into most pension plans is deductible, as is money going into traditional IRAs. When the money comes out, it is taxed.

However, if the money that goes into the retirement plan was not tax deductible at the time, then when *that* money is returned to you, it is not taxed. This is because you already paid taxes on those dollars before they went into the retirement account. When you get the interest earned on those dollars, though, it is taxed as regular income.

To illustrate this, let's take the example of an annuity. Say you have $100,000 and don't want the trouble of investing it. You can buy an annuity. For your $100,000, a bank will promise to pay you a certain monthly amount over the next several years. Because it will have the use of your $100,000 from Day One, it will pay you interest. Assume that at the end of the annuity, it will have paid you $150,000. (Don't go to sleep!)

As to each payment, two-thirds will be return of capital (and not taxed), and one-third will be the interest earned (and taxable).

The new Roth IRA is a bright and shining exception to the rule "dollars will be taxed at least once." Money coming out of Roth IRAs that represents earnings on contributions is *not* taxed. See our discussion at Chapter 4-c.

e. Mark McGwire's 70th Home-Run Ball: A Jurisprudential Quandary

In the fabulous 1998 baseball season, Mark McGwire broke Roger Maris's home-run record. There was great interest as to the tax implications for the fan who caught the record- breaking ball. Now, admittedly, this discussion is not directly relevant to the tax problems most of us face. It does, however, raise the interesting problem of how general rules impact specific situations. Bear with us.

"Income" is defined broadly in the Internal Revenue Code. Like Willie Mays, it catches just about everything: paychecks, capital gains, winnings and, yes, even the valuable objects you find. Thus, if you were the "lucky fan" who caught that ball, you would have a big tax problem. You would have received income in the amount of the fair market value of the ball, several million dollars. You would owe, what, $500,000 or so in income taxes!

Assume with more banker than poet in your soul, you quickly gave the ball to the loudmouth who was sitting next to you, the guy who, after spilling his beer on your shoes, claimed it was your fault and demanded that you to buy him another one. What then?

Have you exacted sweet revenge while avoiding a major tax problem? No. In addition to income taxes, you would have to pay *gift* taxes (amounts you give away over $675,000 are subject to a stiff tax).

The good news is the guy next to you won't owe a nickel!

Shifting from sports to jurisprudence, this story illustrates a major dilemma in law. Legal rules must be general to work at all. But general rules often lead to ridiculous results, as our unhappy fan would attest. This is a central problem in law—the desire to have general laws which promote uniformity and the desire to do justice in the individual case.

Take mandatory criminal sentences. There was a problem that judges might sentence individuals who had committed the same crime to different prison times. It is unfair, if you commit assault, to be sentenced to four years by Judge B but only two years had you been sentenced by Judge A. To solve this problem, state legislatures passed "mandatory sentencing laws," listing, by crime, the penalty the judge must give. For example, armed robbery—five years without parole.

But sometimes "armed robbery" shouldn't bring 5 years without parole.

A slightly retarded 18 year old enters his neighborhood convenience store, where he is known, gets a six-pack of Bud, discovers he has no money, asks the clerk for credit, and, when he doesn't get it, takes out his pocket knife and walks out. Half an hour later, when the police arrive, he is arrested in the parking lot, drinking the beer.

What he did fits the definition of armed robbery. He is now doing five years in the state penitentiary. Without parole.

To return to happier topics, when Mark McGwire broke the record, a young grounds-keeper for the St. Louis Cardinals got the ball. Later, in a breathtaking display of bureaucratic good sense, the IRS did not bill him.

And, in one of the shining moments of the twentieth century, during the celebration following the home run, the young man got on the stage with McGwire, and handed him the ball.

"Mr. McGwire, I have something that belongs to you."

Part Two

Family Concerns

Chapter 10

On the Limits of Law

The chapters that follow deal with family problems—raising grandchildren, financial dealings between family members, divorce and remarriage, and abuse and neglect.

Of course, there will be laws; there will always be laws.

We begin, however, with this short cautionary chapter, with a warning of the dangers of using lawyers and the law to solve family problems. Mediation and counseling promise much better results for you and for your family.

The law isn't good at resolving family conflicts. Lawyers work best in a world of strangers, where they can snarl questions, point fingers, and stamp feet. When the dust settles, strangers pay up and go home. Scars mend or are forgotten.

Kin never walk away; kin are for the long haul.

Lawyers are good in that small portion of the universe where people "start it"—where they run red lights, deliver defective widgets, and pull hair triggers. No one ever "starts it" in the family. Sure, Sis did hit us first, but in our hearts of hearts, we know we pushed her to it with our cruel taunts (which, of course, she richly deserved for what she said last week).

We are a society of *rights*. Individual rights are critical; without them, others would push us around and we would never be safe from bullies. *But a society based solely on rights is likely to fly apart.* Long ago there was a great legal reform movement in China: the laws should be written down so people could know them.

Who could argue with that? The followers of Confucius. If people know their rights, they argued, they will *insist upon them*. They will no longer compromise nor consider the interests and needs of others. Happy societies, and happy families, need compromise and compassion.

In fights with family members, and indeed with neighbors, the question is not who is right according to the law. The question is how the fight can be resolved so as to restore peace. Counselors and mediators, trained in conflict resolution, can help you redirect focus from what happened in the past to what will happen in the future, from casting blame to sharing credit.

And the *earlier* you seek this kind of help, the more effective it can be.

To get counseling and mediation help, a good place to start is by calling your local Domestic Relations Court. Your Area Agency on Aging may have ideas as well.

Chapter 11

Grandchildren

Consider this. After all the years, after all the work, after all the bruises and alarm clocks, after all our successes and failures, it has finally become our time, our time to be that quiet old lady, whispering "Hush."

The nuclear family—Mom, Dad, 2.3 kids—making its happy way in the new suburb, with moments of high humor and mild dangers, was probably more fiction than fact. In any event, we are witnessing the return of the extended family. It's about time. Grandparents have a lot to offer. With young mothers working, high divorce and teen pregnancy rates, grandparents are now critical. Many have assumed the role of parents; others give extended care during summers and periods of family crisis.

At the other end of the spectrum, some grandparents are cut out of their grandchildren's lives entirely. Do they have a legal right to visit?

We begin this chapter discussing grandparent visitation rights, and then we turn to the legal problems triggered by *Kinship Care*—when a grandparent (or other relative) takes over raising the child. We also have some advice if your grandchild is staying with you only for the summer. Then we will discuss what you should do if you suspect your grandchild is being abused or neglected. We close with a list of events that might trigger a trip to the lawyer.

Because these topics often involve family conflicts, we hope you didn't skip the last chapter—it's very short!

a. Visitation Rights

Since the 1970s there has been a major change in grandparent visitation rights. The law previously allowed parents the absolute right to refuse visits; grandparents were at their whim. Now all 50 states allow grandparents to *petition* the court for visitation rights.

The right to petition doesn't mean you will win. Courts are reluctant to get involved in family disputes, and under the laws of most states, grandparents cannot obtain visitation rights if the nuclear family is intact—that is, if the biological parents are still together and both agree on denying visits.

If you are denied visitation, first try to figure out why. Maybe the parents think you are too critical of the way the child is being raised. Maybe you gossip too much. Perhaps there are old family issues that have not been resolved. Don't just assume that you are in the right and threaten lawsuits.

If you were the child's parent, why would you be denying visitation? Is there anything you can do to make things right?

Granted, self-righteous anger is sweet. But your grandchildren need you. Swallow pride. Both sides must compromise and understand the needs and interests of the other. Counseling and mediation help. However, the threat of a lawsuit might convince a reluctant parent to take part.

State laws govern grandparent visitation, and they differ in substantial ways. They usually require a showing of two things: that visitation is in the *best interests of the child*, and that the family situation is *dysfunctional* in certain defined ways, such as a divorce or unreasonable refusal of visitation over several months. If matters get this far, contact a lawyer to discover the specifics of your state law.

Grandparent visitation rights suffered a setback recently. In late 1998, the Florida Supreme Court found certain portions of that state's grandparent visitation law unconstitutional. The case involved a toddler whose mother had died of cancer. The father refused the maternal grandparents visitation. A lower court ordered visitation but the higher court reversed, finding that the order unconstitutionally infringed on the father's privacy rights.

The case applies only to court-ordered visitation in the event of the death of a parent. It apparently leaves intact other portions of the statute that allow for visitation orders in cases of divorce and desertion. Further, it is unclear how far reaching this decision will be. Already an appellate court in Arizona has refused to follow it and has held court-ordered grandparent visits constitutional.

If your grandchild is adopted by strangers, what happens to your visitation rights? Courts struggle. There is a strong argument that there should be a clear break between the birth and adoptive families: grandparent visitation may undermine the authority of the adoptive parents. On the other hand, there is a strong argument that the significant relationships in a child's life should continue.

The general rule, however, favors the adoptive parents. This is clearest when the child is quite young, when neither the child nor the grandparents have formed strong emotional ties. This is less definite in the case of older children, where close ties with grandparents exist. Some courts, notably those in California and New York, have ordered grandparent visits even in the face of adoption by strangers. Given these exceptions, and a general movement away from secrecy and toward "open adoptions," if you are about to lose your grandchild in an adoption, talk with an attorney. The law may be moving in your direction.

b. Kinship Care: Raising Grandchildren

Handing out candy and letting the kids stay up late are only part of the job. While grandparenting is richly rewarding, it can also be tricky and tough. There are books and groups that can help. The AARP has a Grandparent Information Center.

What are the legal issues?

One issue may concern housing. Some landlords may threaten to evict if a grandchild moves in, and some "adult communities" have rules against children. If you find yourself threatened, try to work things out. Although your landlord may threaten eviction, eviction costs money, and it may be hard for him to re-rent your place. If your landlord refuses to compromise, talk to a lawyer. Some state and local laws may prohibit housing discrimination against children and, if you are renting, your lease may not give your landlord the right to evict in this situation.

But housing isn't the major legal issue. The major issue you will face stems from the fact that *physical custody is not legal custody.*

Legal custody is that bundle of rights needed to raise a child: the legal right to determine where he or she lives, what he or she wears, with whom he or she plays, where he or she goes to school and church, and what medical treatment he or she receives. Just because you have *physical* custody of a child, that *does not mean* that you have *legal* custody, the right to make those decisions. Legal custody remains with the child's parents, until and unless you are given it.

Not having legal custody can lead to problems—doctors may insist on a parent's consent to a medical treatment, and school and welfare officials might also require it. If the child's stay with you is to be temporary, say over the summer or until the parents can relocate, then a *Parental Power of Attorney* should suffice. Signed by the child's parent, it will give you power to act in the parent's stead in relation to medical and educational decisions. Even a letter, signed by parent, is better than nothing:

> *To whom it may concern:*
>
> *I am the parent of __________ who will be staying with her grandparents, __________, this summer. I give them the right to consent to any and all medical treatment for my child.*
>
> *Signed (and better still, notarized)*

Things become much more complicated if your grandchildren are living with you more or less permanently.

> *Nancy, 22 and unwed, leaves her six-month-old baby with her parents "until she can work things out." She has an irregular work history, a minor drug problem, and a scuzzy boyfriend.*

Our advice to the grandparents: *consider steps to get permanent legal custody, including adoption.*

We have seen tragic instances where children have been torn from the loving warmth of their grandparents' home. Nancy suddenly reappears and picks up the child, insisting "This time I will make a go of it." Young children need love and *permanence.* Raise your grandchildren without legal custody, and both you and the children will be hostage to the whims of the parent.

A general Power of Attorney does not guarantee permanence. It can always be revoked by the parent.

What about adoption?

If you adopt your grandchild, it need not be forever in the sense that if the parent gets her act together, you can return physical custody to her. Without adoption, however, it is her choice; with adoption, it is yours.

Parents can always agree to allow their child to be adopted by others. If you go that route, realize that the father, if known, will have to be notified. He may intervene and attempt to get custody himself. If this is a real possibility, then you might wish to back off from the adoption since the father, married or not, has a stronger legal claim to his child than do grandparents.

If Nancy and the father do not consent to the adoption, it probably won't happen. Before a parent loses parental rights, it must be shown that he or she is *legally unfit*. At this point in our story, Nancy is not. However, if she does leave the child and has only infrequent contact thereafter, it is possible that a court might sever her parental rights on that basis (abandonment). This allows for adoption over her objections.

Some states have passed legislation authorizing *permanent guardianships*. These are easier to obtain than adoption. They do not require severing parental rights. They give permanence to the guardian relationship. In order to terminate the guardianship, the court would have to be persuaded by the parents that termination is in the child's best interests. (Again, if all you have is a Power of Attorney, the parent can terminate it at any time, for any reason, without going to court.)

If you adopt, you have all the rights and obligations of a parent, including the legal duty to *support* the child until he or she reaches the age of 18 or is emancipated. In some states, for low income individuals, an adoption subsidy is available to help offset some of the expenses.

c. Financial Help in Raising Grandchildren

If you adopt the child, he or she will be entitled to your Social Security benefits as would any of your children. Even without adoption, however, your dependent grandchildren (over 18 if disabled) may be entitled to benefits. The rules are complicated, so call your Social Security Office and explain your situation to them. Concerning the family benefits of Social Security, see Chapter 2-f. See also our discussion of safety nets (Chapter 2-l) and possible help in paying for medical insurance for children (Chapter 7-f).

Adoption support payments may be available for low income families.

You might be able to run down other sources of financial help by contacting your local welfare office or Area Agency on Aging. Welfare and other programs may be available even if you do not have legal custody.

Check with the I.R.S. concerning whether you can claim a child as your dependent and look into the *Earned Income Tax Credit* (EIC), which is a special benefit for low- and moderate- income people, including those raising grandchildren, even if they don't have legal custody. This program provides a cash payment even if you don't owe taxes.

Note: If you are raising your grandchild under a court order as a foster parent, you may be entitled to federal payments for foster care under Title *IV-E* of the Social Security Act. These payments are substantially higher than welfare payments.

d. Abused and Neglected Children

If you suspect that a child is in immediate physical danger, call the police. If you think that a child is being seriously neglected or abused, call the local Child Protective Services Agency to discuss your concerns.

All reports are confidential.

Every state has special courts, usually called Juvenile or Family Courts, which deal, not only with juvenile *delinquency* (crime), but also with child *dependency* (neglected and abused children). Typically a state agency initiates dependency actions. If, after a hearing, the court finds that a child is neglected or abused, it will declare the child *dependent,* a ward of the court. The court might then allow the child to remain at home and simply order the parents to undergo counseling or parenting courses. In more extreme cases, the child will be removed from the home and placed in a foster home or in the home of a relative, such as a grandparent. In extreme cases, the court will sever the parents' parental rights and the child will be placed in a permanent foster home or for adoption.

Let's assume abuse or neglect of a less serious nature. As grandparents, your first step is to think how you can help. But go gentle—offers of help may be mistaken for meddling.

Parenting is hard work. Taking the kids for the weekend may do wonders. There are many sources of help, from Parenting Classes, offered both privately and by local schools, to Parents Anonymous which offers support groups for abusive parents. These kinds of help can be found by calling Information and Referral Agencies.

e. When to Seek Legal Advice

The laws in this area are changing quite rapidly and all are moving toward greater recognition of the importance of grandparents in a child's life. Because of this flux, we recommend that you see a lawyer to discuss any concerns you might have in the following situations:

1. Death of the surviving parent.

When one parent dies, the survivor automatically assumes legal and physical custody of the child, even if there has been a prior divorce which gave custody to the other parent. (This is not necessarily so in the case of an unwed father.) When the surviving parent dies, the Probate Court must appoint a guardian for the child (otherwise there will be no guardian). Usually, but not always, the court will follow the parent's wishes as described in his or her Will.

Encourage your children to nominate guardians in the event of their death. This will likely avoid fights between sets of grandparents or others.

2. Pending divorce of the parents.

If your child is likely to lose custody, your visitation rights may be threatened. Whether or not you can intervene at this stage will depend upon state law.

3. Dysfunction in the Family.

Dysfunction comes in many forms: an arrest of a parent or child; drug abuse and alcoholism in the family; the filing of a dependency petition filed against the parents alleging neglect or abuse; or the placement of the child for adoption. To what degree you have the legal right to intervene in such situations will vary: the point is that because so much is riding on the outcome of these situations, find out.

Chapter 12

Family Financial Dealings

A mountain lake, a rowboat, and two men fishing.
Adult Son, "Dad, you're my Dad... and I love you, man!"
Father: "No, Son, I'm not co-signing for your car."

In this chapter we look at your obligations to support your children and your spouse and their obligation to support you. Generally your children are *not* obligated to support you, but you are obligated to support them until they are 18. Husbands and wives are *generally* responsible for supporting each other, and for paying family debts.

Beware your finer instincts. Don't co-sign notes with your children, don't make their bail, and don't lend them money.

Blame us. (Validate all those lawyer jokes!)

a. Financial Dealings Between Family Members

1. Co-signing Notes and Posting Bail

If you sign any promissory note or contract with your children, you are responsible no matter their age and no matter the purchase. Co-sign for your 45-year-old son on his purchase of a Corvette, and you are legally stuck if he doesn't pay.

But what if we're talking, not Corvettes, but getting out of jail?

If your adult child is arrested, the judge will set bail. If the bail is posted, your child gets out pending trial. Bailbondsmen will post the bond for you for a fee, usually 10%. If the bail is $30,000, the non-refundable fee would be $3,000. In addition, they will require that you give them security in the full amount of the bail: stocks, bonds, savings, and/or real property worth at least $30,000. If your child splits, you lose your security—your stocks, bonds, home.

We don't want to make light of this heartbreaking situation. It is very hard to say no to a child sitting in jail. You will hear a compelling story and heartfelt pledges of the straight and narrow. And perhaps even subtle suggestions as to why it is all your fault.

Don't do it! We know too many parents who have lost their homes and savings. We know too many parents who have posted bail only to have their child, while on bail, commit another and more serious crime. The concept of tough-love comes to mind.

2. Lending Money

Clients ask: "My daughter needs money. Should I lend it to her?"

Our advice: "Never *lend* your children money. If you can afford it, *give* it to them. If you lend it and they don't repay, you won't sue. It may just ruin your relationship."

If you give (or lend) money to one child but not to another, realize that money is a funny thing - it is more than purchasing power; it seems like love. *"Mom loves Sis more than me because she's always giving her money."* Better to explain to all what's going on.

If you have made substantial gifts to one child but not to the others, at the time of your death there will be a question of whether the gifts were advances on that child's share of your estate, or whether they were simply separate gifts. This question may lead to litigation and to hard feelings for sure. You can avoid this by expressing your intent in your Will, or by telling everyone at the time:

> *"I gave Sis $10,000 as an advance on her inheritance, because she is starting her own business. If you other kids do, I'll try to do the same."*
>
> or
>
> *"I gave Sis $10,000 as a separate gift, not as part of her inheritance, because well, frankly, I love her more."*

b. Responsibilities for Minor Children: College Financing

You are responsible for supporting your minor children (usually until the age of 18), unless they have been emancipated. This obligation goes only to the necessaries of life, such as housing, food, health, and education. (When lawyers think of what is necessary in life, we think of hamburgers and tennis shoes, not of poetry, love or community. Whether this is a matter of nature or nurture is beyond our scope.)

So kids are on their own when it comes to Corvettes. If a creditor provides your minor child with a necessity, they can look to you for reimbursement. But if your kid goes out and buys a Rolex, you are *not* obligated to pay for it. Your kid is probably off the hook as well. Children under 18 generally do not have contractual capacity, and hence cannot be sued on contracts they sign—great news if your children are being threatened by CD Clubs or Book Clubs.

> *"Dear Record Club. When I signed your offer, I was under 18 and hence had no contractual capacity. Please stop writing me. Thanks for sharing."*

If your minor children are living on their own and are running up bills for which you may be responsible, you can file an action to have the court declare them *emancipated*. This means you will no longer be financially responsible. Of course, once they are emancipated, you no longer have the legal right to supervise them either (but it doesn't sound like they were paying much attention to you anyway).

Some states (but not many) have expanded the parents' common law obligation to support their children beyond the age of 18. A statute in California, for example, provides:

> *The father and mother have an equal responsibility to maintain, to the extent of their ability, a child of whatever age who is incapacitated from earning a living and without sufficient means.*

This expresses a nice sentiment. However, there are sufficient loopholes if a creditor of your adult child presents you with a bill. First, generally the child must have become incapacitated before age 18. Second, the bill will have to be for a necessity (as your duty is only to maintain the child). Finally, your liability extends only to your ability to pay.

A common question concerns college education. Although you are not responsible for paying for your child's college education, colleges will consider family income in determining the amount of scholarship or financial aid that will be available for your child. Using complicated formulas, colleges will look at the family's income and assets and then determine how much the family can afford to pay toward the child's education. It then decides how much it costs to attend the particular college and, after deducting the amount it deems the family should pay, makes up the difference in loans and grants to the student. In theory this means that the family will spend the same amount no matter how expensive the college attended. How much the student must *borrow* is an entirely different matter.

c. Support Obligations Between Spouses

> *Your spouse is home from the hospital and you receive a bill for $20,000. You don't have any joint savings or checking accounts that could pay this. But you have stock, in your name, that could. Should you pay the bill?*

As to daily bills, the family assets are liable for either spouse's expenses. The issue of who is responsible for what really only arises if one spouse has incurred large medical bills or has received public assistance. Unless you are a co-signor on the bills, we advise against paying them without first seeking legal advice:

1. If your spouse has died, the bills should be paid first from his or her estate. Only if the estate is exhausted, can the creditor go after you.
2. Under the common law necessaries rule, a husband would be liable for his wife's medical care and support. However, some states have thrown out this rule as it denies equal protection (treating men differently from women) while others have leveled the playing field by imposing a similar obligation on the wife. Some states have family expense statutes which make one spouse liable for the debts of the other.

Even though you might eventually be held liable for the bills, our advice remains the same—don't pay them without first seeking legal advice. Most courts, even if they impose spousal obligations, do so only to the extent that it will not leave you broke. A lawyer can probably cut a good deal for you. Further, in the face of large unpaid bills, you should discuss the possibility of bankruptcy. See Chapter 17-g.

d. Your Children's Obligation to Support You

Generally your children are *not* liable for any of your debts or expenses, again, unless they are co-signors. If your children are in fact supporting you, they may be entitled to claim you as a dependent on their federal tax return.

Some states attempt to impose liability on your children if you are likely to become a public charge. These laws are generally called "poor laws" or "general assistance laws." Some may even carry a criminal penalty. However, usually they are used to "attribute" some portion of your child's income to you for the purpose of determining eligibility for public assistance, or in seeking reimbursement for public benefits supplied to you.

e. Note on Nursing Home Expenses

We began this chapter by advising you not to bail your child out of jail. Well, we can be heartless both ways. Your children should never sign to be responsible for your nursing home expenses.

Under a 1989 Federal law, most nursing homes are prohibited from *requiring* relatives to co-sign for their charges. In some states, however, relatives can agree to pay for extra services.

Even though they cannot require co-signing for expenses, nursing homes can *request* it. Some ask a son or daughter to sign as "the responsible party." This sounds like you are signing as the person to contact concerning emergencies; what it means, according to the small print, is that you are responsible for the bills.

Tell your kids not to sign. But after you left them sitting in jail, they probably won't anyway.

Chapter 13

Divorce and Remarriage

Second marriages represent the triumph of hope over experience.

Samuel Johnson

a. Divorce in the Golden Years: Property, Alimony, and Alternatives

Divorce will be a financial disaster. Both of you will have a lower standard of living. You will lose half of your accumulated property and much of your income. Expenses will increase; and then there are hefty lawyers' bills, his *and* hers.

Divorce will be an emotional disaster. There is less opportunity for "new beginnings" (and you are likely grumpier!). And a divorce will not make you any younger.

We'll look at alternatives to divorce after we look at the financial implications of divorce: property settlements, alimony or spousal maintenance, and health insurance.

1. Property Distribution

State divorce laws differ as to distribution of property. Some states follow the old Spanish tradition of *community property,* while most follow the English tradition of *Dower*. While there are nice theoretical distinctions between the two, as a practical matter most judges will try to split the property acquired during a long-term marriage. Let this sink in for a moment. *If you divorce now, likely you will lose half of what you accumulated over your married life.*

Half of it.

Unless there is a lot of cash lying around for buy-outs, you will have to sell the family home.

Assume your mortgage is paid off and your house is valued at $200,000. Dividing its value, each of you is entitled to $100,000. If you have $200,000 in savings, one of you could take your $100,000 share of those savings, and "buy out" the other's share in the house. Of course, one of you is now broke and the other homeless – but you're the ones who couldn't get along. (If you don't have savings of $200,000, most likely the house will have to be sold and the cash divided.)

Pension plans present unique problems of evaluation.

Assume the wage earner is 55. How much is his or her pension plan worth now, given the fact that it will pay, at 65, an amount based on earnings during the last three years before age 65, earnings which won't be earned for another seven years?

We have to project what the pension would pay at 65 and then figure out how much such a plan would cost. That might be the easy calculation. Let's say we figure it out and come up with the figure of $400,000. Fine. But what's the *current* value of a benefit which will be worth $400,000 in ten years? How much would you have to invest now in order to have $400,000 in ten years? This calculation is contentious since it rests upon assumptions as to rates of interest and inflation.

Expert economists love long, leisurely discussions concerning the future worth of pensions, with color charts and computer printouts. And, if both partners have retirement plans, both must be evaluated and then compared.

Expert economists, when they send their bills, figure in *current* dollars.

Pension plans also present the buy-out problem.

Assume that the husband's retirement plan has a current value of $200,000 and that the wife has no pension plan. Under the principle of division, the wife is entitled to $100,000. If the husband has the cash, he can buy her out. If he doesn't?

To solve these difficult evaluation and current value problems, some states allow the judge to simply order that the wife receive, at the time of her husband's retirement, a percentage of that retirement. Federal law allows this to be done for Military benefits as well.

These problems do not arise with Social Security. Even after a divorce, at the age of 62, the non-wage earner can collect on her ex-husband's Social Security account if

1. They were married at least ten years, and
2. If she has not remarried. (If she remarried after the age 60, she does not lose eligibility.)

Note: If you are divorcing and have been married less than ten years, it might be smart to wait a while in order to create Social Security eligibility.

2. Alimony

You can't go back to Constantinople and you can't go back to alimony. As we rush toward our brave new world, we discard old sexist traditions such as "alimony." We now call it "spousal maintenance." The basic notion is to "maintain" the non-working (or less-earning) spouse at relatively the same standard of living, while she (it is almost always she) can bring her skills up to speed to allow her to make her own way at a comparable level. While *alimony* might be permanent and thus "demeaning," *spousal maintenance* is to be temporary and thus "empowering."

This philosophy makes no sense at all in the case of elderly women. Their chances of entering the labor force and earning enough money to support themselves at comparable levels is almost nil. Recognizing this, many judges are now ordering permanent spousal maintenance. In setting the amount of that maintenance, the court will consider the assets that the spouse receives at divorce, as they may produce significance amounts of income.

3. Health Insurance

Many married people have health insurance only under their spouse's work policy. When both work, the couple will decide whose health policy is best and go with it. Upon divorce, one will lose coverage. However, a federal law, called *COBRA*, gives ex-spouses the right to maintain that insurance for three years. They must pay the premium, thus *increasing* their expenses. If they do not become eligible for Medicare within this three- year period, they will be severely disadvantaged, as it will be difficult and expensive to obtain other insurance. These expenses should be reflected in the amount of support ordered.

4. Alternatives to Divorce

Counseling is a good place to start. Often, the problems really aren't with each other. They are with the pressures of aging and retirement.

Divorce won't make you younger, nor will it give you things to do. Divorce doesn't solve many problems; counseling might.

You can try living together but separately. Separate bedrooms, with occasional angry glares over the kitchen table, solve most of the legal problems we have been discussing in this chapter. There is no need to divide property, to obtain additional health insurance, or to pay lawyers. And just maybe if you fell out of love, you might fall back in.

Another alternative is a *legal separation.* It can provide for a formal settlement of economic issues, while allowing for the continuation of health and death benefits. Under a legal separation, the parties are still married.

If you don't want a divorce and your spouse does, contact a lawyer. Don't let the matter go by default. Even in no-fault divorce states, marriage dissolutions can be delayed and sometimes counseling ordered.

There are two situations where elderly divorce does make sense:

1. If one plans to get remarried; or
2. As a device to save the family assets from Medicaid nursing home expenses.

Nursing home expenses can bankrupt families. Medicaid will pay them but only after the family has "spent down" to a certain level. In addition to other exemptions, such as the family home, the law allows for the non-institutionalized spouse to keep $75,000 of other assets. Say the couple has a large estate, say $300,000 in nonexempt assets, if they divorce, the non-institutionalized spouse will be able to keep his or her share, probably $150,000, rather than only the $75,000 which would be allowed under Medicaid rules. See Chapter 8-b.

b. Marriage in the Golden Years: Prenuptials and Wills

First, our enthusiasm: Congratulations!

Second, our wisdom: Get a prenuptial and change your Will.

Redoing Your Wills

A new marriage requires a new estate plan. Do you want your new spouse to inherit all of your property? Perhaps, given his or her financial situation, you want to bypass your new spouse and leave everything to your children. If you do not rewrite your Will in light of your new marriage status, expect a Will contest and expect that your wishes will not be carried out.

There is a special problem if both of you have children from prior marriages. You will probably want to provide for your new spouse after your death, but at the time of his or her death, you would like to see your assets go to your children. But how can you be sure your new spouse will keep his or her end of the bargain? Maybe your kids will get cut out.

A *living trust* is a good solution. (See Chapter 23-h.) The assets of both spouses are placed in trust for their use during their lives. Upon the death of one, the spouses have agreed that the trust will become irrevocable and provide that income will go to maintain the survivor (with liberal principal invasion terms to cover such things as medical emergencies). At the death of the survivor, the assets can be distributed as provided by the original trust instrument, i.e., divided among the couple's children from prior marriages.

If a living trust is not for you, a lawyer can help you set up other devices to accomplish the same goal, such as joint Wills.

Prenuptial Agreements

The hardest part about prenuptial agreements is broaching the subject. Blame us.

A "prenuptial" is simply a written agreement between the happy couple. It can cover such things as:

1. Who is responsible for the debts brought into the marriage?
2. In the event of divorce, what happens to the property brought into the marriage *and* to property acquired during it? What of support obligations?
3. Who is to inherit what?
4. Who takes out the garbage?

Number four is not a joke (at least not much of one). We all tend to get a tad set in our ways. Marriages require adjustments. It might be well to hammer some things out—such as vacations, hobbies, relationships with ex's, and things of that ilk. These concerns may seem petty, but they are the stuff of life.

A prenuptial (even without number four) is a good idea in and of itself. It will help you focus on issues that may otherwise be ignored, issues that can create real friction later.

However, the potential for overreaching and misunderstanding is great. *Each of you should be represented by separate lawyers.* Given the potential conflicts between you, one lawyer should not endeavor to represent you both. Both lawyers should sign the agreement – don't just recite in the agreement that each person consulted with their own lawyer before signing. Recitals may not stand up in the event of a challenge.

Full disclosure of assets, debts and other matters that might bear upon the agreement, must be made. Otherwise, a court will most likely throw it out.

If you are currently married and don't have a prenuptial agreement, postnuptial agreements are possible, as are contracts to make Wills.

Without a prenuptial agreement, your new spouse may be entitled to half the property earned during the marriage and, in some cases, some of the property brought into the marriage. Support may also be ordered. Prenuptials can hammer out the respective rights of the parties.

Of course, if a lot of money is involved, expect a fight as to the validity of the prenuptial agreement. Unlike death and taxes, the validity of prenuptials isn't certain.

But planning to remarry at your age, you are obviously not averse to taking chances. Good for you. We always applaud the triumph of hope over experience. (In an over-cautious world, there would be very little joy and very little need for lawyers.)

Chapter 14

Abuse and Neglect

The clinical history of abuse suggests that it gets worse, not better, both in terms of frequency and severity. It does not self-correct—intervention is imperative.

If there is serious physical abuse:

Call 911.

Don't wait until the last minute. Police, who know the course of violence, advise to err on the side of calling them too early, not too late.

Call Adult Protective Services.

Most states have agencies that deal specifically with elderly abuse, usually called "Adult Protective Services." They can help you sort out your options. Calls are *confidential.*

Call 1-800-677-1116.

This is the number of the *Eldercare Locator.* It can give you the numbers of agencies and sources of help in your area. Your Area Agency on Aging can help as well as local Information and Referral.

Lawyers, doctors, ministers, and other professionals are good folks to talk to as well.

In this chapter, we look at

- Why relatives don't recognize abuse and neglect
- Why victims don't complain
- The signs of abuse and neglect
- Helping those who can't help themselves
- Self-help for victims
- Self-help for perpetrators

This is a serious matter. To repeat:

The clinical history of abuse suggests that it gets worse, not better, both in terms of frequency and severity. Intervention is imperative.

a. Why Relatives Don't Recognize Abuse and Neglect

If we acknowledge, even just to ourselves, that a relative is being abused, we will have to do something about it. And, Lord knows, we are too busy as it is. And how do we know what to do?

We too easily accept cuts and bruises as being the result of falls; we too easily dismiss complaints as evidence of senility or the "natural grumpiness of old folks." We too easily look away.

Even when we don't look away, it may be hard to see. It is very hard to accept the fact that abuse is occurring in our family. Abuse happens in the best families, and it happens in the worst families; it happens on Boardwalk, and it happens on Baltic Avenue.

"Yeah, but Mom and Dad were always so happy together."

Sixty-five percent of elderly abuse occurs between spouses. Frequently, it is of recent origin. Surprisingly, husbands are twice as likely to be victims, although wives receive greater injuries.

Many couples get along famously when they see each other only at night and on weekends. Retirement changes that relationship radically.

Be open to the possibility that abuse is occurring in your family. Be aware of your desire to turn away.

b. Why Victims Don't Complain

Victims have very good reasons not to report abuse and neglect. If you suspect a relative is being mistreated, before he or she will open up to you, you must address those reasons.

"I'm concerned that someone may be mistreating you. I know this is very hard for you to talk about. Before we get started, let me tell you a few things that might address some of your fears."

Figure out why the person might reluctant to complain and then to address their fears. People generally have "good reasons" for what they do, even if what they do is harmful to themselves or others.

"If I tell you I'm being hurt, you will blame me, think less of me, think I'm getting senile."

Talk about how abuse is found in all kinds of families and that it is not the victim's fault. The question is not blame; the question is prevention.

"If I tell you about the abuse, you will call the police. I don't want the person to go to jail."

Promise that you will not call police unless the person wants you to. Can you keep this promise? Generally yes, if you want to. There is no general obligation to report crime. If you are the person's legal guardian, then you should report. In many states, medical, legal, and mental health professionals must report physical abuse, not to police, but to a designated agency, most likely Adult Protective Services.

Unless the victim presses charges, police will not arrest the abuser, except in the case of extreme physical abuse.

"The person abusing me is the person caring for me. If I tell, what will happen to me?"

This is the tough one. But there are solutions. Perhaps the abuser is just overworked and help can be found. Alternative living arrangements are possible.

"If I tell, I'll get beat up."

Short-term shelters are available, as well as the option of hospitalization. Many jurisdictions allow for easy-to-obtain domestic court orders of protection which will prohibit the abuser from coming to the victim's home. Locks can be changed.

Once you have addressed the victim's fear of talking, you still must convince the victim that it is in his or her interest to talk.

"Abuse gets worse, not better. Even if the person has promised never to do it again. There is help available for you and the

person mistreating you. I want to help you. I can't, unless you tell me what's going on."

Once the victim opens up and starts talking, you can begin working out a solution. We'll give you some ideas momentarily. But first, a quick description of the signs of abuse and neglect.

c. Signs of Abuse and Neglect

There are four common kinds of elder abuse:

- Physical abuse—slapping, bruising, sexually molesting, restraining.
- Psychological abuse—threatening, humiliating, ridiculing.
- Neglect—abandonment, denial of food or health services.
- Financial exploitation—spending an elder's money on others, or *not* spending it on the elder (saving it up for the inheritance).

What to Look For—Signs of Abuse

Isolation

Abusers keep victims isolated. *"Mildred's a little too tired to come to the phone just now."* A relative's refusal to allow home visits by nurses or friends may indicate problems. Insist on occasionally visiting in private. Be aware that abusers will likely try to turn their victim against other relatives. *"Mildred, isn't it a shame your son never calls."*

Injury and Withdrawal

Abusers, and often victims, explain injuries and bruises as the result of falls caused by poor balance. Ask for *details* of the accident and don't just assume it occurred.

Signs of possible abuse include:

Physical mistreatment—bruises, burns, welts, cuts, punctures, sprains and broken bones; dehydration and weight loss; hair pulling; venereal disease and genital infections; signs of physical restraint (e.g., rope burns); missing eyeglasses, hearing aids, dentures, or prostheses; or unexpected or unexplained deterioration of health.

Psychological mistreatment—insomnia, excessive sleep, unusual weight loss or gain, a change in appetite, tearfulness, paranoia, low self-esteem, excessive fears, ambivalence, confusion, resignation, or agitation.

Financial Exploitation

Watch for the sudden inability to pay bills, withdrawals of large amounts of cash, and living well below one's means. Another possible sign of exploitation: the elder deferring all responsibilities for finances to a third person.

The elderly are often financially exploited by children ("Well, I'll get the money later anyway"), home shopping channels (offering companionship) and, surprisingly, political action committees (targeting "senior issues" and alerting as to need for immediate action).

See also Chapter 16 on common scams.

d. Helping Those Who Cannot Help Themselves

Mentally impaired individuals and folks in nursing homes may not be able to help you help them. You may have to take direct action.

Individuals Lacking Mental Capacity

Your senile aunt who lives with her daughter is being abused or neglected by her. You can seek a guardianship and then remove her from the abusive situation. (See Chapter 28.) Check with Adult Protective Services if you need help.

In the case of financial exploitation, a conservatorship can be sought on an emergency basis to protect an incompetent person's money and property. See Chapter 28-d. Before that, banks, credit card companies, and financial institutions should be notified of your suspicions. If you suspect that the individual's guardian or conservator is the abuser, notify the court which appointed the guardian and seek an Accounting.

Mentally Ill Individuals Who Are a Danger to Themselves or Others

Most states have civil commitment laws which allow forced hospitalization and treatment of certain mentally ill individuals, those who present a physical danger to themselves or to others. If the individual is creating a danger to himself (not eating) or others (not careful with fire), contact your lawyer or Adult Protective Services, and inquire about Civil Commitment. (See Chapter 28-g.)

Individuals in Nursing Homes

Abuses in nursing homes range from inadequate care to the use of physical or chemical restraints to control patients. If a home receives Medicare or Medicaid funds, the Federal Nursing Home Bill of Rights applies. It prohibits the use of physical or drug restraints except to protect the patient or other residents and only upon the written order of a physician.

The best way to prevent abuse of relatives in nursing homes is simply to stay involved. Visit often and at different times of day. Ask questions of nurses and doctors. Periodically ask to review the person's chart. Under the Nursing Home Bill of Rights, as the patient's representative, you have the right to examine current clinical records (within 24 hours after request) and to make copies of them.

If you suspect abuse or neglect, report it to the administration, and to any federal or state agency that oversees the home. Signs should be posted in the nursing home as to how to file a complaint and how to contact these agencies.

See Chapter 27 for more on nursing homes.

e. Self-help for Victims

If you are abused or neglected, most likely it's by a loved one. It is may be heartbreaking to take action, yet realize:

- Taking action to protect yourself does not mean that the person will be arrested and taken to jail. *Unless you file a criminal complaint,* only in extreme cases of abuse will the police arrest the person.

- Sources of help are available to the abuser. Abuse may stem from overwork or lack of knowledge about community services that are available. These can be remedied. Counseling may address other problems.
- You shouldn't have to live that way. Abuse isn't your fault and it doesn't single out you or your family: abuse and neglect are all too common.

Most likely you'll need an ally, someone on the outside who will help. In emergencies, use 911. Talk to your doctor or lawyer. Call a relative. Information and Referral will have other sources of help. Most locales have Adult Protective Services which specializes in protecting the elderly. Again, the national clearing house: 1-800-677-1116.

Coping with Spouse Abuse

The law has been moving quickly to deal with spouse abuse. Local police are being trained to be more sensitive and are less likely to treat abuse lightly. In most jurisdictions, it is possible for a battered spouse (not always the wife) to go to court, fill out a simple form, and get a court order which will require the aggressor to stay away. This is true even if the person lives in the same house; he or she will have to move out. If the abuser shows up where he or she has been ordered not to, he or she can be arrested for violating the order; he or she need not do anything more in terms of threats or abuse.

In most cities and towns, there are shelters for battered individuals to stay in during emergencies. These are at secret locations and abusers cannot find them. Friends and relatives can also offer shelter although in extreme cases that might put them at risk as well. To get help, call police, your Area Agency on Aging or the Information and Referral Agency.

Abuse by Adult Children

Almost one quarter of elder abuse is committed by adult children. Most mental health hospitals have closed, and now many mentally ill live with their parents. Their continuing dependent relationship may fire violence and abuse.

Be cautious. It is easier *not* to let children move back in than it is getting them out. If they have moved in, you have the legal right to have them removed. Call police and change the locks. Protective orders, like those against spouses, are likely to be available.

Financial Exploitation

Dishonest children, friends, or nurses may simply forge your name to checks or, on their way to the bank to deposit your checks in your account, suddenly see a better alternative.

Get hold of your monthly bank statement. Check to see if all deposits were made and whether any of the returned checks have been forged. If you report a forgery within 30 days of receiving your statement, the bank *must* make it good; otherwise, probably not.

If your bank statement is missing, bells should go off. Dishonest relatives may have stolen it. If you suddenly stop getting your bank statement, check with the bank as to when it was sent. Duplicates can usually be sent, although it takes time.

If you are under guardianship, you have the right to demand an accounting of your financial affairs. Contact an attorney.

Nursing Home Abuse

Nursing homes that receive Medicare or Medicaid funds (and most do) must comply with the Nursing Home Bill of Rights. Your most important rights include:

- The right to be free of physical or drug restraints unless needed to protect you or other residents and only then upon the written order of a physician.
- The right to receive and send unopened and uncensored mail.
- The right to reasonable access to a phone and to make calls in private.
- Area Councils on Aging maintain an office of Ombudsman to take and investigate nursing home complaints.

f. Self-help for Abusers

If you are abusing someone, fess up. You're a criminal.

The following are *not* defenses to a criminal charge:

- the victim was hard to deal with;
- the victim abused you in the past; or
- the money, down the road, would have been yours anyway.

Abuse is hard to self-correct; the natural course of abuse is downward, toward greater frequency and severity.

Confront the fact that you are abusing someone. It is easy to lie to yourself. Ask the cause and *seek help* dealing with it.

Read our discussion on caring for others. (Chapter 26.) It offers tips on how to cope with caring for the elderly. It is a very tough job. Frustrations and lack of sleep can lead to abuse. But there are several sources of help.

Alcoholism and Drug Abuse

A police officer friend, who has responded to over 300 cases of domestic violence, reports that all but one involved alcohol. All but one.

Alcohol gets more toxic as we age. Our bodies lose the ability to process it. We may slip into alcoholism or drug abuse and these conditions may trigger us to abuse others. Programs are available, such as Alcoholics Anonymous (AA). Many AA chapters are exclusively for seniors.

Psychological Resentments

Abusers are often financially dependent upon their victims and, resenting that dependency, resort to abuse. Sometimes spouses, over the years, begin to resent each other. Counseling may help. Separation, and even divorce, are possible solutions.

g. For More Information

Elder Abuse: Questions and Answers, An Information Guide for Professionals and Concerned Citizens

Available in Spanish. Information of the origins and causes of elder abuse and neglect; victim and perpetrator characteristics; descriptions of programs.

Send $4.00 check payable to NASUA for NASUA Publication #7, and send to:

National Association of State Units on Aging
1225 I Street, N.W. Suite 725
Washington, D.C. 20005
202-898-2586

Part Three

The Bad Guys!

Chapter 15

Bigots

Supervisor: *Henry, don't bother signing up for training on the new computer program. Old dogs can't learn new tricks and, besides, you would just forget it anyway.*

Boss: *Mary, we have this great new early retirement program, but you must sign up by the end of next week or face layoff.*

Recruiter: *You are just too qualified for this job.*

Boss: *Real sorry about your disability, but we have to let you go because you can no longer do the job.*

Supervisor: *Come on over and give me a big hug.*

Bank: *Sorry, no credit.*

Boss: *Sorry, old goat.*

Landlord: *Sorry, no goat.*

Discrimination comes in many forms: triggered by the victim's age, disability, race or sex. We have two main topics:

1. A discussion of the various laws that prohibit discrimination; and
2. Tips on how to recognize discrimination and then how to prove it.

a. Overview of Anti-Discrimination Laws — Good News!

The law is pretty good in prohibiting discrimination.

Employment Discrimination

Age discrimination, beginning at age 40, is illegal. This applies in hiring, termination, and job treatment, such as promotions or job reclassifications. Similarly, you cannot be discriminated against merely because you become disabled and have a more difficult time doing the job. The employer must work with you, trying to find "reasonable accommodations" which would allow you to go on working.

Credit Discrimination

Legislation prohibits age and sex discrimination in the credit industry. Widows, who may be forced to apply for credit after the death of their husbands, should *suspect* discrimination if they are denied.

Disability Discrimination

While *age* discrimination, at least at the federal level, is prohibited only in employment and credit, protection for the *disabled* is far more extensive. Disability discrimination is generally prohibited in the following areas:

Housing
Public accommodations
Government services
Employment

Racial and Sexual Discrimination

These kinds of discriminations are outlawed in employment and in many other areas as well. The "hot" area is sexual discrimination in employment. The law recognizes two forms of sexual discrimination: direct (supervisors demanding sexual favors) and indirect (employers allowing a "hostile work environment" to exist, such as where co-workers are allowed to post explicit sexual pictures or to make crude remarks). The law prohibits same-sex harassment (male on male or female on female).

The protective legislation we will look at had its genesis in the Civil Rights Movement. The root notion is that the law should act to protect citizens against irrational discrimination, whether based on race, national origin, religion, sex, age, or disability. There are a few other general comments we can make:

- While we focus on federal law, many states have parallel anti-discrimination laws. State laws may provide for broader judicial relief (a polite way of saying "more money").
- Most Civil Rights laws provide that, if you win your lawsuit, the defendant must pay your lawyer. Thus you *can* afford a lawyer.
- Most Civil Rights laws are enforced by governmental agencies. It is easy to report discrimination and let them investigate and take appropriate action. These agencies will contact the other side, hear their side of the story, and then try to conciliate the matter without going to court.
- In all cases of discrimination, it is important to act quickly. If you wait too long, your complaint may be barred by the Statute of Limitations. Further, much of your evidence might be lost. People move and forget.
- Your local Area Agency on Aging can give you information on how to make claims of discrimination and may even intercede on your behalf and try to negotiate an agreeable outcome.

We begin our discussion with pet discrimination.

b. Cat Discrimination

No, this is not a clever gambit to catch your interest. Well, not entirely. Discrimination against pets can have devastating impact. Pets provide substantial physical and mental benefits to their owners, particularly older people who live alone. Recognizing this, Congress passed a law in 1983 prohibiting owners of federally assisted housing, designated for the elderly or disabled, from having flat rules against pets, including cats, dogs, and fish. Thus you can keep your cat unless the landlord shows that it is a nuisance or a threat to the health or safety of others. (Lions, crocodiles, and T Rex, all have to go; old goats fall in the grey area.)

Although this law has a narrow application, if you are renting from a private landlord, you might point to it if you want to keep a pet. A creative lawyer might be able to convince a judge that it would be against public policy to allow a private landlord to evict an elderly tenant because the tenant kept a cat.

c. Credit Discrimination

The Equal Credit Opportunity Act prohibits creditors (stores, credit card companies, and banks) from discriminating against any applicant on the "basis of race, color, religion, national origin, sex, marital status, or age," or because the applicant is receiving public assistance.

Creditors can turn you down if your are not credit worthy – if you have a history of late payments or if your income and assets do not justify the amount of money you wish to borrow.

Thirty days after you apply for credit, you must get a decision. If you are turned down, the creditor must tell you why. Don't be satisfied with explanations such as "Bad credit risk" or "Bad credit record." Insist on details, and if the creditor remains vague, call the local office of the Federal Trade Commission, which enforces the Equal Credit Opportunity Act. Again, widows and older persons should suspect discrimination.

d. Disability Discrimination: Housing

In the area of housing, it is illegal to refuse to rent or sell to a person because he or she is disabled, while it is legal to discriminate on the basis of age. Federal law does not outlaw age discrimination (as opposed to disability discrimination) in the sale or rental of housing. If you have been turned down because of your age, the only recourse you may have is state law; check with your State Attorney General's Office to see if your state prohibits age discrimination in housing.

On the other hand, federal law does outlaw housing discrimination against the disabled (as well as discrimination based on race, color, religion, sex and national origin). This protection is afforded by the "ADA"—Americans With Disabilities Act.

A disabled individual is a person who has a "physical or mental impairment that substantially limits" one of the major life activities, such as walking.

A covered owner or landlord cannot *refuse to sell or rent* to an individual simply because the person is disabled, unless the handicap is such as to threaten the health and safety of others or would lead to substantial property destruction. The only housing that is exempted from the ADA are single dwelling residences rented or sold without a Realtor; small housing complexes of four or fewer units where the owner occupies one; and housing run by religious organizations and private clubs.

An Important Note to Disabled Renters

> You have a right, at your expense, to make *reasonable modifications* (put in ramps) to your rental to accommodate your handicap. Your landlord cannot refuse to allow you to do so, although the landlord can insist that you agree to restore the place to its original condition when you leave.

Disabled victims of housing discrimination can either file their own lawsuit or contact the federal Department of Housing and Urban Development (HUD), or a state or local housing enforcement agency. The State Attorney General's Office can point you in the right direction.

e. Disability Discrimination: Employment

The Americans with Disabilities Act (ADA) also protects disabled individuals in employment. The first reported case under the ADA concerning employment discrimination involved a 56 year old executive who was discharged after being diagnosed with terminal brain cancer. He sued and won $250,000.

If a physical or mental disability prevents you from doing your job, you have no recourse against an employer. However, your employer cannot *assume* that you cannot do the job simply because you are disabled. If you become disabled, your employer must allow you to try to do your job and cannot simply assume you can't.

Further, your employer must work with you in figuring out how to change the job so you can do it. An employer must make "reasonable accommodations for known physical or mental limitations of an otherwise qualified individual." If a disability is interfering with your performance, are there things you or your employer can do to remedy the problem? Changing the height of desks, getting additional training, or taking more frequent rest breaks may help. How far employers must go in making "reasonable accommodations" is unclear. On the one hand, they must make good faith efforts and not just go through the motions; on the other hand, they need not incur unreasonable expenses.

The requirement of reasonable accommodations throws new light on an old dilemma: *If you are having a hard time doing your job because of a disability, should you tell your boss?* The fear is that, if you do tell, you will be fired. However, if the employer doesn't know of your disability, he or she is under no obligation to offer reasonable accommodation and, if you are fired for bad job performance caused by your disability, you will not be able to claim the ADA's protection.

Only small employers are exempt from the ADA: those with fewer than 15 regular workers. However even small employers may be covered by state or local statutes.

Disabled individuals may also face discrimination in government programs (no programs for the deaf in school) and public accommodations and facilities (no ramps in retail stores). These aspects of the ADA are beyond our scope, but if you feel that you have suffered because of your disability at the hands a government agency or private business, you should contact the federal Equal Employment Opportunities Commission (EEOC), which enforces the ADA, or your state's Attorney General's Office. You can also seek private counsel.

f. Age Discrimination: Employment

An Aside on the Common Law

Before we give you the details of employment law, let's take a brief look at "common law" and one of history's very first cases – *Barney Rubble v. Fred Flintstone*.

Common law is judge-made law. This is opposed to *statutory law*, which is made by the tobacco industry. In the early days of our country, we followed the law of England (despite the fact that we didn't think much of the King). The law of England at the time was mostly judge-made. Here is an example of how the common law works:

Let's take the first employment case, long, long ago. There are no records but we are convinced that it involved Fred and Barney. Fred had hired Barney to help him fix up the cave, but, after a couple of days, fired him. Barney went to court and complained, "Fred fired me without any good reason. I was doing a real good job."

The *factual question*, to be decided by the jury if there were a trial, would be "Was Barney doing a good job?" But, before the matter could get to this point, a *legal* question would have to be answered by the judge, "Does an employer need good cause to fire someone?" If the judge held "Yes," then there would be a trial as to whether Fred had good cause; if the judge held "No," there would not be a trial because, as a matter of law, employers could fire for any reason they chose.

Some are critical of the judiciary, arguing that judges should not "make law." But note that to decide the case, the judge had to decide the question – the judge would be making law either way.

The first judge, perhaps a secret admirer of Wilma, said "Sorry. Barney, I hold that an employer can fire anyone for any reason or for no reason." Thereafter, other judges, wishing to "treat like cases alike," followed the ruling of the first judge. Over time, it became "law," the *common law.*

This is the concept of following *precedent,* also known as *stare decisis,* and it, at least in theory, creates predictability. Employers and employees will know the rules and will be able to plan their lives. Important decisions will not turn on the whim (or politics) of individual judges.

Some have argued that the doctrine of precedent cannot hold, cannot keep its promise that like cases will be treated alike. This is because judges can "distinguish" prior cases. Assume a judge is dealing with a case involving a ranch-hand fired from a dinosaur ranch. She can write: "The rule laid down in the case of *Fred v. Barney* only applies in cases of individuals working in caves; the case before me involves employment at a dinosaur ranch, and I will adopt a different rule to govern this kind of case."

The more flexible the law, the more judges can fine tune it for unique situations. Maybe there are important differences between cave work and ranch work that would justify a different employment rule. However, the more flexible the law is, the less predictable it becomes. If it is flexible enough to deal with every unique situation, the law may collapse into the individual whim of the judge.

We could neatly solve this timeless jurisprudential dilemma for you. But if we did, the price of this book would skyrocket, so let's return to employment law.

* * *

Common law starts with the notion that an employer can fire you for any reason at all. Even if you are doing a great job, you can be fired to make room for the employer's third cousin from Toledo.

Rather than call this "The Third Cousin from Toledo" rule, lawyers labeled it the "at will" doctrine. It left employees quite vulnerable. Unless you have a contract or your employer has an employment policy to the contrary, the employer is not even obligated to tell you why you are fired. Many are told by their lawyers not to. "The less they know, the harder it will be for them to sue," the lawyers say, as the audience hisses, and throws popcorn.

So where can employees find protection? Perhaps in employment contracts and, if not, in various kinds of legislation modifying the common law "at will" doctrine.

Contract Rights

If you are one of those rare individuals with an employment contract, the "at will" doctrine does not apply to you. The contract has to be for a specified period of time such as a year. The contract can be oral. With such a contract, an employee can be fired only for "good cause" – which includes sleeping on the job, but not making room for folks from Toledo.

Even if you don't have an employment contract, you may have contract rights you don't know about, and they are the first place to look if you have problems at work.

Labor Union Contract

Labor unions enter into collective-bargaining agreements with the employer. These spell out a worker's rights concerning termination and conditions of employment. *Unions have a duty to represent you* if your job is covered by a collective bargaining agreement, even if you are not a member of the union and even if your shop foreman has lost a major bet with you on the Super Bowl. Further, labor unions cannot discriminate on the basis of age.

Employee Manuals as Contracts

Some employers have an employee manual or a set of work policies which may describe the circumstances in which an employee can be fired or laid off, and what kind of notice must be given. Creative lawyers have argued that these policies in effect become part of the employment contract and hence are legally binding on the employer.

Legislation: The Age Discrimination in Employment Act (ADEA)

If you have no recourse to contract rights, turn next to legislation. It has made major inroads into the "at will" doctrine by prohibiting discrimination based on race, sex, and age. Our concern is with age discrimination, so we turn to the provisions of the Age Discrimination in Employment Act (ADEA) which was passed by Congress in 1967.

A major aspect of this legislation is to outlaw mandatory retirement. The narrow exceptions deal with matters of public safely; for example, airline pilots must retire at age 60.

The other major aspect of this legislation is that it protects people 40 and older from discrimination in terms of hiring, firing, promotion, and pay. This applies to both part time and temporary workers as well. What employers cannot do is to treat people over 40 differently because they assume that, because of their age, they cannot do as good a job as younger individuals. Employers can, however, fire individuals for bad job performances, even if those poor performances are due to the aging process and can also reduce the work force, as long as they do not single out the elderly.

This law applies to almost all employers (private and public, profit and non-profit) but only if the employer has 20 or more employees. Certain high-ranking employees aren't covered, nor are top managers.

g. Proving Discrimination

Occasionally there may be direct evidence of age discrimination. In one case, the defendant fired the plaintiff, calling him an "old goat." The old goat sued and won big bucks; with a nod to Winston Churchill, *"Some goat!"*

> *Our lawyers did not get the Churchill reference. Fearing that it is somehow actionable, they demand that we explain it.*

At the beginning of World War II, Hitler bragged that Germany was about to grab England like a chicken and break its neck. Churchill, in one of his great speeches, repeated Hitler's threat, and then paused....

"Some chicken!" he roared.

Thunderous applause. After several minutes, the audience fell silent. Another pause....

"Some neck!"

Alas, most lawyers are historical illiterates and most employers are too cagey to call you an old goat. (This awkward construction in no way suggests that *we* are calling you an old goat.)

Employers are likely to claim they just love older folks but that you, alas, cannot do the job. How can you prove that they are in fact discriminating against you because of your age? To win an age discrimination suit, you don't have to prove that age was the *only* factor in an adverse employment decision, only that it was a factor. How? We recommend three basic steps:

1. Ask yourself: Does my employer have a reason to discriminate against me?
2. Demand explanations of conduct you believe might constitute discrimination.
3. Sit down and write out why you think you have been victimized.

Why Employers Discriminate

1. To cut insurance costs.

Seniors get sick more and hence have higher bills. To avoid higher premiums, a company might refuse to hire or might fire (or force into retirement, or make life hell so that they quit) older workers. This is against the law.

Employers cannot discriminate against seniors on the basis that they trigger higher benefit plan costs. Employers can, however, insist on spending the same amount on all employees. This may result in lesser coverage for older workers; the same premium will get more coverage for a younger worker than for an older one.

2. To cut payroll and to weasel out of retirement commitments.

New hires are paid less than folks with experience. Some employers are tempted to cut costs by replacing more senior workers.

As to weaseling out of retirement commitments, federal law provides that, once you have worked for a company for five years, you have a vested right to be in the company's retirement plan (if they have one). This means that the employer cannot get back its contributions to your account. Be very suspicious if you are fired as you approach the five-year mark.

3. To let stereotypes do their thinking (it is easier that way).

Some employers simply assume that over a certain age people won't be able to do the job. *Most of us can.* Studies suggest mental function remains high well into the seventies.

Civil rights legislation protecting minorities, women, the disabled, and the elderly can be thought of as anti-stereotype legislation. Employers cannot simply assume that, for example, no elders can do a job simply because some elders cannot. Individual decisions must be made. Further, these laws force employers to think through job qualifications. Employers may simply assume that people need to have certain skills to do a certain job when they really don't. It is a violation of law to have a job requirement that is not really needed if it acts to discriminate against the elderly. For example, if a job requires no heavy lifting, employers cannot insist employees pass strength tests that would discriminate irrationally against the elderly.

After thinking about whether there was a motive to discriminate against you, the next step is to *demand an explanation.* If you weren't hired because you "aren't qualified" or are "too qualified," ask "In what respects?"

University professors, for example, are not over-qualified for repetitious, boring and mind numbing jobs. Just look at their publications!

If you were fired because you "can no longer do the job" or "no longer get along with customers," demand specifics. Be suspicious of vague answers and the refusal to respond.

If you are going to talk your employer, take someone with you. You might need a witness later.

Writing down why you think you have been victimized should prove worthwhile. Writing is simply a great way to slow your mind to allow you to sort things out. Things will come to you that you would overlook if you just thought about it.

Now some tips for specific situations:

If you weren't hired, consider:

* Was there anything the interviewer said or asked that indicated age bias? Did the interviewer tell you the job qualifications and did you meet them? Vague qualifications coupled with "You aren't qualified" are suspicious.
* Did the interviewer tell you why you weren't being hired? If they were to "get back to you later" and later you were simply told "Nope," write a letter: "Why didn't I get the job? In what ways wasn't I qualified?" A failure to respond to this inquiry increases suspicions.
* Was the job kept open? You could have a friend call or even apply. If the employer is hiring a lot of folks, are any of them your age?

If you think that your employer is setting you up to be fired:

* Watch the paper trail of bad evaluations. Respond to them in writing.
* Talk with co-workers your age and see if the same thing is happening to them.
* Record the incidents that you feel are suspicious.
* Seek legal advice early on, *before* the axe falls.

h. Court Procedures: Administrative Exhaustion, Disparate Impact, and Remedies

Administrative Exhaustion

Typically, if someone runs you over, you can go directly to court (at least after you get out of the hospital). Not so with most civil rights legislation or with age discrimination legislation. The law requires that you first file a complaint with the governmental agency whose job it is to enforce that particular law. The idea is that the agency will investigate your complaint and try to resolve the dispute. If it cannot, and it believes you are right, it *might* go to court on your behalf. Even if the agency finds you are wrong, you still can go to court after you have given the agency time to investigate.

If your state has an age discrimination law, you must first file a complaint with the agency that enforces it. If your state does not, then you have to file with the local office of the Federal EEOC (Equal Employment Opportunities Commission). Things can get complicated and these offices will guide you through the ropes.

What you need to know now is that you need to *act quickly.* If you wait too long to file a complaint, it may be barred by the Statute of Limitations. (The length of Statutes of Limitations varies from state to state.)

Disparate Impact

If your case goes to court (most are settled), it will be your job, as plaintiff, to prove that the employer intended discrimination. The law helps you in the following fashion. Once you have put on a prima facie (basic) case of discrimination (you show, for example, that you were qualified and someone younger, with the same or lesser qualifications, was hired or replaced you), the burden of proof shifts to the employer to prove that they were not discriminating. Neat trick. Lawyers, no matter what you think, are clever.

There is more help. Under the disparate impact doctrine, it is *not* necessary to prove intentional discrimination. If it is shown that an apparently neutral employment practice has a disparate impact upon a protected group (the elderly), then that practice violates the law *unless* the employer can prove that it is necessary in furthering a legitimate business need.

Say what?

Let's return to where we started, the *No Pets* rule in an apartment house. Now, on the surface, it is a neutral rule that applies to every tenant the same. But say that the evidence showed that the rule impacted most heavily on elder tenants: they had less choice in where to live and they needed their pets more. Even though the landlord had no wish to discriminate against the elderly, once the disparate impact is shown, the *No Pets* rule would have to be justified. Does it further a legitimate concern of the landlord? Are there other ways, less harmful to the protected class, in achieving those goals?

The classic statement of disparate impact was captured by a French philosopher who, praising law's neutrality, mused, "The Law is perfectly fair. It prohibits both the rich and the poor from sleeping under the bridge."

But they can keep their cats!

Remedies

Your possible remedies under federal law include payment for lost pay, reinstatement, front pay (if reinstatement isn't appropriate) and injunctive relief (a stern judicial warning not to do it again). Awards for pain and suffering are not allowed. However, if there was a *willful* violation, your recovery can be doubled. Punitive damages are not allowed under the federal law although they may be if you pursue other theories of recovery.

i. A Concluding Note on Early Retirement

If an employer has a pension plan, it will provide full benefits when a worker retires, usually at the age 65. (It cannot *require* retirement because, again, mandatory retirement is almost always illegal.) Employers can, however, offer workers the opportunity to retire early and offer such incentives as

- paying full retirement benefits now; and
- supplementing payments with additional cash ("bridge payments") to help out until the worker becomes 65 and thus eligible for Social Security and Medicare.

If offered early retirement, *you don't have to take it.* While early retirement plans can be good things (we're waiting by the phone), don't be pressured into agreeing. Think long and hard about retirement and the loss of income, daily direction and status it may entail. Consult a financial adviser. And, if you are interested, there may be room to negotiate better terms. One big item will be health insurance and who is to pay the premium.

And who is to buy the pet food.

Chapter 16

Con Artists

"I never met a man I didn't like."

—T. Tiger

"I never met a man I couldn't trick."

—C. Chiseler

Crooks don't look like crooks; they look like Will Rogers. They're good at what they do: friendly, caring, and, guess what, *"You remind me so much of my own parents."* Of course, crooks are only interested in making things better for you—improving your health, getting you the right insurance, increasing your income, fixing your home.

Once they steal your money, crooks know you will blame yourself: *"What a fool was I. I should have known better. I must be stupid or getting senile. I'm not going to tell anyone."*

Young people, sophisticated people, brilliant people, all fall victim. MBAs from Harvard simply lose more money. If you get taken, pick yourself up, dust yourself off, and go after them. We'll tell you how at the end of this chapter. But first, we'll tell you how to avoid being taken.

You're most vulnerable when you answer your phone, open your door or turn on your TV. We'll tell you your best defenses. Then we'll describe common schemes and finally turn to protecting your most valued assets: your checking accounts, your credit cards, and your home.

Herein man's inhumanity to man; tigers at least snarl first.

a. Phone Solicitations, Door-to-Door Sales, and "Home Shopping" Channels

Telephone Fraud

Consumers are bilked to the tune of $40 billion annually by telemarketing scams. (Again, you're not alone.)

When the phone rings, *don't be polite*. You didn't ask to be called. The person at the other end of the line is not an orphan, not a burn victim, not someone working their way through college, and not someone planning to help others by giving them puppies. The person on the other end of the line is working on commission, reading a script and, we hate to tell you this, has absolutely no interest in whether you are having a good day. The person has been trained to cheat you. They rehearse! They count on your decency and plan to use it against you.

> *Don't be polite. If you hang up, you won't hurt their feelings. They'll light another cigarette, scratch, burp (or worse), and then, with a smirk, call the next mark.*

There is a great scene in the movie *In Cold Blood*. Two killers are hitchhiking in the desert and a guy in a convertible speeds by, stopping about 50 feet down the road. The two killers run toward the car but, at the very last minute, and most impolitely, the car speeds away. One killer shouts "Smart move, jerk. We were going to kill you."

Remember that scene.

How can you sort out the legitimate charities that raise money by telephone?

> *"You seem to have a very worthwhile cause but I never give money over the phone. I promised my lawyer. Please send me some material on your project and after I see it, but not before, I might send you some money. Have a nice day. My lawyers sends regards as well. Goodbye."*

New rules of the Federal Trade Commission help control telephone fraud.

- Telemarketers must promptly identify themselves, who they represent, and what the purpose of the call is, such as seeking funds or selling a product.

If you aren't told this information at the beginning of the call, the caller is violating the law. So, too, if the caller is hiding the sales pitch behind "You've won a free trip to Hawaii." Hang up.

- The law prohibits calls before 8:00 a.m. and after 9:00 p.m.
- If you ask not to be called again, it is a violation of the law for them to call you again. You can report violations by phoning 1-800-876-7060 (National Fraud Information Hotline).

Remember the following points:

- Never agree to make a purchase or give money on the first call. Insist on thinking it over. Resist the "Limited time" offer. Legitimate sellers will give you time to think.
- Never give your credit card number to a caller.

A common scheme is to phone and pitch a low cost item and ask that it be paid for by credit card. With your name and credit card number, the con can easily max out your account in a matter of hours. (Often they are in cahoots with dishonest retailers who help run up the bill.) Even though the extent of your liability will be only $50, likely your card will be canceled and might not be returned.

- No one *ever* wins a free trip to Hawaii.

Door-to-Door Sales (and Three-day Cooling-off Period)

What do we know about door-to-door purchases?

- Before you answered the door, you didn't even know you needed the product.
- You have little idea as to what is a fair price or as to whether competing models have better features. (*Consumer Reports* would come in handy.)
- You don't know anything about the seller or even where to find him if the product never gets there or breaks when it does.

As to the "substantial savings" you get because the seller doesn't have to maintain a retail store or engage in advertising, the commission structure on door-to-door sales offsets these amounts. Salesmen pocket a large part of the purchase price.

Bottom line, *never,* well almost never, buy from door-to-door sellers. (Two thumbs up, however, for Girl Scout Cookies.)

Three-Day Cooling-Off Period

The Federal Trade Commission adopted a three-day cooling-off period rule for door-to- door sales. You have the right to cancel any *credit* purchase (as opposed to *cash* purchase) *for any reason you want.* This rule applies even though the goods have been delivered to you. You simply have to write the seller by midnight of the third business day after the contract was signed. The seller must give you a "notice of cancellation" to use for this purpose.

The seller then has 10 days to return any down-payment you made and 20 days to pick up the goods (after that, they're yours!). Don't give the seller the goods until he has returned your money.

The cooling-off period does *not* apply to cash purchases, sales that were first discussed at the seller's place of business, telephone orders, mail orders, or emergency home repairs.

Most states have statutes which parallel the federal rule.

"Home Shopping" Channels

Here the problem is not getting cheated; it is spending too much.

"Those nice folks on TV seem to be talking to me; and when I call them, they do."

Buy a movie channel. Get on a web chat room.

If your parent or spouse continues to overspend, phone their 1-800 number and follow up with a letter.

> *Please be advised that my mother is 83 and has made several substantial purchases from you which she does not need. She no longer has contractual capacity. From this time on, I will refuse to allow her to pay you on credit card charges. When the bill comes, I will dispute it by enclosing a copy of this letter to you.*
>
> *P.S. Great show!*

b. Common Scams

Here is a list depressingly long and, more depressingly, incomplete:

"Loan" scams
"Good cause" scams
Health care scams
Health insurance scams
Home repair scams
Investment and franchise scams
Inheritance scams
Home mortgage scams
Scams at the time a loved one dies
Pyramid Schemes

"Loan" Scams

These are getting more common. The pitch is that person can arrange for a very favorable loan for you but you have to pay the "loan fee" up front. Never do this. The person will simply run off with your money.

"Good Cause" Scams

Never, never take cash from your checking or savings account to give to a stranger, no matter how compelling his or her story.

> *In the "bank examiner" scheme, the con approaches you, claiming to be a bank official and asking you to help the bank catch an embezzler by making a substantial withdrawal. Once the money is withdrawn, the con takes it and is gone. In the "falling on hard times" scheme, the con comes to the door with a compelling story, usually involving his wife or child and their immediate medical needs, which can be met with a small loan, to be repaid tomorrow and, as collateral, "Here's my bike." Here you are not only out your money but also have a stolen bike on your hands.*

If you must give strangers money, *write a check* or, if you don't have a checking account, *purchase a money order*. Make it payable to the person and *note the purpose of the transaction* on the check or money order. If you give someone cash, they can deny that you gave them money; if you just write a check without a notation, they can claim that it was a gift. Finally, if things go the way we think they will, having a name will help in tracking the person down.

Health Care Scams

Sick people want to get well; if traditional medicine doesn't seem to work, people seek other avenues. *Be extremely careful.* Many promised cures are lies. Laetrile doesn't cure cancer, Compound Q doesn't cure AIDS, and Snake Oil doesn't cure much of anything. Fraudulent cures not only cost money but may delay an actual cure through traditional medicine.

On the other hand, it is your money and your life and some people swear by non-traditional methods. Not so long ago, traditional medicine used "bleeding." Whatever your medical decisions, just realize that snake oil sellers are still out there and that the human condition is such that we don't always get better.

The American Medical Association suggests that you be careful in the following situations:

- Where the quack claims a "secret" formula or machine to cure disease;
- Where the cure is claimed to be quick and easy; and
- Where the quack scoffs at traditional methods and claims that his are superior.

No matter your ailment, from cancer to wrinkles, from alcoholism to ulcers, someone will offer you a cure. Others push defective (or not needed) eyeglasses, hearing aids, dentures, drugs and prevention programs.

Two points to remember:

1. Before taking any new form of medicine, talk to your pharmacist! and
2. Be leery of the word "natural."

Drugs can interact in bad ways. Pharmacists have a broad knowledge of medical matters, and, unlike the person pushing the sale, are disinterested in your decision.

You can also get advice from local offices of the American Medical Association, the American Dental Association, the American Cancer Society, the Arthritis Foundation or similar organizations.

Without getting into a philosophic discussion of what is natural (and the fallacy that "natural must be good" - cancer is natural), just realize that before a drug is approved by the FDA, it goes through millions of dollars worth of tests, looking for side effects and effectiveness.

"Natural remedies" generally have not been tested for either effectiveness or side-effects. Personal testimonials mean little because you don't know (1) whether anything was ever wrong with the person; (2) whether what was wrong with them is wrong with you; and (3) even if they got better, why they got better; it could have been for a host of other reasons.

As for purchasing hearing aids, see Chapter 26-d.

Health Insurance Scams

There are three kinds of health insurance offered to most seniors:

- Medigap policies which cover some of the gaps in Medicare. See Chapter 7-d.
- Long-term care policies which cover nursing home care and certain in-home services. See Chapter 8-a.
- Disease-specific policies covering such things as cancer, liver disorders, and heart disease. See Chapter 7-d.

Recent Congressional hearings found that insurance fraud is widespread.

- Deal only with those insurance agents you have been dealing with on home and auto insurance.
- Be suspicious of unsolicited insurance advice coming in the form of letters, door-to-door sales, or even TV. Don't believe those friendly familiar faces of aging stars—they are being paid to sell insurance, and we know that they are great actors. Of course, had they been better actors, they might still have day jobs.
- Don't believe what the agent *says*. Whatever the agent says may be denied later; what is *written* in the policy is what counts. Policies are very hard to read. Ask questions regarding coverage, deductibles, filing requirements, and so forth. When you ask these questions, if you don't know and trust the agent, have him or her *point to the language in the policy* that confirms the answer.

- Don't get too much coverage. Medicare covers a lot (Chapter 7-b) and if you buy a policy that provides double coverage, Medicare provides you cannot recover twice, *no matter what your agent says.*
- Call the State Insurance Office to get information about specific companies.
- See our general discussion on buying health insurance, Chapter 7-f.

Home Repair Scams

Mario Puzo, in *The Godfather,* tells of the Holland Furnace Company. It would go door to door, offering free furnace inspections. After tearing the furnace apart, the burly repairmen would explain "It's broke. Pay us $500 and we will fix it and put it back together. Otherwise, we're out of here."

The scam worked well until the day fate took them, unbeknownst, to the home of the Godfather.

What a marvelous moment!

Crooks come to your house, often pretending they are from the city or county, to inspect your roof, electrical system, or furnace. Even if there is nothing wrong, they will claim there is and then force you into expensive repairs.

Don't let them in your house. No government official has a right to enter your home without a search warrant. (That was what the American Revolution was about, that, and if I recall correctly, tea.)

Take their card and phone the city to see if they are for real. If they are for real, they can come back.

Investment and Franchise Scams

The pitch here is that you can earn substantial amounts, usually in your spare time, often from the convenience of your own home. Of course, to show your good faith, your interest, or to help offset some of the costs, a relatively small investment on your part is required.

See you later, Alligator.

Be leery of work-at-home offers that require you to invest in equipment or in start up kits. U.S. Postal Service Officials claim that they are not aware *of one* of these offers that actually lives up to its claims of profits. Not one!

Higher end investment frauds include franchising and distributorship frauds. Under a franchise agreement, an individual gets the right to distribute the franchiser's product or service in a local area. In return, the individual (the franchisee) pays fees and, usually, purchases equipment and supplies from the franchiser. These are common in fast-food restaurants, vacation and travel agencies, and other service agencies. Distributorships are quite similar, involving an individual purchasing the right to distribute certain products, such as vending machines, in particular areas.

Many of these are great investment opportunities, *but go slowly*!

Hundreds have been bilked out of their life savings in phony or shaky franchise and distributorship deals. The Federal Trade Commission requires that as a potential investor you be given a great deal of information. You can get a copy of what is required from them in the publication:

Disclosure Requirements and Prohibitions Concerning Franchising and Business Opportunity Ventures.

Inheritance Scams

An official-looking letter informs you that you are about to receive a large inheritance but that you must send in an advance on legal fees to receive it. Wrong! Lawyers are paid by the estate, not by the heirs.

Home Mortgage Scams

Many of us need to borrow against the equity in our homes. You may receive offers to borrow money against your home that sound too good to be true. They are.

"Lenders" have been going to various states and lending money in exchange for a mortgage on your home. They tell you that you will have payments you can easily afford. But when it comes to signing the papers, there are extras – insurance, fees, commissions, etc. They will often include a provision for a "balloon payment" due after 3, 5 or 10 years. A balloon payment requires you to pay off the entire balance at once. Of course, you can't. These lenders will offer to refinance the loan and eventually, you owe so much that you cannot make the payments and you lose your home.

When borrowing against your home, always use reputable, established lenders and have any loan or mortgage agreements reviewed by someone independent, such as an attorney. On getting money out of your house, see Chapter 5.

Scams at the Time a Loved One Dies

Some bottom dwellers read the obituaries (or perhaps have them read to them). They may come at you with their traditional scams or they may use one of the special ones designed for this time. They may send a phony bill in the name of the deceased spouse claiming that the bill is long overdue and that dire consequences will follow if it is not paid. A particularly repulsive variation is where the bill purports to be for pornography.

Don't pay any of your deceased spouse's bills. See Chapter 12-c.

Pyramid Schemes

In the 1680s, Halley discovered a great comet; in the 1930s, Ponzi discovered a great scheme.

At first, these schemes seem to work. They begin with a plausible plan to make money. Ponzi claimed he could make huge profits trading foreign currencies across the international dateline. You are asked to invest, usually not much. You may be asked to let two or three friends in on the "fantastic deal."

It's *not* "See you later, Alligator." In fact, here it's

"Here's a check representing what you have earned so far on your investment. Notice that you have made 50% in the first month. Want to invest some more?"

The money returned comes from the money your friends put in. You leave your money in and put in more. Your money is now offered to your friends, and they too opt to stay in.

Only after hundreds or thousands have invested is it time for "See you later, alligator."Some pyramid schemes are straightforward. You are asked to send money to someone and give the names of friends who will then send money to you and so forth. Great returns are promised. These schemes are *criminal* in most states, not only to set up, but to *play*!

* * *

And, of course, the list doesn't end there.There are "burial frauds" and "living trust" frauds; there are stock brokers who "churn" your account (each transaction putting commissions in their pockets), nursing homes which overcharge, and advertisers who use "bait and switch" tactics (they advertise a super deal but, when the customer arrives, the item is disparaged—or is "sold out"—and then the customer is switched to a higher priced item).

But we don't want to depress you.

Let's discuss crooks who steal money the old-fashioned way—forging your checks or stealing credit card numbers.

c. Protecting Your Checking Accounts and Credit Cards

Check Your Monthly Bank Statements

If someone steals a check and forges your name, under the Uniform Commercial Code, if you report the forgery within 30 days after you receive your statement, the *bank will pick up the loss*. After 30 days, the bank need not pick up the loss unless you can prove that it was negligent. This will be an uphill fight.

Check Your Credit Card Bill

Under the federal Fair Credit Billing Act, you have 60 days to report billing errors, including unauthorized charges, situations where the goods or services were not delivered or accepted, clerical errors, and failure to indicate payments made. Unless the error is corrected, the creditor has 30 days to notify you that your complaint has been received.

Never give your credit card number to someone who phones you (it is okay if you phone them and are ordering tickets or making reservations).

d. Protecting Your Home

If a creditor has a security interest in your home, you might lose it if things go bad for you. Otherwise, your home is relatively safe.

Federal law gives you a three-day cooling off period in which to cancel any transaction that triggers such a security interest. Consult a lawyer before signing papers relating to your home. Be especially cautious with home repairs. Usually the contract you sign for roofing, paving, siding, or other repairs creates a lien on your home.

e. If You Are Suspicious

Getting Information About Sellers

Ask other customers about it. If the business won't give you the names of other customers, walk away. Doctors, lawyers, dentists, psychologists, realtors, and a host of other professions are regulated by professional associations. These associations answer questions, take complaints, and make investigations.

Many businesses, such as auto dealers and home builders, also have trade associations that might provide good information. As to Better Business Bureaus, they do not license businesses nor do they vouch for them. However, most will tell you if a particular dealer has had complaints filed.

Getting Information About Products

Try the library. The person behind the desk is there because they want to help and know how.

Consumer Reports has in-depth reports comparing almost all kinds of products. Libraries have back issues. Many of these services and publications are on the Internet. Going on-line can get you vast amounts of information from your own desk.

f. If You Think You Have Been Cheated, Raise Hell!

Start with the Consumer Affairs Office of your state's Attorney General's Office.

City Attorney Offices and District Attorney Offices often have similar offices. Explain your problem. Often they will help you resolve it;

if not, they will point you in the right direction. You'll need a guide since there are multitudes of state and federal laws that apply to consumer frauds, all with different coverage and methods of enforcement. To wit:

- State Unfair and Deceptive Practices Laws
- Section 5 of the Federal Trade Commission Act
- U.S. Post Office (mail fraud)
- FDA (foods and drugs)
- Securities Exchange Commission (stock and bond frauds)

Consider visiting a lawyer. Laws prohibiting consumer fraud may give victims not only the right to get their money back, but also to sue for money damages, punitive damages and statutory penalties. Attorney fees may be recoverable if you win. Even if you were not cheated out of a great deal of money, a lawyer might take your case if a lot of other people were also cheated by the same person or company: class actions are possible.

Your Area Agency on Aging has an Ombudsman who can be very helpful in mediating consumer disputes.

If the amount is small, consider filing a complaint in Small Claims Court. The forms are easy to fill out and you don't need a lawyer. You just go to court and tell your side of the story and the other side does likewise. Then the judge rules. On your way out, you stand before a TV camera and are asked what you think of the judge's decision. (Oops, wrong show.)

Chapter 17

Bill Collectors

> *Hamlet advised Ophelia, "Get thee to a nunnery."*
> *If it ever comes down to buying needed medications or paying the Finance Company, we advise, "Get thee to a Pharmacy!"*

Okay. *Hamlet* is something of a push and the rhyme isn't all that good, but we make a very serious point. We have had clients who have cut back on needed medications in order to pay other bills. Don't do that.

This chapter will help if you've got financial woes and, even if you don't, it may help you avoid them down the road. First, what *not* to do. Don't dig yourself in deeper by borrowing more money. And don't stick your head in the sand and hope your creditors will forget about you. Second, what *to* do. Get debt counseling, consider bankruptcy, keep in touch with all your creditors, and buy your meds!

> Debt counseling agencies can help you with a budget and can contact creditors on your behalf. Some are even free. Contact your Area Agency on Aging or your local Information and Referral.

The remainder of this chapter backs up this advice. We first look at what creditors and collection agencies can do—their barks are worse than their bites. Then we will look at why you shouldn't get a "bill payer" loan and why you should *not* allow creditors to repossess furniture or car. Next we discuss which bills to pay first. Finally we look at bottom line concerns: what happens if you get sued and the option of bankruptcy.

a. Barks and Bites

Don't panic! *Creditor barks are worse than their bites.*

- There is no imprisonment for debt—you won't go to jail.

- Social Security checks are safe, so you won't starve.
- You won't get thrown out in the street (only the bank which holds your mortgage or, if you rent, your landlord, can throw you out).
- Your car and most of your personal property are safe (TV, household furniture, kitchen appliances). These items are generally exempt for execution, which means that only creditors who have contractual security interest in them can take them.
- Collection agencies cannot go around telling your neighbors or employers that you are a "deadbeat."
- Creditors cannot sue your children (unless they co-signed).
- You are not liable for the debts of your adult children (unless you co-signed).

Most creditors are willing to deal. Most will give you more time and perhaps cut interest charges and even some of the principal *if* they are convinced that you are in good faith and are willing to work with them. Going to court, turning the matter over to a collection agency, or trying to foreclose on their security interest all cost creditors money. Plus you might go bankrupt. Thus there is room to negotiate.

Work with your creditor *before* the matter is turned over to a collection agency. When this happens, the creditor loses between 30% and 50% off the top. This means, if you pay *most* of your bill, the creditor comes out ahead by not turning it over to an agency.

b. Collection Agencies

The Federal Fair Debt Collection Practices Act protects you from harassment and intimidation.

- Collection agencies *cannot* contact other people (except to learn where you are) and cannot tell them that you owe any money.
- Collection agencies *cannot* harass you by calling late at night, by using obscene or threatening language, or by threatening to publish your name as a deadbeat.
- If you tell the agency you are not going to pay the bill or that you don't want further contact with it, it must stop contacting you, except to advise you that it is filing suit. If you

get a lawyer, then the agency can only communicate with your lawyer.

If you get a letter from a collection agency and *if you dispute the debt,* write the collection agency. It must then obtain verification of the debt and communicate that verification to you before taking further steps to collect it.

If you think you have been mistreated by a collection agency, you can contact a lawyer since a federal act gives you the right to sue it. Or you can file a complaint with the Federal Trade Commission. To find out how to do so, check with your local U.S. Attorney's Office.

c. Avoid "Bill Payer Loans" Like the Plague

Actually plagues are very hard to avoid; otherwise they would never be plagues, only a few dead rats in the harbor.

Bill Payer Loans, consolidation loans, seem too good to be true – pay off all of your bills at once and still have *lower* monthly payments.

Where's the catch?

Longer Repayment Schedules

Most credit card bills treat the loan as a loan for 36 months: your minimum monthly payment is 1/36 of the outstanding balance. Most small loan company loans are for 72 months: your minimum payment is only 1/72 of the outstanding balance. Because the pay back period is much longer, monthly payments go down *even if the interest charged is significantly higher.*

Why avoid these loans?

- The interest rate may be higher. If not, you will still end up paying more interest as you will pay it for a longer time.
- Many of these loans have *prepayment penalties* which mean, unlike credit cards, you can't pay them off all at once to avoid further interest payments.
- These loans turn *unsecured debt* (credit cards, doctor bills) into *secured debt.* This means that your home, car, and fur-

niture are more at risk if you fall behind making payments. More on this as we go along.

- With lower monthly payments, you may be tempted to run up other bills.

d. Never Agree to a Repossession

If you fall behind paying for your car, the seller might try to take it back (repossess it). If you fall behind with the small loan company, they might try to pick up your furniture.

If they come, what should you do?

Don't let them. Although they have a contractual right to repossess (you gave it to them in the small print), *they cannot commit a breach of the peace in doing so.* This means if they come to your house to pick things up, you *don't* have to let them in.

The problem is that once they take your car or your furniture, that might not be the end of the matter. They will sell it and deduct what they get from what you owe. You may *still* end up in debt. To see how this works—and it is an ugly picture—see our discussion of deficiency judgments which comes in a page or two.

Lock the door and get advice, a lawyer's if possible. It may be best to call their bluff. Yes, they can go to court and get a court order (which the Sheriff may enforce), but will they? It will cost them money—sure, you may be liable to pay those costs, but can they be sure of collecting it from you? You always have the Bankruptcy Card, and, as we shall see, you might be "judgment proof."

e. Which Bills Should You Pay First?

In George Orwell's parody of the Russian Revolution, *Animal Farm*, the animals rose up, took over the farm, and created Animal Paradise. Their Constitution spoke to their idealism: "All Animals are Equal."

Alas, this utopia was not to last. Soon the pigs took over and grabbed the good stuff. They were, after all, pigs. Noting the apparent contradiction between their behavior and their Constitution, the pigs realized one would have to change. They opted to amend their Constitution:

Some Animals Are More Equal than Others

So too with creditors. While paying something on all your bills, give priority to some. Priorities are based on how badly the creditor can hurt you. Briefly, the highest priority are court ordered and government creditors, next those folks who will cut off necessary services, then secured creditors who might repossess your car or home, and finally unsecured creditors, such as doctors, hospitals and credit cards. Of course, you should also consider paying off higher interest debts before others. Now some of the rather technical details of consumer law.

Court Ordered and Government Creditors

Child support and alimony (spousal maintenance) are *top* priorities. If you don't pay them, *you can go to jail.*

Government creditors have a high priority as well. Debts owed to the IRS are *not* dischargeable in bankruptcy, and interest and penalties on IRS debts can be substantial. Don't ask what your government can do *for* you; ask what it can do *to* you.

Creditors Who Can Cut Off Services

These have the highest priority too. If you don't pay these folks, they cut off needed services. Don't pay your car insurance, your health insurance, or your fire insurance, you lose your coverage; don't pay your electric bill, you lose your lights.

If you are renting, your landlord can *evict* you for non-payment of rent. To do so, however, the landlord must first go to court and serve you with papers. Some have been known to lower rent if approached by a long time resident. Further, landlords, depending on the market, may have less of a hair trigger than other creditors. If you are evicted, the landlord must find a new tenant or the place stands vacant, bringing in nothing.

Secured Creditors: Acceleration Clauses, Repossession and Deficiency Judgments

If you buy a car on time, the seller keeps a security interest in it. If you don't pay your bill, the seller can repossess (take back) the car. If you borrow money from a small loan company, it will take a security interest in your household furniture. If you don't pay your bill, they can pick up your furniture. If you buy a house, the bank that lent you the money will take a security interest in the house, here called a mortgage or a deed of trust. Again, if you don't pay, you will lose your house.

There are several things you need to know about these arrangements and none of them are particularly cheery: repossession clauses, acceleration clauses and deficiency judgments.

Most loan contracts contain, in the small print, a clause that allows the creditor, if you miss your payments, to repossess the secured item without going to court. Automobile lenders often come in dead of night. We have already advised you not to allow the repossession if you can prevent it without violence. It is far better to force your creditors to go to court where you have a chance to defend yourself.

Another typical hidden clause is the *acceleration clause*. It provides that if you miss one or more payments, the creditor can declare all the rest of the payments due now. The *entire* amount you owe becomes due.

> *If a creditor tells you that you are in default because of late payments and demands that you now pay the entire outstanding balance or he will repossess the secured item, see a lawyer. There are defenses to a creditor's use of acceleration clauses.*

Finally, there is the matter of deficiency judgments. Let's use the example of Smilin' Sam, Used Car Dealer. If you miss a few payments, Sam can *repossess* your car *without* going to court; then he can sell the car and apply that amount to your unpaid balance. If you still owe more than they received from the sale of your car (a likely situation), Sam can come after you for the remainder *plus* the attorney fees you agreed to pay in the small print. This is known as a *deficiency judgment.*

Say you purchased a car for $10,000. You put $500 down and made another $1,500 in payments, leaving a balance owed of $8,000. You miss a few payments and the finance company declares a forfeiture and has someone pick up your car. They then sell the car for $6,000. As you still owed $8,000, there is a $2,000 deficiency. The company can sue you for it, plus their attorney fees, say an additional $500. Things could actually be a little worse. But note the bottom line: you have paid $2,000, still owe $2,500, and are taking the bus!

One is reminded of a scene in Dicken's *Oliver Twist.* A man is told that he is responsible for the criminal acts of his wife, as the law presumes that the husband controls his wife. "If the law presumes that," he responds, "the law is a ass, a idiot."

The bank that has your home mortgage is a secured creditor. It will probably be easier to work with than small loan companies or automobile lenders. There are two factors at play. First, under the laws of most states, a bank must go to court before it can sell your house (compare the repossession of your car) or give you scads of notice. This costs them money and takes time. (Some banks, rather than take a mortgage in your property, use a *deed of trust.* This legal device allows them to sell your house *without* going to court. You are more vulnerable in this situation.)

The second reason home lenders might be reluctant to foreclose is that in some states there is anti-deficiency legislation. Say you owe $70,000 on the house and, upon foreclosure, all they can sell it for is $60,000. If there is anti-deficiency legislation, they *cannot* come after you for the $10,000. This is a sobering thought to bankers. They also don't like being in the business of selling houses.

Be extremely cautious in giving anyone a security interest in your home. It opens the possibility that you may lose it. When you give someone a security interest, under federal law, you have a three day cooling off period to get out of the deal.

Note, in this regard, many companies offering bill payor loans take a security interest in your home.

It seems, thus far, that all of your creditors can inflict great harm. There is a final category of creditors, however, that do not have the same teeth and, thankfully, many of your bills are no doubt owed to them. These are your unsecured creditors.

Unsecured Creditors

Unsecured creditors include credit card companies, hospitals, other medical providers, and service providers such as lawyers and accountants. While perhaps being the most virtuous, these folks have the lowest priority. Before they can reach any of your property, they must go to court and get a judgment (see our discussion immediately below on how this works). Further, as we will see, they are most vulnerable to losing part of their claims in bankruptcy. On the other hand, in the case of credit cards, unpaid balances pile up interest charges.

f. If You Get Sued: Defenses and Exemptions

Most of what you own is safe from creditors unless and until they sue and obtain judgment against you. Before that, they cannot take any of your salary, bank accounts or other property. The only exception to this is that, as we have seen, secured creditors might attempt to repossess their security interest (e.g. your car) without going to court. Before suit and judgment, most creditors can only bark. Threatening letters don't make it nor does filing suit: they need to get a judgment.

If a creditor sues you, it will serve you with an official looking document known as the Complaint. Service, with rare exceptions, must be by hand; the creditor cannot simply mail you the Complaint. Usually a process server will show up at your house or your place of employment and ask you your name and then hand you the papers. It is not a great experience. The Complaint will state why the creditor (known now as the "Plaintiff") thinks you owe it money. The Complaint will then pray for judgment and state how much it claims you owe. This will include the amount owed on the debt and, most likely, attorney fees and court costs. These can run up quickly.

It is important to read the Complaint to see if the Plaintiff got things right. Often they don't. Common consumer defenses include:

- Fraud or misrepresentation on the part of the seller
- Failure of consideration: what was purchased broke
- Waiver of payment dates: If a seller allows you to pay late several times, generally they cannot suddenly claim you are late as to one and then accelerate the balance.

If you get served with a Complaint, you gotta see a lawyer *quickly.* Legal Aid offers help to low income defendants. Most local Bar Associations have referral programs which allow you to talk to a lawyer for a minimal payment, say $25 for a 30 minute consultation.

If you and your lawyer decide to fight the Complaint, your lawyer will write an Answer which will be filed with the court. Thereafter, the lawyers will negotiate a deal. Often, even at this late stage, creditors are willing to compromise. If a deal cannot be made, the matter will be set for trial, often far in the future.

If you ignore the Complaint, hoping it will go away or waiting for a better time to deal with it, after about 30 or so days, the creditor will get a *default* judgment against you in the amount asked for. Once this happens, it can get court orders allowing it to attach your property.

Once the creditor gets a judgment, what next?

Execution of Judgment

Once a creditor gets a judgment against you (either by default or after a trial) it becomes a "judgment creditor" and can:

- Attach your wages—up to 25%. ("Attachment" is a Court Order directing your employer to pay up to 25% of your salary to the creditor rather than to you. It can continue until the judgment is paid in full.)
- Attach, by court order, your stocks, bonds, vacation homes, and bank accounts. Once an asset is attached, it can be sold and the proceeds applied to the judgment. Monies left over go to you.

The good news is that a judgment creditor cannot get any of your exempt assets. Exemptions are generally governed by state law, but let's take a look at the common ones.

Assets Exempt from Judgment

Your Home

Most states allow you to file a "Homestead Exemption" which will protect your home from execution. Homestead laws protect homes only of a certain value; check with your County Clerk for more information.

Usually state law allows you to file your exemption at the very last minute, even after a creditor has sued you, but before they have obtained a judgment. Because you can wait until the last moment, we advise against routinely filing homestead. Most folks will never need it, and it will take paperwork to remove it when you sell your house.

Your Furnishings and Car

Most states make most home furnishings and one car, below a certain value, exempt from execution. Furnishings include your furniture, general household goods, and your clothing. In addition, your tools needed for work are exempt. Some states have more liberal exemption rules than others, and it is a good idea to consult with a lawyer if you find yourself in this position.

Social Security Checks

These cannot be attached (executed upon). Bank accounts can be. So once social security payments are placed in bank accounts with other funds, they may lose their exempt status. *Keep them in separate accounts* or use cash.

For a lot of people, most of what they own is exempt from execution. Lawyers call this "judgment proof." If you are living on social security, have homesteaded your modest home, and have no stocks and bonds or large bank accounts, there is nothing your unsecured creditors can go after. If you are in this situation, consider writing your creditor: "Stop bothering me. I will pay when I can. But I am judgment proof."

g. Bankruptcy

Bankruptcy works wonders with unsecured debts:

Credit card bills
Doctor and hospital bills
Tort judgments (auto wrecks)

It doesn't work well with:

IRS debts
Child support/alimony
Secured creditors (the bank that holds your mortgage)

One major problem with bankruptcy is that you can do it only once every seven years. It is a great card, but don't play it too quickly. There are two popular forms of bankruptcy: Chapter 13 (wage earner) and Chapter 7 (regular).

If you are still employed, consider Chapter 13. Basically it does not discharge debts so much as get creditors off your back. You will pay them according to a plan that is made, one which usually gives you 36 months to pay off your debts. The Bankruptcy court may order some creditors to reduce finance charges and even to knock off part of the principal.

If you are no longer working, Chapter 7 Bankruptcy is your only alternative. It will actually discharge some of your debts.

It works this way. Once a petition is filed in Federal Bankruptcy Court, a court trustee is appointed. Your creditors will be notified, and they then must cease all collection activities, including contacting you; any court proceedings against you are immediately put on hold. The court trustee will gather your non-exempt assets together, sell them, and then pay the creditors their pro rata share (if you have $20,000 worth of bills and only $10,000 in non-exempt assets, each creditor will be paid 50% of their bill).

Your exempt assets are generally those discussed in the last section. You do not lose these if you go through bankruptcy.

After this payment, the debts are discharged; your creditors cannot come back and try to get more.

What About Secured Creditors?

These too will be discharged *if* you give up the property and throw it into the pot. Maybe you won't want to do that. Let's take your car as an example. Let's say you still owe $8,000 on it. If it is worth $10,000, you won't want to throw it in the pot: you will be losing $2,000. To prevent this from happening, you can reaffirm the debt. At the first meeting of creditors, the judge will ask you which debts, if any, you want to reaffirm. By reaffirming, these debts are kept out of the bankruptcy process. You still owe the money, but you still have the car.

Once a debt is discharged in bankruptcy, *don't promise the creditor to pay it.* If you do, you may have waived your protection. You may, however, still pay on it if you wish. But you need not pay all of it, unless you promise to do so *after* it was discharged. Don't believe a creditor that tells you different story and, again, don't make any promise to pay the entire amount.

Bankruptcy will not discharge secured creditors (unless you threw the property into the pot) or government creditors, such as taxes or other government obligations. It does not discharge child support obligations or debts resulting from fraud on your part.

Not that we think you would, but you cannot go out, have a spending spree, and then file bankruptcy—debts incurred in anticipation of bankruptcy are not dischargeable.

Although many stores sell bankruptcy kits, trying to do your own bankruptcy is penny wise, pound foolish. A good lawyer can make sure you get all of your exemptions and will make sure that you get all of the debt relief you are entitled to. Even though you will pay a fee, most likely you will come out way ahead. Paying the lawyer the fee pre-bankruptcy is money you would otherwise pay your creditors—think about it.

* * *

All of that was pretty heavy going. We should have stuck with *Hamlet*:

"*Neither a lender or borrower be!*" (At least we tied it up!)

Part Four

Putting Your House in Order

Chapter 18

Keeping Control of Your Medical Decisions

Dismal news. A recent study published in the *Journal of the American Medical Association* focused on the terminally ill in several leading hospitals.

> *50% experience moderate to severe pain, half the time.*
>
> *38% spend ten or more days in a coma, attached to a ventilator, or in intensive care.*
>
> *31% spend all, or most, of their family's savings during their final illness.*

Surely we would not choose this. How can it be? The law is clear:

> *Every human being of adult years and sound mind has a right to determine what shall be done with his own body; and a surgeon who performs an operation without the patient's consent commits a battery.*
>
> Justice Benjamin Cardozo

The law protects our right to make our own decisions. We can:

- leave the hospital against doctors' orders and
- decline medical treatment, even if it kills us.

So why is the American Way of Death so needlessly expensive and painful? You may be incapable of exercising your right to reject treatment or your right to go home to die. Slipping in and out of consciousness, wracked with pain, confused as to time and place, medical personnel simply can't trust what you say. Doctors, trained to save lives (and fearing legal liability if they don't), will keep you alive even though everyone knows that the end is inevitable. You can protect yourself. You can protect loved ones. *If you act now.*

a. The Needed Documents

Two documents must be prepared and signed:

1. Living Will
2. Durable Power of Attorney for Health Care

A *Living Will* tells medical providers the kinds of treatment you want, and those you don't, during your final illness. It takes effect only if you are incapable of making those decisions at the time.

A *Durable Power of Attorney for Health Care* allows you to appoint someone to make health care decisions for you if you are incapable of doing so. It is broader than a Living Will, which takes effect only during terminal illness. A Durable Power takes effect any time you need medical assistance and are incapable of giving consent. It can cover such things as consenting to surgery or moving you into a nursing facility.

Alas, these documents might not be enough. They may be ignored by doctors, nurses, and family members. Doctors are trained to view death as a defeat and hence are predisposed to take "heroic measures."

- Talk to your *doctor* about your Living Will and Durable Power and the decisions you have made. Make sure your doctor agrees to follow your instructions. Have your doctor put copies in your medical file. There is one problem with this advice. In most urban centers, your family doctor will not be caring for you in the hospital. You are turned over to specialists. You must somehow have them contact your doctor to confirm your wishes

- Talk to your *family* about the decisions you want made. (In Chapter 34, "A Family Conversation," we'll offer tips on how to get this conversation started.) Your family's agreement to your wishes is vital. If even one of your family insists that doctors take all heroic measures, they generally will even though your Living Will says not to do so. As one doctor friend explains, "Only the living can sue."

- Talk to the *agent* you appointed in your Durable Power about your decisions. Again, make sure your agent agrees to carry out your instructions.
- *Keep the original documents* with your important papers. Make certain that people know where you have kept the documents. You can even notify the local 911 response team.

b. What Happens If You Do Nothing?

"Yeah, all of that sounds good and I definitely should get those things for both me and my parents. But I have miles to ride before I sleep. I'll do it next week."

Suddenly, it's always suddenly, something happens. A car wreck, a stroke, a trip on the stairs.

If you haven't signed the necessary documents, your family and doctors will have to agree on your medical treatment. If the treatment is major or if there is disagreement, then your family will probably have to go to court to get a formal guardianship which would give it legal power to make your decisions. We describe the process in Chapter 28-d. For now, know that it is time- consuming, expensive, and heartbreaking.

To avoid the hassle and expense of guardianships, some states have passed *Family Agency Acts*. These list those who can make medical decisions when you can't, usually your spouse first, then your adult children, and thereafter other relatives and, in some states, domestic partners.

Even if your state has a Family Agency Act, don't let it do the walking.

- You might not like the person the statute selects: families fight and spouses may be too sick or too depressed to take on this added burden.
- In some cases, the most significant person in your life may not be "officially approved." This has been painfully illustrated during the AIDS crisis where longtime companions have been refused entry into hospital rooms.
- Finally, the person designated by the Act *may not make the decisions you would want made*. Their power may come as a total surprise, at the worst possible time.

You need to have documents that reflect your wishes.

c. Avoid Store-Bought Documents

Don't buy them at an office supply store and don't use a self-help book. A lot is at stake. Have your lawyer do them for you, probably as part of the Will package. (We'll discuss Wills soon.)

A simple Will Package including Wills and health care documents for both spouses should not cost more than $300 to $500. Why is this worth it?

- Lawyer drafted documents are more likely to be effective.

State laws vary and change. Store-bought documents might not conform. Even if they do conform to state law, as we have seen, health care workers still might ignore them and override your wishes. Lawyers are good with bells and whistles, and an individually prepared document, with a lawyer's name and number on it, simply has more clout.

- Lawyer drafted documents will reflect better decisions on your part.

These are very serious matters. It is important to talk about your options with a disinterested professional and not just check appropriate boxes. A lawyer can tailor your documents to reflect your individual, and sometimes weird, wishes.

> *Under no circumstances shall I be placed in a nursing home that plays Country and Western music.*
> Well, maybe not so weird.

d. The Time-Frame Problem

To prepare health care documents, you must project into the future. The problem is that, when you are healthy, your view of what you want done if you are sick will likely be much different from your view when you get sick.

We may say, "I would rather die than be in a wheelchair, unable to feed myself." But most who find themselves in that position disagree. And it is not just their fear of death that keeps them going. They find that they still enjoy their lives.

It is one thing to experience disability from the outside; it is quite another to experience it from the inside. We are all more resilient than we think. Some of us have even come to love Willie Nelson.

The law handles this time-frame problem by providing that neither a Living Will nor a Durable Power takes effect as long as you can make your own decisions. You can amend or revoke them any time, by simply telling your family or doctor.

e. Issues Concerning Your Durable Health Care Power of Attorney

1. Who do you want as your health care agent?

It probably isn't a good idea to appoint your spouse. He or she may be sick at the time decisions must be made or may be too depressed or confused to do so. Usually children or long time friends are better choices. If you select one child but not another, wisdom would dictate explaining your choice to both of them. Appoint a back-up agent. This is important as often the first choice is unable or unwilling to serve.

2. What powers do you want the agent to have?

Should your agent have the authority to move you to a nursing home?

Should your agent have the authority to remove you from a hospital against doctors' advice? This really gets down to the decision of *where* you want to die, at home or in the hospital. Elsewhere we describe the wonderful Hospice Movement and all the in-home services it can provide a terminally ill patient. See Chapter 30-b.

We advise our clients to give their agent the power to take them home.Your agent may be called upon to make very difficult decisions. You can give as explicit instructions as you like. Consider the matters in the next section.

f. End of Life Directives

In preparing your Durable Power, consider a checklist most grim.

– *Do you want to die at home or in the hospital?*

A hospital has no legal right to keep you against your will. You can always leave, even if your doctors recommend against it. If you become incapacitated, do you want a loved one to have the power to take you home against medical advice?

Many elderly people want to die at home but fear that they will be rushed to a hospital by 911 personnel. A few states have authorized "Out of Hospital Do Not Resuscitate Orders." If properly prepared and executed, this document will direct 911 personnel not to take emergency steps to keep you alive in order to get you to the hospital. If you sign such a document, make certain that caregivers are aware of your wishes and of the location and existence of the document. Call the local emergency response team in your area and let them know of your decision.

Another solution to the problem of well-meaning paramedics is to tell your relatives *not* to call 911 immediately. As this may lead them into difficulty with authorities, best to write out your wishes (and probably advise them not to admit to the delay).

– *Do you wish to be kept alive by a ventilator?*

Breathing machines can keep you alive long past when your body would otherwise shut down on its own.

– *Do you want artificial feeding and hydration?*

Even if you are in an irreversible coma, you can be kept alive almost indefinitely with artificial feeding and water tubes. Would death from dehydration and starvation be particularly painful? Not according to one study. Terminally ill patients were allowed to refuse to eat or drink and eventually died from dehydration and starvation. Only 13% were judged to have experienced discomfort during their dying period. Efforts were made to relieve dry mouth, thirst, and other symptoms. Check with your doctor for more information.

A Note on Not Hooking Up Machines

As a practical matter, it is much easier to refuse to have the tubes inserted than it is to have them removed. If a relative is in a nursing home and you are asked to approve a feeding and hydration tube, think long and hard. You may have to get court permission to get it out.

– *Do you want a "Do-Not-Resuscitate Order"?*

Hospital personnel watch the TV hospital shows, too. They can jump-start hearts and lungs. Without orders from you, or your health care agent, not to do so, they will.

– *Do you want treatment for curable but otherwise fatal illnesses, such as pneumonia, if you are suffering dementia (from Alzheimer's or from stroke) or have another terminal illness such as cancer?*

– *Do you want pain relief even if it means shortening your life?*

Morphine is a terrific pain killer but at higher dosages may cause death. Most physicians, without express instructions from you, will play it safe and keep dosages low even though you are still in pain.

g. Living Wills

Why have a Living Will if you have a Durable Health Care Power of Attorney? Good question.

Again, a Living Will is a document telling your doctors the kinds of treatment you want (and those you don't) *during your final illness.* A Durable Health Care Power is much broader as it is effective *any time you are incapacitated* (not just during your last illness) and can involve matters other than medical treatment, such as authorizing nursing home care.

Even in the situation of your last illness, it is good to have both documents. First, your appointed agent might not be around; second, under the laws of some states, agents may not have the power to order the termination of life-sustaining treatment.

Many people think of Living Wills as devices used to reject certain kinds of life-sustaining treatment. They frequently are. But they can be used for just the opposite effect: to insist that all heroic measures be taken. Even from a medical viewpoint, this is not an irrational choice. Medical science does make progress and what used to be a terminal illness may no longer be so, with the shining example being AIDS.

All states recognize Living Wills. Although states vary as to format, a few general things can be said.

- Living Wills become effective only if you are *incapacitated* (if you can still make your own decisions, they don't apply) and they can be revoked at any time, simply by telling your doctor. *You can always change your mind.*
- They allow you to direct your doctors to discontinue "medical treatment" if
  a. you have a terminal illness (usually defined as one giving you less than six months to live), or
  b. you are in an irreversible coma, or
  c. you are in a "permanent vegetative state" (that is actually the legal term and not the punch line of a gallows-humor joke).

A carrot steps from the curb and is hit by a truck. After several hours of emergency surgery, carrot awakes in the recovery room and is told by the doctor, "The good news is that you will live; the bad news is that you will be a vegetable."

If you are in an auto accident and are rushed unconscious to the hospital, your Living Will *does not take effect unless you are in one of these conditions.* If you can be saved, health care workers will do all they can.

There will be fights about what constitutes medical treatment and they can be crucial. Surely surgery and drugs designed to fight a disease are medical treatment, but what about feeding tubes? If feeding tubes are not medical treatment, your Living Will may not prevent them from being used on you. Because of these kinds of uncertainties, you are well advised to consult a lawyer who will know the specifics of your state law.

Finally, Living Wills and Durable Powers can only direct the withdrawal of medical treatment—they cannot direct that affirmative steps be taken to shorten life. That is euthanasia.

h. A Note on Euthanasia

We discuss this issue in Chapter 30-e. After all of this heavy going, we could use a joke or two.

> Yogi Berra, on the way to a friend's funeral, *"If you don't go to theirs, they won't come to yours."*
>
> Woody Allen, on Deeper Questions, *"I don't mind the idea of dying. I just don't want to be there when it happens."*

Chapter 19

Keeping Control of Your Finances

If you own a house or land or a car, and the title is in your name only, it cannot be sold or borrowed against if you become legally incompetent. Your family will not be able to make withdrawals from your bank account or sell your stock. If, through accident, stroke, or disease, you become legally incapable of exercising financial control, how will your loved ones reach your assets to pay your bills? How will your dependents support themselves?

We see two kinds of clients:

- Sons and daughters who want to make sure they have the legal authority to use an incapacitated parent's income to pay the parent's bills.
- Clients who come in for an estate plan and ask, "Who will manage my assets if I get Alzheimer's?"

If nothing is done to prepare for these possibilities, relatives will be forced to go to court to get formal guardianships or conservatorships. Not a happy choice. See Chapter 28-d.

Without going to court, there are three ways to set things up so one person can manage the finances of another:

1. Special Bank Accounts
2. Powers of Attorney
3. Trusts

We will defer our discussion of trusts as they are viewed primarily as a way of passing property at time of death. They can also be used as a method of planning for possible legal incapacity. If a large amount of money is at stake, definitely take a look at our Chapter on Living Trusts, Chapter 23.

Whatever legal device you choose, *get it signed while the person is competent.* States vary as to their definition of legal competence, but all tend to boil down to the ability to understand one's situation, to weigh and evaluate one's alternatives. This is a fuzzy line, so have the needed documents signed when competence is obviously clear. (If you expect that someone might challenge the document, get witnesses to the signing. Video tape works miracles. "Do you know what you are signing?" "Do you know what the document provides?" "Are you mentally alert today?")

a. Representative Payee Accounts for Incapacitated Parents

Even if a parent is already incapacitated, there is a special account you can set up to handle Social Security checks. Contact the Social Security Administration to set up a Representative Payee Account which will allow you to manage your parent's money. You will have to establish your parent's incapacity. Such accounts may also work for Supplemental Security Income, civil service, railroad retirement, Veteran's benefits, and some state pension checks. They will *not* work for the other assets your parent owns (dividends, other pensions).

b. Joint Accounts

Joint accounts must be set up while the individual is still competent. If the income consists mostly of Social Security checks, pension checks, and dividends, it is fairly easy to set up a joint checking account (arranging to have the checks deposited directly into it). As co-owner of the account, you simply write checks to pay your parent's bills.

Most joint accounts also come with the right of survivorship. That means the co-owner owns the account at the death of the parent.

Joint accounts are easy. But life never is.

The dangers of joint accounts from the parent's point of view:

1. Without putting too fine a point on it, the co-owner (son or daughter) may use the money for their own expenses.
2. Further, their creditors might come after the money. Because the co-owner *owns* the bank account, his or her cred-

itors can take it *all*. Creditors include persons who sue for such things as automobile wrecks.

You can avoid these dangers by:

1. Not putting too much in any one joint account. You can, for example, have several accounts and have different relatives as joint owners on each.
2. Or you can ask your bank about a designated signer account. With such accounts, the other person can sign checks on your account to pay your bills but does not own the account. That person's creditors cannot reach it. These accounts do not protect against dishonesty. These accounts do not include the right to survivorship.

You can avoid the problem of someone else's creditors by using a Living Trust or Power of Attorney. Creditors of the person handling your affairs (the trustee or the agent) cannot get at your money. Of course, you are still at risk of the dishonesty of the manager.

If you are using a joint account as a way of passing money at your death, check into the possibility of a *payable on death account*. The beneficiary you list will be able to close the account at the time of your death but, before that, neither he nor his creditors can reach it - thus protecting you from theft and creditors. A variation of this is used for brokerage accounts: these are called *transfer on death accounts*.

If there are a lot of assets involved, setting up joint accounts and joint ownership to cover them all will prove too cumbersome. You will need to give someone a more general power over the assets. A Living Trust, discussed in Chapter 23, is one solution. Here we discuss the other—Powers of Attorney.

c. Powers of Attorney, in General

With a properly executed Power of Attorney, the person designated can manage the other person's bank accounts, stocks, and other assets. A Power of Attorney is simply a specially prepared piece of paper that allows one person (called the agent) to act as a deputy and make legally binding decisions (buying and selling real estate, for example) for the principal.

Powers of Attorney can help in many situations; for example, you will be out of town and it is necessary for your daughter to sell your car.

However, it is a *very bad idea* just to give anyone a *general* power of attorney. They can use it to get everything you own. Yes, we know you trust the person, that it shows love, and that it will "avoid complications down the road," *but* we also know that some of our closest friends and relatives may be compulsive gamblers or drug abusers or, deep down, simply jerks.

We have seen too much heartache; too much fraud. How can you protect yourself? Limit the power to the agent to do certain things, such as *"Sell my 1999 Ford Explorer"* or *"Withdraw money from Savings Account 1234 at People's Savings."* You should also limit the time frame: *"Good only to August 1, 2001."*

Of course, if you are thinking of using a Power of Attorney to cope with your possible legal incapacity, you face two problems.

First, a traditional Power of Attorney is valid only as long as the person giving it remains legally capable. To prepare for incapacity, you must create a *durable* power, one that remains effective even if you are incapacitated.

Second, you want the power to be effective only when, and if, you become incapacitated. To accomplish this, use a Springing Durable Power. It "springs" to life when you become incapacitated. Your lawyer can draft triggering devices, such as certification by your attending physician. Or your lawyer can simply keep the Power and not give it to your agent unless and until you become incapacitated.

A downside to springing powers is that third parties might be more reluctant to honor them, insisting on documentation that the spring has sprung.

d. Issues Concerning Your Durable Financial Power of Attorney

In the last chapter we discussed Durable Health Care Powers of Attorney. Here we discuss similar documents that allow a third party to make your financial, as opposed to medical, decisions.

1. Whom do you want your agent to be?

Name a backup just in case. Tell that person of your decision as well as folks who might be upset because they weren't chosen (other children, for example). You can name two people as agents. Must they agree or can they can act separately? A lawyer can draft a document that allows separate decisions as to minor matters, joint decisions as to major.

Be aware of possible conflicts of interest. If your agent will inherit your estate, he or she will have an interest in keeping as much money in your estate as possible. If you end up in a nursing home, for example, your agent may refuse to spend your money for things you really want or need.

2. What powers do you want your agent to have?

State law will determine the agent's powers under a general power. It is best to discuss with your lawyer what precise powers you want your agent or agents to have. Consider giving the agent the power to

- sign IRS and state returns
- open bank accounts and safe deposit boxes
- change beneficiaries of pensions and life insurance
- make loans and gifts to others
- pay oneself for work as an agent

A brief word as to the power to make gifts. Giving away some of your assets while you are alive is a good way to reduce your estate in terms of probate and perhaps help you avoid some taxation. (See Chapter 21-a.) Without specific authorization, your agent may not have that power.

If your agent will be making investment decisions for you, you may wish to write out general directions as to aggressiveness or security. ("Buy low, sell high" won't do.) We discuss this issue further in our chapter on Living Trusts, as the trustee will also have broad powers over your assets. There are some limits to an agent's powers. They can't divorce your spouse nor can they write your Will.

e. Note: If You Are an Agent Under a Power of Attorney

Chapter 29 is devoted to the thorny issue of "deciding for others." Here are two pieces of quick advice:

- When you are signing a document on behalf of your principal, don't just sign your own name; indicate that you are signing for another. "J. Cricket, as agent for D. Rodman." Otherwise you might become personally liable and be forced to give more than a little whistle.

- Never *comingle* funds. If you put some of your principal's funds in your account, your creditors might seize them or you might forget them and, down the road, be charged with fraud.

f. Durable Powers of Attorney Compared to Living Trusts

Compared to a Living Trust, a Durable Power of Attorney is cheaper and quicker. There is no need, as there is in the case of a living trust, to take the necessary legal steps to transfer your assets; the Durable Power covers whatever you list.

However, a Living Trust is more certain: whereas some banks and businesses may refuse to honor a Durable Power, most will honor the directions of the trustee of a living trust.

Further, a Durable Power is *not* an estate planning tool: at your death, the power of attorney ends, and your property simply remains in your estate. So what happens to your stuff when you die? *(Editor's note: Nice segue.)*

Chapter 20

Wills and Estate Planning

In the movie Twilight, *Gene Hackman's character, talking of his cancer, says, "As Samuel Johnson once said, 'Nothing focuses the mind like the prospect of dying.'"*

Later in the scene, Paul Newman's character, who is somewhat disgusted with Hackman, says:

"The quote is, 'Nothing focuses the mind like the prospect of hanging.' Do you think you're the only one to watch Jeopardy*?"*

To focus your mind: What's going to happen to your stuff when you die? How can you provide for your family?

Before we get into the goals of estate planning and the bewildering array of choices you have, a quick look at the excuses we all have for waiting until tomorrow, or maybe next week.

– *I don't even want to think about it.*

What this gains in honesty, it loses in insight. Of course we think about death. In fact, we spend great amounts of energy pretending we don't think about it. Face facts, make plans, and get on with your life.

– *I can't do anything until I get my records in order.*

You don't need to know what you have in order to write your Will. It can read "My spouse gets everything" or "My three kids each get $20,000 and the remainder goes with me" or even "I don't care what happens as long as Uncle Joe doesn't get anything."

– *I'm not exactly sure what I want to do with my property.*

Trust us: Until you actually start writing your Will, you will never be sure. Writing things focuses the mind. And remember that nothing is in stone. You can always change your Will (rather than call them "changes" or "Second Thoughts," lawyers call them codicils; we are, after all, a learned profession).

- *I don't have time to meet with a lawyer.*

Nope. You can write out your own Will. Right now.
In estate planning, what might you want to accomplish?

a. Goals of Estate Planning and Some Ways to Achieve Them

Over the years, our clients have used estate planning:

- To provide for a personal guardian of their minor children;
- To provide for the short-term financial needs of those they have been supporting;
- To provide for the long-term support of disabled relatives;
- To provide for their own possible mental disability;
- To get their assets to certain relatives and charities quickly (and to cut out others);
- To keep their home in the family;
- To keep their businesses running smoothly;
- To minimize expenses and taxes; and
- To avoid creating family hostility based on perceived unfairness.

Estate planning involves a wide range of legal choices:

- Wills
- Joint Ownership
- Life Insurance
- Gifts
- Pension plans and IRAs
- Living Trusts

Before turning to a detailed discussion of these legal choices, a few brief words as to how best to achieve some of the goals listed above.

Guardians for Minor Children

You can nominate whom you want to raise your children. You can do that right now, before you go to bed, by writing a holographic Will—we'll tell you how momentarily.

Immediate Cash Needs of Dependents

There will be a period of months or longer before your heirs will get the bulk of your estate. Meanwhile, there will be bills to pay (including funeral expenses). Here are some options:

Joint savings or checking accounts. In the last chapter we described some of the dangers of such accounts – your co-owner may run off to Brazil or his creditors may attach the account. If your only goal is passing money at death (and not having someone manage your money in the event of your disability), set up Payable at Death Accounts (which delay, but do not prevent, trips to Brazil).

Lifetime gifts. You can just give your dependents sufficient cash to get them through the short term. We discuss this option later. Outright gifts to minors, however, can create problems. We'll give you the solutions.

You can set up your retirement benefits and IRAs to pay your beneficiary at the time of your death. Beneficiary designations are one of the most important and most overlooked elements of estate planning. Enormous unpaid taxes are hiding in retirement plans and IRAs; beneficiary designations, when done correctly, can defer such taxes for many years. A Living Trust also solves the problem of getting money to your spouse immediately after your death.

Providing for Minor Children and Disabled Relatives

Consider setting up a Trust, either now or at the time of your death (as part of your Will). We'll be telling you soon all the marvelous things Trusts can accomplish.

Keeping Your House in the Family

Should you give your house to the children now or as part of your Will? We'll tell you the best way at the end of this chapter.

Providing for Your Own Possible Mental Disability

We've discussed some options in the last chapter, joint accounts and Durable Powers of Attorney. We will discuss another popular choice, a Living Trust.

Cutting Folks Out

Unless you have a Will, Dreaded Relative might just get some of your loot through the laws of Intestacy (which we will describe momentarily). We'll tell you how to draft your Will in order to settle old scores. However, you cannot cut out a spouse entirely.

Keeping Your Business Going

A cartoon shows the decedent lying in state in his hotdog stand. It has been converted into a coffin. One of the mourners is telling another, "He told us, again and again, that the business would die with him."

Estate planning which involves active businesses is quite complicated and we won't even try to tell you what to do. Suffice to say, if you own a business, it will be extremely difficult for your relatives to keep it going unless you have an estate plan which addresses the numerous problems which will arise. Consult a lawyer.

Cutting Taxes

If you don't have an estate plan, your estate may get whacked by estate taxes. Federal estate taxes don't kick in unless the gross value of the estate is $650,000 (in 1999—going up to $1 million by 2006). These taxes are steep, beginning at 37% and quickly rising to 55%. Your estate is probably larger than you think; for example, it will likely include life insurance policies, the value of your home, and the full value of all of your retirement plans and IRAs. You can save substantial estate taxes by having an estate plan. Through a rather simple device, you and your spouse can pass up to $1.3 million ($2.0 million by 2006) to your beneficiaries tax free (this represents a tax savings of about $230,000).

Preventing Family Fights

Did the money Dad gave Sis for college count against her share of Dad's estate? If not, why did she get more? Wills and family conversations (Chapter 34) can be used to clarify ambiguities and explain choices.

Here's our plan from here on out. We will describe Wills in the remainder of this chapter. In Chapter 21, we'll look at other ways of passing money and property at the time of your death: Joint Ownership, Life Insurance, and Life Time Giving. These are ways to avoid Probate. Should you? In Chapter 22, we discuss the marvelous things you can accomplish by setting up trusts and, in Chapter 23, we discuss the popular choice of a Living Trust. It might not be for you. First, however, what if you do nothing?

b. The Law of Intestacy

If you die without a Will, your property will pass by intestacy. Worse things have happened. State intestacy laws represent the legislature's best guess as to how most people would want their property distributed, generally first to their spouse, then to their children, and then to more distant relatives. There are problems:

- Your property may not go to whom you would want it to: Many states provide that at the death of one spouse, only half of his or her property goes to the surviving spouse, the rest going to his or her children. You may want all of your assets to go to your spouse.
- Intestacy laws treat everyone the same: children take in equal shares even though some may be younger, some may have special problems, and some may be brats.
- Under intestacy, none of your friends, distant relatives, or favorite charities receive anything.
- You won't be able to nominate guardians for your minor children. It will be up to a judge to decide who takes care of Junior.

- If you die without an estate plan, you won't be able to use trusts to avoid the problems of outright gifts to minor children and disabled relatives.
- If you die without an estate plan, you can't pick the person who will administer your estate. This may lead to family fights about who that person should be. Convinced? Let's get started.

c. Holographic Wills

Holographic Wills are the first choice of nervous flyers everywhere.

If I die before I land,
This is the stuff I do hand:
. . . .
. . . .

A Holographic Will is one which you write out entirely in your own handwriting (no typing, no Word Perfect, no Holiday Inn letterhead, and not just signing what someone else wrote for you). No substitute for a formal Will, a Holographic Will can fill the void until you get back home. (You will.)

If you have, for example, arranged for a good friend to be guardian of your child if you die, or if you have decided to give a certain amount to charity, write a holographic will now and store it in a safe place. There's no set form:

Holographic wills don't have to rhyme,
Just be sure to date and sign.

For example:

Date. . . . .

I intend this to be my Will to be effective upon my death. I am of sound mind and am writing this of my own free will. Upon my death, I want the following:

a. That my sister, Sherina Cadnum, of Albany, California, become the guardian of my two minor children.

b. That $2,000 of my estate go to the Humane Society.

c. That my children get the rest of my estate when they turn 22 but before that time my sister will keep the money for them to pay the reasonable and necessary expenses for their care, comfort, maintenance, and support, including education.

Signed. . . . .

No witnesses or notaries are necessary (but they can help). Date the will as later ones void prior ones.

The problem with Holographic Wills is that they are recognized in only certain states. However, even if your state does not recognize them, until you execute a Formal Will, there is no harm in putting your wishes on paper. Even where they are recognized, it is best to use them only as a stop-gap measure. Formal Wills are preferable to get things right.

The states that recognize Holographic Wills are: Alaska, Arizona, Arkansas, California, Colorado, Idaho, Kentucky, Louisiana, Maine, Michigan, Mississippi, Montana, Nebraska, Nevada, New Jersey, North Carolina, North Dakota, Oklahoma, Pennsylvania, South Dakota, Tennessee, Texas, Utah, Virginia, West Virginia, and Wyoming. In Maryland and New York they are available only for members of the armed forces. Note that Florida, a popular retirement state, is not on this list.

d. Wills

Next to the funny Birthday Cards at the drugstore, you'll find the Will forms. There will be blanks to be filled in, boxes to be checked, and language designed to impress – "per stripes" "aforementioned clause III (b) (2)" and, of course, "being of sound mind" (The latter is known as a "Sanity Clause" and, in *Duck Soup*, Harpo says of it: "I don't believe in no Sanity Clause.")

You can buy a form Will. But be sure to pick up a condolence card as well.

Granddad wanted to leave me a lot of money but he was too cheap to get a lawyer to do it right so all he left me was this Stupid Card!

Lawyers don't make their money writing wills; they make their money upsetting wills. (Actually they make their money in administering your estate at the time of your death. As they say, nothing is certain but death and lawyers.) The cost of a simple Will, drafted by a lawyer, can go for as little as $100 to $200.

Once you have your Will, keep it with your important papers. Your lawyer will keep a copy; this will insure that it is found at the time of your death and that it has not been altered. Some lawyers are willing to retain the original. If your lawyer loses the original, a copy can be admitted to probate; if you lose the original, the law presumes you revoked the will.

What to include:

- Consider creating Trusts for children or relatives with special needs. Trusts allow you to delay and condition gifts. They can be created in a Will or separately. Such trusts, when properly drafted, allow the individual to continue to receive public benefits while the trust assets can be used to meet supplemental needs. (See Chapter 22.)
- When your Will is probated (bills paid and gifts distributed), the person in charge is known as the executor or personal representative. You can name that person in your Will. It's important. There will be discretionary calls; pick someone your family will trust. In the case of remarriage, where two families will be involved, fights over probate can be bitter. Consider joint executors, one Hatfield, one McCoy.
- You can make Specific Bequests such as "My wedding ring to my niece Jessica" and "$2,000 to Public Radio." What is left of your estate is the Residual Bequest and it is usually the largest. It can go to specific individuals or into a Trust. Bills are paid out of this Bequest—if the bills are large, the residual beneficiary might not get anything. This might mean you should cut back on your specific bequests.
- What if someone you name in your will dies first? Assume you have three adult children and want to divide what you have into three equal shares. What happens if one of the three dies before you? Should the other two now divide your estate or should the children of the deceased child divide the one-third? Or should they take a share equal to your two surviving children—if there are two children, then your estate would be divided into four parts. Your lawyer can draft language to accomplish what you wish.
- Sometimes you might not wish to treat your children equally. One might have special needs or maybe you have already

given one money or property. To avoid bitterness (there is nothing worse for a child than to think their parent loved a sibling more), consider putting in your Will why you are treating your children unequally.

Note on Recitals in Wills and Other Documents

There are certain dangers in reciting in your Will why you are doing what you are doing. While that might make it easier for your heirs to understand your choices (and hence resent them less), you make your Will more vulnerable to attack. "Dad said in the Will that he was cutting me out because I smoked dope and that's not true—or at least I never inhaled—and putting that in shows that he was incompetent at the time he signed the Will." We have even known defamation suits arising out of Will recitals.

Another way, probably a better way, of explaining your choices is a family meeting. (Maybe he wasn't smoking dope after all and this will allow him a chance to defend himself.) (See Chapter 34.)

e. Defeating Disgruntled Heirs: Taking Arms Against a Sea of Troubles

Your Will can be contested by disgruntled heirs—individuals who would take some or all of your estate under intestacy laws. If they succeed in having your Will thrown out, it will be as if you died without one. How can you protect yourself from this group of sore losers? (Of course, as lawyers, we work both sides of the street. We'll have some advice for disgruntled heirs later on. Chapter 32-b.)

Will contests are usually based on one of three theories:

1. You forgot a natural object of your bounty (such as a child or spouse);
2. You were subject to undue influence by one of the Big Winners; or
3. You were legally incapable of executing your Will.

Protect your Will from these attacks.

- Make sure you name in your Will all of your children (legitimate or not), and spouses (current or not), even if you don't want to leave anything to them. If you do not name them, they can later claim you forgot them.
- Make sure that no one who will inherit signs as a witness to your Will.
- If your gifts will not seem natural, to meet the undue influence claim, but subject to the disclaimer above, explain in your Will why you are doing what you are doing.
- As to legal capacity, first make sure you have it. This is a reason for not putting off doing a Will. You could be in an accident tomorrow which would leave you mentally unable to execute a Will.
- The requirement of legal capacity explains why all Wills begin with "Being of Sound Mind." Of course, that language will not stop someone from claiming you weren't. If you are fairly sure your Will will be challenged, consider videotaping your signing it. (One of our colleagues suggests getting Leading Citizens to be witnesses. They are found under "L" in the Yellow Pages.)

Again, family conversations can help reduce misunderstandings and hurt feelings. If your family knows why you did what you did, there will be less chance of challenge. More importantly, it will prevent family members resenting other members who seemed to get more.

There is another area of Will litigation that need not concern you so much as your attorney. If your attorney messes up drafting your Will, and the folks who you wanted to get your money don't, those people may be able to sue the attorney. (They should probably hire another one.)

f. Keeping Your House in the Family

If you want to pass on the family home to your children, how? Give it to them now, as a lifetime gift, or give it to them as part of your Will? It is generally better to give it to them through your Will. Why? They will get a stepped up basis.Your basis is the amount you paid for your house (plus capital improvements). It is important when the house is sold.

Say you paid $100,000 for it several years ago, put in a pool ($10,000) and a new kitchen ($10,000). Your basis is $120,000. Now assume that the house has a fair market value of $250,000.

If you leave your house to your children under your Will, they will get a stepped-up basis, its fair market value at the time of your death—here $250,000. If your children now sell the house for $250,000, there is no capital gain and hence no taxes. If you give your house to them during your life, they will not get a stepped up basis. They will take yours, here $120,000. If they then sell the house for $250,000, they will recognize a gain of $130,000 and probably have to pay a tax in excess of $25,000. There would, of course, be no tax if they used the home as their residence prior to sale as described above in Chapter 5-b.

There may be situations, however, where, as part of a complicated estate plan, it is best to make the gift in your lifetime.

Don't you just love lawyers? You finally get a straight answer and then they quickly add nitpicks and quibbles.

We now turn to the issue of avoiding probate and other estate planning devices.

Chapter 21

Avoiding Probate and Estate Planning Alternatives

A few years ago Jay Leno went to the Post Office on the night of April 15th. Last minute taxpayers were lining up. A tax protester stepped forward.

"They're never going to get any of my money," he boasted. "I got rid of my house and my car and my savings. I even quit my job!"

Leno nodded with admiration, "You sure showed them."

Show Probate! Die broke!

Probate is simply the court process designed to gather your assets, pay your bills, and distribute what's left according to your Will or, if there isn't a valid one, according to the state's intestacy law. Court authorization may be required before your heirs can change the title to real property you own and, until they do, they cannot sell it or borrow against it. Similarly, your heirs will not be able to gain access to stocks and bank accounts until the name on the title is changed.

All of this, we shall see, can be avoided. You can avoid probate! Should you?

The case *for* avoiding probate is that it can be quite expensive and lengthy. However, things have improved considerably and now many states have informal, inexpensive and fairly quick probate processes. With smaller estates, surviving heirs simply file a document with the proper court and the clerk will walk them through the steps. No lawyers! In these states, the costs and hassles of avoiding probate are worse than probate itself.

In some states, however, probate remains expensive and lengthy: New York, California, Illinois, Florida and Hawaii. In those states, it is a good idea to take steps to avoid probate.

Some say Probate should be avoided because probate records are public, and you probably don't want every Tom, Dick, and Harry knowing what you had. Putting your money in a trust avoids public disclosure. However, probate is not as public as some may claim. While your Will must be filed with the court, in most states your executor need not file the list of your assets as long as it is mailed to the heirs.

In the movie *Ghostbusters,* Bill Murray had the job of removing ghosts from haunted houses. This often brought him into close contact with ghosts. He had one rule—"Never have sexual relations with a ghost." Then he met a very seductive ghost. "Well, it really isn't a rule. It's more of a guideline."

"Avoid probate" is, at best, a guideline. However, even if avoiding probate is not your goal, you should become familiar with the estate planning devices we will discuss in this chapter. They may prove useful to you even if most of your estate will pass under a Will.

The estate planning devices we will discuss are:

- Lifetime Gifts
- Gifts to Minors and Disabled Individuals
- Life Insurance
- Joint Ownership
- Retirement Annuities, Roth IRA's and traditional IRA's
- Trusts and Living Trusts (discussed in Chapters 21 and 22)

One point to start. *Avoiding probate is not the same as avoiding estate taxes.*

The only way to avoid estate taxes is to give your property away before you die—either to individuals or irrevocable trusts. Even then you might have to pay Gift Taxes. (See Chapter 24.) If you use other devices to avoid probate, such as joint ownership or revocable Living Trusts, these assets will be counted in your estate for estate tax purposes.

The basic way to avoid probate is to get your assets (money, stocks, property) *out* of your estate before you die. The huge problem with this is that your money is gone... *and you aren't.* More of this, anon.

There are four main ways to rid yourself of a lifetime of success and shopping:

1. Give assets away.
2. Convert assets into life insurance.
3. Put assets in Joint Ownership.
4. Put assets in Trust, perhaps a Living Trust.

We will look at the pros and cons of each.

a. Lifetime Gifts

With large estates, gifts are a very good way not only to avoid probate, but also to reduce estate taxes. (See Chapter 24.) One problem in making gifts is that you can't take them back. A less obvious problem takes us to tax law.

In the case of *appreciated assets,* such as property and stocks, it is often best to pass them by Will rather than by lifetime gift. Why? Because if you pass them at death, the beneficiary gets a *stepped up basis*. In the case of gifts, the beneficiary takes your basis.

> *Assume you paid $50,000 for stock now worth $200,000. If you give it to your daughter as a lifetime gift, she will keep your basis of $50,000. If she sells it for $200,000, she will have a taxable capital gain of $150,000. On the other hand, if you pass the stock to her under your Will, she will get a stepped up basis when she takes it at your death. The stepped basis is the worth of the asset at the time of death, here $200,000. If she now sells it for $200,000 she will have no capital gain.*

If how to dispose of great sums is *not* your problem, consider another problem with gifts: they can delay your eligibility for Medicaid and SSI (Supplemental Security Income). See Chapter 8-b.

Gifts can also create uncertainties. Was the money you advanced to your daughter to reduce the amount she takes under your Will? If you are not clear about this, one way or the other, there will be fights.

b. Special Problems with Gifts to Children and Mentally Disabled

Outright gifts to minors and mentally impaired adults create a host of problems. If you give stock to your 12-year-old granddaughter, it will now be in her name. Although she is the owner, she can't sell it, even to pay for emergencies (minors do not have contractual capacity). Most likely, her parents will not be able to sell the stock either. A guardian will have to be appointed for the child and this will take a court proceeding.

There are problems at the other end as well. When the child turns 18, the child is outright owner of the stock and she can squander it.

Many grandparents want to leave money to their grandchildren to be used for medical emergencies while they are minors and for their college education thereafter. With estate planning, this goal can easily be achieved; without planning, it cannot be.

Consider *Uniform Gifts to Minors* or *Uniform Transfers to Minors* laws which allow you in essence to appoint a parent to be the child's financial guardian for the gift. The downside of this approach is that the income of the gift will be attributed to the parent for tax purposes (until the child is 14).

Special trusts are now available for educational expenses as well. Check with your bank or broker; they will happily take your money.

The same kinds of problems involve gifts to mentally disabled individuals. They do not have contractual capacity to manage their affairs and may squander money if they get the cash. Again, trusts are a solution.

A further note on the mentally disabled recipient. If the person is receiving some form of public assistance, money received from a gift or trust may make the person ineligible or at least reduce their benefit. Carefully drafted trusts can avoid this problem. Legal help is required.

c. Life Insurance

Beneficiaries of your life insurance policies collect upon your death by simply presenting your death certificate to the insurance company. This feature makes life insurance an attractive estate planning tool if the concern is to get some money to your heirs quickly. Probate, even in the best of cases, takes time— and proceeds from life insurance policies may come in handy.

The proceeds from your life insurance do not pass through your estate and are not subject to creditors of your estate. Generally, however, death benefits will be included in your estate for estate tax purposes. This is true *if* you retain the right to change the beneficiary. You can avoid estate taxes (but maybe not gift taxes) if you put the policy in an irrevocable trust. This means that you retain no ownership rights, such as the right to change beneficiary or borrow against the policy.

Sorry, you'll need the advice of a tax lawyer.

Life insurance can be a good method of avoiding probate. You take money from your estate *now*, using it to pay the premiums, to have it paid out on the other side, so to speak. However, because life insurance proceeds likely will be figured as part of your taxable estate, it should not be used as a device to avoid estate taxes unless special steps are taken.

d. Joint Ownership

Some tout joint ownership of property and stocks as the best way of avoiding probate. We disagree. The basic idea is that when you die, the joint owner simply files the right piece of paper and the title will be rewritten in that person's name alone. No need to go to Probate Court.

But except for smaller items, such as a car and relatively small bank accounts and stock holdings, we recommend against joint ownership. We have our reasons:

- There are several forms of joint ownership; only some have a "right of survivorship" which vests title in one joint owner at the time the other dies. *Without* such a survivorship aspect, joint ownership does not avoid probate: at the death of one joint owner, his or her share stays in his or her estate.
- Even with survivorship, joint ownership doesn't avoid probate, only postpones it. When the surviving owner dies, the property will be in his or her estate. Trusts can avoid this.
- Joint ownership presents problems if both die at the same time, and may have adverse income, gift, and estate tax consequences.
- Joint ownership means you give up control over the asset; while it is easy to add someone's name to a title, it is hard to get them off.

Many married couples hold title to their house as joint tenants with the right of survival. Assume a couple has been separated for several years, with the wife living in the house. In her Will she leaves everything to her daughter. When she dies, however, the daughter may not get the mother's inter-

est in the house: it passes, without probate, to the surviving husband. The husband is now free to sell the house or leave it to anyone he wishes.

- As long as property is in joint ownership, the creditors of the other person can attempt to reach it. And, of course, joint owners can always cash in and run off to Brazil. For possible solutions to these problems, see Chapter 19-a.
- In some states, joint ownership won't even speed transfer of assets upon death, and some states automatically freeze these accounts until tax officials can check things out. (Banks assign employees to read the obits.)
- Joint tenancy assets are still included in your estate for purposes of calculating your estate tax, at least to the extent that you were the one who put the money into the asset.

e. Retirement Annuities, Roth IRAs and IRAs

Don't overlook the possibility of using your retirement nest eggs as a method of providing for your loved ones after your death. For example, if you had a pension plan and have decided to take an annuity, consider appointing a loved one as your beneficiary. Your monthly check will be reduced but, if you can afford it, your beneficiary will go on getting a monthly check for years or for life, depending on how it is set up. (See Chapter 3-d.)

The new *Roth IRA* is definitely worth a look. A major advantage the Roth IRA has over a traditional IRA is that you need not begin drawing on it after age 70. This means the entire amount, with its earnings, will be available to your beneficiaries. It will create a lifetime stream of tax free income for them. They will have to begin drawing on it at the time of your death. (See Chapter 4-c.)

It is possible to convert any IRA you currently have to a Roth IRA. You will have to pay any taxes due on it at the time of conversion, but this might be well worth it. You should talk to your accountant.

Finally, you can pass money to a loved one by designating him or her as your beneficiary under traditional IRAs.

f. Living Trusts

A very popular device to avoid probate is the *living trust.* One advantage it has over the other estate planning devices (such as Wills and various forms of joint ownership), is that a living trust also solves the problem of having someone else deal with your financial affairs if you become incapable of doing so. That is, a living trust has many of the advantages of a Durable Power of Attorney which we discussed in Chapter 19-d.

But before we turn to living trusts (and decide, once and for all, whether to capitalize them), we will describe the most wonderful legal device of all — the Trust!

Chapter 22

Trusts for Special Needs

Remember the "Funnies"? In Little Abner, *the Shmoos were unique beings that did just about everything—shopped, cleaned, set the table —and then cooked themselves for dinner.*

Trusts are like that. They do about anything—except cook themselves and live forever. In basic form, trusts are quite simple. They are written agreements between the trustor and the trustee, providing that the trustee will use the money or property the trustor puts into the trust for the benefit of a third party, the beneficiary. Say what?

You (the *trustor* or *settlor*) give money or property to a *trustee* (a bank, a friend, or, as we will see, yourself) to be managed and used in trust for the benefit of the *beneficiary* (a minor child, a disabled relative, or, as we will see, yourself). The money or property is to be used as directed by the *trust instrument* ("for the college education of my grandchildren" or "for the medical care of my niece Joanna").

Trusts cannot live forever, although they can hang in there a very long time. When their time is up, the trustee distributes the remaining assets to the individuals named in the trust instrument. Thus, trusts are like Wills in this regard; they are a way of passing money and other assets after death. Many people use trusts as part of their estate plans.

a. The Marvelous Trust

The basic virtue of trusts is that they allow you to delay and structure your gifts. You can provide money for your grandchildren's education without fear they will drink it all up, and you can provide lifetime support for a disabled nephew. Trusts are quite flexible and can be tailored almost any way you want:

"The trustee shall accumulate interest until my grandchild enrolls in college and then the trustee will pay for tuition, room

> *and board, and necessary books for four years of college and any graduate education thereafter. After my grandchild finishes his education, the trustee shall pay him the interest on the trust until he turns 40 years old, and then the principal shall be distributed, one half to him and one half to the Humane Society of Greater Boston."*

You can create trusts during your life (called *intervivos trusts*) or you can create them as part of your Will (*testamentary trusts*). Or you can create one now, but fund it only in part, and then have other assets pour over into it from your estate at the time of your death (*pourover trusts).*

Why can't you keep your property in trust forever? English landowners tried.

> *My beloved country estate I leave in trust for my first-born son, for his use during his lifetime, and thereafter for the use of his first-born son and thereafter for the use of his first-born son, etc. etc. etc.*

English judges, who gave us much of our common law, were not fools. If these trusts stood up, neither they (nor their first-born sons) were likely to get very much of anything. (It was, by the way, *always* the first-born *son.*) So these judges, clever old codgers that they were, came up with the *Rule Against Perpetuities*. It is so complicated that it drives law students batty. The California Supreme Court went so far as to hold that lawyers don't even have to understand it. (We kid you not!)

Basically, the Rule means that at some point you will have to let your incompetent heirs finally get their hands on the property. Trusts can last only for *a life in being plus 21 years*, which is much easier to say than figure out.

If you are considering using a trust, the first thing to do is to ask your lawyer to explain the Rule Against Perpetuities. That will signal that you are not to be trifled with. Then get down to brass tacks.

b. Revocable or Irrevocable?

If you create a trust during your lifetime, the basic choice is whether you want to make it revocable or irrevocable. (In the nature of things, trusts created at the time of your death are irrevocable unless, of course, *Ghostbusters* was right.)

A revocable trust allows you to change your mind and tell the trustee to return your property. Times change and you may need your property back to make ends meet. Or you may change your mind as to whom you want to get your property (you move to Los Angeles and now, rather than give anything to Boston's Humane Society, you want to give everything to some weird cult).

The big *disadvantage* of revocable trusts is that the law deems the money in them as yours; just as you can get your money back, so, too, your creditors.

Tax Issue. Transfer of assets to a revocable living trust is not a "transfer" for tax purposes. Income it earns is reported on *your* individual tax return. A transfer to an irrevocable trust is a taxable event since you are forever giving the stuff away. It may be subject to the Gift Tax. (See Chapter 24).

The pros and cons of *irrevocable* trusts are:

- Once you put assets in, you can't get them back (but then again, neither can your creditors).
- The trust is an independent entity. It must get its own Taxpayer ID Number and must pay its own taxes. Further, making lifetime gifts to irrevocable trusts may reduce your estate taxes. On the other hand, major gifts to irrevocable trusts may trigger *gift* taxes. (See Chapter 24.)

c. How Should Your Trust Be Administered?

If you have ever read an English novel, you know trustees tend to be conservative (at least when they're not falling in love with their shy, beautiful ward, who is, in turn, madly in love with a poor but noble, handsome youth).

Address how you want your trust to be administered.

> *I intend that the provisions of this trust be liberally construed and that the term "education" include trade and art schools, educational travel and all necessary expenses related thereto, including the purchase of a car.*

I intend reasonable medical care to include the costs of non-traditional pain relief such as hypnotism, bio-feedback, and massage, and I authorize medical treatment at home even if it costs more than institutional care.

d. What Powers Do You Want the Trustee to Have?

- No power to buy speculative stocks?
- Authority to invade principal to handle emergencies?
- Power to make gifts?
- Power to settle claims?
- Power to hire accountants and others to help administer the trust?

e. Who Should Be the Trustee?

Banks and other financial concerns will not get involved unless the trust is large, in the range of $150,000 to $500,000 in discretionary assets.

For smaller trusts, relatives are often used. First you should check with them to make sure they are agreeable. Should they receive a fee for their services? Honesty is important—a trustee can run off with the money. Also consider the trustee's

- relation to the beneficiaries
- financial skills and stability
- age in relation to beneficiaries
- geographical proximity
- co-trustees are possible, perhaps a bank for wisdom and a relative for compassion.

Always name an alternative or successor trustee, just in case.

f. Funding the Trust

There is no need to *create* and *fund* a trust at the same time. When you actually put money or other assets into the trust will turn on tax issues and on whether you still need the assets for your own needs.

If future emergencies are a concern, you can create an irrevocable trust but simply not put that much money in it. For maximum flexibility, you can make the trust revocable or make it a testamentary trust, one funded at the time of your death.

There is one form of trust that is very popular, the so-called Living Trust. It deserves its own chapter and its own Movie Moment.

Chapter 23

Living Trusts

In the movie comedy Raising Arizona, *a baby is kidnaped and the father is approached by one mean-looking bounty-hunter who offers to find the baby for him.*

"Why should I hire you?" the father asks. "I have the police working on it."

"If you want to find your baby, ask me. If you want to find Dunkin Donuts, ask the police."

Nice gag. But how does it fit?

"If you want a Living Trust, ask a lawyer. If you want a free donut, go to a Living Trust Seminar."

Today's hot item is the Living Trust, sold by traveling salesman at free breakfasts, lunches, dinners, and seminars. The price ranges from $900 to $1,500 and up. *Don't buy!*

- While a Living Trust may meet your needs, other legal devices will, too, often at a *lower* cost.
- To get a Living Trust that conforms to state law in your state, have it drafted by a lawyer, not by a traveling salesman.
- There is more to a Living Trust than signing the papers. You must transfer your property to it and legal advice will be needed as to how.

In our experience nine out of ten people who purchase living trusts *don't need them*. But what are they?

a. An Example Living Trust of Mildred and Joseph Durbin

The assets of this trust shall be used for the benefit of Mildred and Joseph, husband and wife, and shall be administered by them. In the event that they become incapable of administering this trust, it shall be administered by their son, Matthew, or, if he cannot, by the First National Bank.

At the death of either Mildred or Joseph, this Trust shall become irrevocable. Thereafter the assets of the trust will be used for the benefit of the survivor. At the death of the survivor, the assets remaining in the trust shall be distributed in equal parts to the then surviving children of Mildred and Joseph (or, for example, "shall be held in trust for the then surviving children, with the income to be distributed to them yearly, with the remaining assets distributed to them when the youngest turns 25").

With a few more bells and whistles, that's about it! What has been gained? Not much, at least until the incapacity of the couple or until the death of one (when the trust becomes irrevocable).

- Earnings on the trust's assets must be reported on Mildred's and Joseph's individual or joint tax returns. A Living Trust is *not* an independent tax entity. It does not need a federal tax number. Putting (or taking out) money and property into this kind of trust is *not* a tax event.
- Creditors of Mildred and Joseph can still go after the trust's assets as long as the trust is revocable, as most of these trusts are. Assets in these trusts will be counted as owned by Mildred and Joseph for Medicaid purposes. (See Chapter 8-b.)
- Mildred and Joseph can always change their minds and take their money out of the trust.

So what's the case for having a Living Trust?

b. The Virtues of Living Trusts

Living Trusts can accomplish many important goals: help you avoid probate, provide for financial management in the event of disability, and act as a Will substitute distributing your property after death. Whether a Living Trust is for you will depend in part on how important these various goals are to you and in part on whether you can better achieve them with other legal devices.

Living Trusts, as we shall see, may have special advantages to those of you who have property in several states and for those of you in second marriages where both parties have children from prior ones. One disadvantage we will discuss is that some people enter into them too casually, without realizing their true significance.

c. Living Trusts Help Avoid Probate

If you put everything you own in a Living Trust, in the eyes of the law, you die penniless. There is nothing to go through probate as your property is in the trust. You win! But don't forget that all the assets of the Living Trust are still subject to estate tax.

How important is it to avoid probate? In the old days, probate was a very expensive and lengthy proceeding. Something to be avoided, like the Plague.

In many states, probate is no longer the plague; at worst, it's a bad cold. For most estates, survivors simply file an Application for Probate, stating the death, the assets and, if there is one, attaching the Will. There will be no court hearing and no lawyers. Court clerks will walk you through the process.

But even in states where probate remains a plague (such as New York, California, Illinois, Florida, and Hawaii) consider *probate-avoiding options* to the Living Trust we discussed elsewhere: irrevocable trusts, gifts, life insurance, and joint tenancy, discussed in Chapter 21.

d. Living Trusts — Financial Management in Event of Disability

The assets of this trust shall be used for the benefit of Mildred and Joseph, husband and wife, and shall be administered by them. In the event that they die, or become incapable of administering this trust, it shall be administered by their son, Matthew, or, if he cannot, then by the First National Bank.

A person may become mentally or physically incapable of managing their finances. If their assets are in a Living Trust, this presents no problem: the designated trustee just takes over.

As we have seen in Chapter 19, however, there are other legal devices which can be used to accomplish the same goal, such as a Durable Power of Attorney.

e. Living Trusts — Will Substitutes

At the death of the survivor, the assets remaining in the trust shall be distributed in equal parts to the then-surviving children of Mildred and Joseph (or, for example, "shall be held in trust for the then-surviving children, with the income to be distributed to them yearly, with the remaining assets distributed to them when the youngest turns 25").

Of course, you could pass your property by Will instead and, if you wish, create trusts at that time.

f. The Pros and Cons of Informality

There is one major advantage a Trust has over a Will, which, upon analysis, may be a terrible disadvantage. Living Trusts are less vulnerable to attack by disgruntled heirs than are Wills. This is because Wills require more formalities — witnesses and notarized signatures — and with more formalities, the more points to attack.

On the other hand, the reason the law requires formality in the case of Wills is to alert folks that they are making very important decisions. Signing a Trust agreement may not alert you to the far-reaching implications of the terms and language of that agreement. There is something sobering about

"Being of sound mind, this is my Last Will and Testament."

Bottom line, our advice is to *consider* a Living Trust but don't assume it is the best for you. If you do decide upon one, consider the issues we flagged in the previous chapter dealing with the powers of the trustee and so forth.

g. Living Trusts — Property in Several States

If you have real property (land or houses) in other states, it may be necessary for your heirs to open probate proceedings in each of those states. Courts in California, for example, have no jurisdiction over land in Colorado (otherwise they would have all the water). However, if your trust owns all the property, the trustee can simply sign the deed and give the property to your heirs.

h. Living Trusts — The Problem of "Blended Families"

You remarry. You have three children from a previous marriage; your new spouse has two. You decide that at the death of one of you, the other should get all your assets; at the death of the survivor, the remaining assets should be split among the five children. You visit your lawyer and write your Wills. All well and good, but what if you die first? Can you trust your spouse not to rewrite the Will, cutting out your kids?

Some states will enforce mutual agreements not to change one's Will. These must usually be written and signed by both parties. Another solution: the Living Trust. Again, these can be written to become irrevocable at the death of either spouse. Written this way, the survivor usually has access to all of the income and perhaps can invade principal for listed purposes. The survivor cannot, however, distribute the balance; that distribution scheme has become irrevocable.

Finally, after all these dull legal pages, a matter of high drama! Temptation! Greed! Betrayal! We close this chapter, and this part, on a Shakespearean Moment!

Enter, Stage Left, the three witches, tempting:

Eye of newt and toe of frog,
Wool of bat and tongue of dog...
Double, double toil and trouble
Fire, burn; and cauldron, bubble.
Tear your Will, a thousand pieces,
Give everything to **your** *selfish nieces.*

Chapter 24

Estate and Gift Taxes

"Handle Your Own Death Penalty Appeal—Don't Pay a Lawyer. Save Your Money for Cigarettes!"

If you have a large estate, get competent legal help. You will save much more money in estate taxes than you will pay in lawyer fees.

Besides, cigarettes aren't good for you anyway. Here we give a basic overview of estate and gift taxes.

Federal Estate and Gift Taxes only apply to larger estates.

Estate and gift taxes kick in only if you give away (by lifetime gift or by Will) $650,000 (1999). This figure will increase to $1 million in 2006.

Note, however, your estate may be larger than you think as it will likely include real estate, investments, joint tenancy property, tax deferred assets such as IRAs, 401k's, pension plans, personal property and life insurance unless owned by an irrevocable trust.

Federal Estate and Gift Taxes are steep.

For amounts you give away in excess of the above limits, the tax rate begins at 37% and quickly rises to 55%.

Federal Estate and Gift Taxes are the same thing!

Federal law allows individuals to give away up to $650,000 (1999, increasing to $1 Million by 2006) without paying any taxes. This is called the *Lifetime Unified Estate and Gift Tax Exemption.* If you give away more during your life, the excess will be subject to a "gift tax"; if you leave more at your death, it will be subject to "estate tax." The rates are the same.

Gifts you make during your lifetime will reduce the lifetime exemption. Let's say you give away $200,000. No gift tax will be due (and the happy recipient need not pay taxes either). However at the time of your death, you only have $450,000 left of your exemption. If you leave more than that, the excess will be subject to estate taxes. Give away $500,000 during your life, you will have only $150,000 left in your exemption. Give away more than your lifetime exemption during your life, you will have to pay gift taxes on the amounts over the exemption.

Yearly gifts of $10,000 per person don't count.

You can give away $10,000 per year to as many individuals as you want without it counting against your Lifetime Exemption. You can get a lot of money out of your estate (and away from the taxman) by this device. Each year, a husband and wife can EACH give each of their children $10,000, each of their children's spouses $10,000, each grandchild $10,000 and each of the authors of this book $10,000. And you can make $10,000 gifts to trusts as well.

Check with your accountant concerning whether or not tuition payments made for a grandchild's college or medical payments made to a hospital count against your lifetime exemption.

However, if you want to give away a lot of your estate by making exempt gifts, don't wait too long. Any gift you make within three years of your death will be deemed a gift in contemplation of death and will be counted as part of your estate. Thus a series of gifts, all under $10,000, might be swept back into your estate if you die within three years of making them.

Bequests to your spouse are not taxable.

You can leave as much as you like to your spouse without triggering tax liability. However, when you spouse dies, there will be taxes, unless you have consulted a good tax lawyer.

Gifts to Charity are not taxable and reduce the size of your estate.

Any gifts that you make to charities by will or by trust distribution are not includible in your estate for purposes of calculating estate taxes.

Such gifts allow you to determine how your money will be spent after your death. But there are some additional benefits available by charitable gifting. It is possible during lifetime to transfer assets to a charity and get the benefit of the charitable donation on your income taxes while having the charity agree to pay you a lifetime income from the earnings it receives on the gift. This gets complex, but a gift of appreciated assets (such as that IBM stock that you bought for $10 that is now worth $100) can give you a deduction for nearly the full value while giving you an income from the charity for life based on the value at the time of your gift. These are called *Charitable Remainder Trusts* and they come in many flavors and are well understood by experienced estate planning attorneys. The point is, if you have charitable intent, get advice—*it may be far better for you to be donating assets than it would be for you to write a check.*

Estate tax planning is very complicated and the more you have, the more complicated it gets. Estate tax planning is not for amateurs and requires professional help. Those who have substantial amounts of land or a big interest in a family business have lots of options that only the specialist in the mysteries of the Internal Revenue Code can implement and sometimes explain. If you have ever heard of Family Limited Partnerships, Discounts for Marketability, etc., get thee to a estate planning attorney, a specialist.

In the 1980s, there was a popular bumper sticker:

> *The person who dies with the most stuff wins!*

The 1980s were hopelessly naive. It should have read:

> *The person who dies with the most stuff has the biggest tax problems!*

Part Five

Bad Times

This part walks you through the hard times, beginning with when you first recognize that a parent or spouse is becoming disorientated and ending with the probating of a loved one's Will.

Chapter 25

On Training for Ill, Pumping Iron and Sending Dylan Thomas to Bed

Since the world has still
Much good, but much less good than ill,
And while the sun and moon endure
Luck's a chance, but trouble's sure,
I'd face it as a wise man would,
And train for ill and not for good.

A. E. Housman

Train for ill.

The next chapters deal with disability, terminal illness and death in the family. *Read them now*, before you need them. Why?

Trouble's sure.

Talk with your family. Tonight—by the weekend, for sure—even though you have a thousand good reasons to wait. We have a chapter at the end of this book on how to begin that conversation. (Chapter 34.)

Of course, *training* conjures grunts and sweats. And that's a nice transition into an optimistic aside. While death may be sure, disability isn't. In fact, the rate of disability, defined as the loss of one major life function (such as the ability to dress or feed oneself) has been falling among the elderly: among folks over 85, it is only one in five. Improved medical care has played a role, as has improved nutrition and, indeed, so have grunts and sweats.

On the Virtues of Pumping Iron and Working Crosswords

If you stop exercising, you get weaker; if you stop pushing yourself mentally, you get dumber. Studies show that learning is good exercise for the brain. Consider adult education, not only for its intrinsic fun, but as a method of maintaining mental agility. Don't be a passive student.

Question what you learn ("How could a study show that learning new things keeps you alert? Are these folks just making up studies as they go along?").

> *What's the cube root of 27? Who said "Fee, fie, foe, fum, I smell the blood of an Englishman"? Explain chaos theory. Coherently.*

As to *physical* exercise, yet another study showed that surprisingly little can produce surprisingly much. A hundred men and women in their 80s and 90s, most so frail that they needed walkers, increased their strength 118% during a ten-week exercise program. They could walk faster and climb stairs more easily. Some, so taken with their new persona, even began snarling: "Fee, fie, foe, fum..."

For some ideas as to exercise, you can order *Exercise: A Guide from the National Institute on Aging*. Call 1-800-222-2225. (1-800-222-4225 hearing impaired; Web: www.nih.gov/nia/)

* * *

But even if severe disability comes your way, it is not as bad as it seems. Now, viewing it from afar, it seems terrible, worse than death.

Nancy Mairs is paralyzed from the waist down and has lost total control over one arm, partial over the other. She has fallen from her wheelchair and has been unable to get up, lying there until someone happened by. She cannot feed herself, and someone must dress her.

A fate worse than death? In *Waist-High in the World* she writes:

> *There are readers who need, for a tangle of reasons, to be told that a life commonly held to be insufferable can be full and funny. I am living that life. I can tell them.*

A different life than we have now—but a life worth living, full and funny. Even death, from afar, is not as it seems. In a searing couplet, Dylan Thomas shouts to his dying father:

Do not go gentle into that good night.
Rage, rage, against the dying of the light.

What a powerful phrase—the dying of the light. One almost chokes. But that's young Dylan's view of death; was it his dad's? What do those who have almost died tell us? They report feeling a sense of calm and acceptance; many report on seeing a bright light rushing toward them. A surgeon visits his patient and is told:

> *"Lying on the operating table, I knew I was dying. You and the others were trying to save my life and that was O.K. But it was also O.K. if you didn't."*

As a young man Montaigne, the famous sixteenth century French essayist and philosopher, was involved in a serious riding accident. Thrown from his horse, he lay crumpled on the ground, bloody and writhing in pain. His friends lamented, convinced that their dear companion was dying a terrible death. Montaigne later recalled:

> *It seemed to me that my life was hanging only by the tip of my lips. I closed my eyes in order, it seemed to me, to help push it out. I took pleasure in growing languid and letting myself go. I was not only free from distress but felt that sweet feeling of sliding into sleep.*
>
> *I believe that this is how people feel whom we see in the agony of death. We pity them without cause.*

So what of Dylan's father?

> *"That's O.K. Dylan. Everything will be fine. Now wipe away your tears and go back to bed. I want my rest."*

The fear of death, the denial of death, prevents us from living to its fullest. In the fabulous book *tuesdays with Morrie*, Mitch Albom writes of his Tuesday afternoon visits with his old professor, Morrie. Morrie is dying of Lou Gehrig's Disease. One afternoon he talks about denial.

> *"Everyone knows they're going to die, but nobody believes it. If we did, we would do things differently.... To know you're going to die, and to be prepared for it at any time. That's better. That way you can actually be more involved in your life while you're living.* Once you learn how to die, you learn how to live."

* * *

In the poem with which we began, A.E. Housman advises us to face reality directly, even though it may be painful. We should not let alcohol, or even poetry, blind our vision. The poem begins with the castigation of Terrance, who, as young men are apt to do, sits in a bar, eating munchies and reciting bad poetry lamenting the tragedy of life.

"Terrance, this is stupid stuff,
You eat your victuals fast enough;
There can't be much amiss, 'tis clear,
To see the rate you drink your beer."

Housman advises that we train for ill; he gives us the example of Mithridates, king of ancient Pontus in Asia Minor, who made himself immune to poison by swallowing small doses every day.

Does training for ill work? You bet! His enemies tried to kill him.

They put arsenic in his meat
And stared aghast to watch him eat;
They poured strychnine in his cup
And shook to see him drink it up;
.....
—I tell the tale that I heard told.
Mithridates, he died old.

So let's get started!

Chapter 26

Disability in the Family

There are three bad aspects to getting older. First, physically you aren't as sharp. Second, you tend to forget things.

A loved one is becoming disorientated and confused. What should you do?

a. Look for Curable Causes

Don't assume that disorientation or memory loss is irreversible.

Mary lived alone. Over several months, she just fell apart: her yard went to weed; her house and kitchen became cluttered and filthy. She sat and sat and sat. Finally, she went to the hospital. Doctors found a massive vitamin E deficiency. The condition was corrected and she again is living on her own.

Disorientation and memory loss can result from improper medications, alcoholism, and depression.

Have a pharmacist review prescriptions:

– *Are the dosages proper?*

Dosages which worked fine in middle age may become *toxic* later. Some doctors fail to adjust dosages.

– *Is the mix proper?*

Medications from different doctors and different drug stores may cause disorientation and memory loss.

– *Are the prescriptions being misused?*

Could prescription abuse cause the symptoms you have noticed? If it's not the medications, next eliminate alcohol abuse. It is quite common. Are you dealing with a secret drinker? Check for bottles in the garbage and remember that Vodka is "breathless."

Expect: "I don't have a problem with alcohol, and it isn't any of your business anyway."

AA can advise you how to get a person in denial into treatment.

Finally, check for depression. The signs of depression include:

- Feeling depressed, down, sad, or blue
- Change in sleep and appetite
- Extreme tiredness
- Trouble concentrating
- Feelings of guilt or worthlessness
- A sense of hopelessness or helplessness
- Thoughts of death or suicide

Depression is common and treatable. A physician can prescribe antidepressant drugs. In the remainder of this chapter we look at memory loss, bad driving, hearing loss, and home care.

b. Memory Loss

More than grey hair and wrinkled skin, memory loss is the real shocker. And it's scary.

"Who wrote that book? I just read it last week and she's one of my favorites. This is terrible. I'm getting senile."

Memory loss is not the same thing as dementia. Although dementia usually entails memory loss, it is much more: it is the inability to think things through, the inability to recognize options and choices and the inability to make sound decisions.

As we age, we can generally expect at least some memory loss. The first to go is short term memory, "What did you have for breakfast yesterday?" And names tend to escape our grasp. While this kind of loss is embarrassing and, indeed frightening, it does not interfere with our daily lives. We retain the ability to make good decisions and lay sound plans. Further, memory loss does not inevitability lead to dementia or senility. It does not necessarily get worse. While most of us will suffer some memory loss, few of us will become senile. Indeed, if you are concerned about memory loss, that is a good sign. Geriatric physicians will ask patients "Are you worried about memory loss?" and, if the answer is "yes" they are relieved. The answer that troubles them is "No, my memory is fine."

If you are concerned about a relative, you might want to test their "executive function" by asking questions like "If you wanted to take a trip to Europe, how would you go about it?" If the answer touches upon travel agents and airline tickets, fine. Be concerned with "I don't know" or "I would ask my daughter to take care of things." Consider a medical checkup.

c. Bad Driving

> *"You might as well shoot me," said a nurse when told she could no longer drive. "It's like telling a patient they have a terminal illness."*

Having to stop driving can be a horrible passage. Driving is a whole lot more than trips to the store. It is independence, vitality, and self-control.

Unfortunately, driving entails danger to the driver and others. Although elder drivers have fewer accidents (because they spend less time on the road), their accident rate is higher.

Again, check for *correctable* causes. The AARP offers a refresher course ("55 Alive"). It stresses defensive driving. Commercial driving instruction companies do as well. Special equipment is also available, such as rear mirrors that provide a wider view of the road. Cars and vans can be outfitted to cope with many disabilities.

Certain medications can affect driving ability. Check with the doctor or pharmacist. Failing eyesight may be corrected. Night vision usually goes first (making the true retirement home rogue the guy who can still drive at night).

Rush hours, left-turns, and frequent trips should be avoided. Co-pilots help. If the driving doesn't improve:

> *"Mom, I'm worried about your driving. You don't want to get in an accident. I know you think you are fine. You are probably right. But I want you to take a driving test."*

Most State Departments of Motor Vehicles will conduct field driving tests to confirm or reject your fears. Private companies are also available.

Talk to Mom's physician. If necessary, the physician can play the heavy (not you) and pull the plug on driving.

This is a pressing issue. You don't want to make Mom dependent; on the other hand, you don't want to get the call that she has hit the neighbor's child.

If Mom's Irish—or for some other reason strong-headed—take off the plates, hide the keys, or disable the car by disconnecting the spark plugs.

A Warning to Legal Guardians

You may be liable for any damages caused by your ward while driving. Your existing insurance policies probably will not cover these losses. Call your insurance agent.

d. Hearing Loss

Remember how cool it was to crank up the radio real loud?

Presbycusis, age-related hearing loss, is becoming more common, what with rock concerts, jet airplanes, and jackhammers. Vanity often keeps folks from getting help. If a loved one is losing hearing (or if you are), get help now.

Hearing loss, even partial hearing loss, can be devastating. It isolates; it distracts from family and social life; and it puts an emotional strain on all involved. And once you get used to partial deafness, it may be harder to correct later.

Hearing loss tends to sneak up, and ironically you will be able to hear certain sounds perfectly. The warning signs:

- People seem to mumble and voices get lost in background noise.
- The TV must be turned up; movies are less enjoyable.
- You must look at people to understand what they are saying.

Check with your physician first. A good hearing test costs around $200 and may rule out diseases that can cause deafness. *Hearing tests must be conducted in soundproof rooms,* not in your home, one of many good reasons not to buy a hearing aid from a door-to-door salesman.

Otolaryngologists and audiologists are hearing specialists. Be sure they are licenced. The American Speech-Language-Hearing Association (1-800-638-8255) will send you a list of licensed audiologists in your state. (E-mail: actioncenter@asha.org.) If the audiologist is also in the business of selling hearing aids, it is best if he sells a variety of brands.

Be sure to get a copy of the test results (an audiogram) so you can buy from someone else if you wish. Federal law requires, for good reason, that hearing aids can be sold only after the buyer has gotten an evaluation from a licensed physician. However, folks over 18 can waive the evaluation.

There are three popular models — behind-the-ear (usually most effective), in the outer ear, and in-the-ear canal (usually the least effective). New technologies have greatly improved hearing aids and there are new digital designs. A good behind-the-ear model will run from $500 to $2,000 while new digital designs can go for over $2,000.

Some points to consider:

- Get a 30-day trial period in which you can return the hearing aid for a full refund, less a small service charge. State law may require this. Count on some time to get used to the hearing aid and realize that none will capture sound as well as your own ear.
- Ask about upkeep. Are the batteries hard to change? How long do they last? How often are repairs needed?
- Make sure what you buy fits your lifestyle. Some hearing aids, with extended frequency ranges, are better for music; others are good at reducing background noise. Discuss your needs.

Consider too an *Assistive Listening Device*, a small amplifier with headphones, like a small cassette player. Try a cheaper model first (around $50) and, if it works, you can go higher (to around $500).

Hearing aids are not covered by Medicare or by most insurance policies. If you are selecting a Medicare HMO, coverage in this area is important. You can get information on state and federal help from the Better Hearing Institute (1-800-Ear-Well). Hear Now (1-800-648-HEAR or 303-695-7797 hearing impaired) may help those in financial need.

e. Home Care

Almost one in four families provides unpaid care for an older relative or friend. This is a sharp increase, over threefold in only ten years. People are living longer. Also, hospitals, to cut costs per government regulations, now release people much sooner. Medicare is saving money by throwing the expense to families.

We begin with advice and solace. We then discuss home care. The next chapter focuses on nursing home care.

On Being a Caregiver

> *"In the unlikely event we lose cabin pressure, an oxygen mask will drop from the compartment above you. If you are traveling with small children, put yours on first; only then, put on theirs."*

If you're a nervous flyer, likely you never got past "In the unlikely event." Now that you're safely on land, appreciate its soundness: *Caregivers need to take care of themselves.* Caring for others is hard work. Expect resentment. Expect exhaustion. And expect guilt.

> *"I'm not doing enough. My dad did so much for me. And I just want to go the movies."*

Taking time out is putting on your oxygen mask. Get help.

- Adult Day Care programs are available.
- Support groups can help; many are formed around specific illnesses, such as cancer, diabetes, heart disease, arthritis, or Alzheimer's.
- If you work, your employer might be agreeable to flex time.

Help on Call, Information and Referral, and your Area Agency on Aging are good places to start. If you're a surfer, check out the Web for specialized chatrooms.

Recently the Federal Trade Commission, in partnership with the AARP, created a series of 10 articles to help caregivers help their aging loved ones. They include "Making the Home Senior Safe," "Caring for the Caregiver," "Community Based Services," and "Selecting a Geriatric Care Manager." Call (202) FTC-HELP (382-4357) or www.ftc.gov/bcp/conline/pubs/services/apact.

There are many books on caring for the disabled (and on caring for yourself). Ask your library or bookstore.

Thoughts on Home Care

- *Make your house safe.* Install grab bars in bathrooms, lower hot water temperatures, and buy appropriate emergency alert systems.
- *Home nursing services* are available. Many services are covered by Medicare and other insurance.
- *Respite care* is available to give you a break. Some is offered in the home; some as temporary stays in a nursing home. Insurance and Medicare may cover the costs.
- Local agencies can help you: they offer Meals on Wheels, home nursing services, day care programs and periodic in-home respite care. Handicapped van service for doctor's appointments may be available; there is even talk in medical schools of returning to the *home visit.*
- *Some expenses* of home care might be picked up by Medicare, Medicaid, or long-term care insurance. For example, Medicare Part A, with a 20% co-payment, will cover the cost of "durable medical equipment" such as wheelchairs, hospital beds, traction equipment, walkers, and similar devices. Medicare Part B will cover emergency ambulance services. Many of the costs of hospice care (care given to the terminally ill) will be picked up by Medicare. (See Chapter 30-b.)
- Caring for a parent may allow you to claim an additional income tax exemption.
- Home care, if you count value of the time given by family members, is not that much cheaper than nursing home care, which is, surprise, our next chapter.

f. A Note for Alzheimer's Families

Individuals with Alzheimer's can wander off, causing their families great consternation and putting themselves at risk. There is a "Safe Return Program" that can help. For a one-time $40 registration fee, a bracelet and clothing tags will be provided. The items have a toll free number on them: if someone finds the person, they call the number and the operator will then contact the caregiver listed in the database. This service is 24 hours a day. For more information, call the Alzheimer's Association at 1-800-272-3900. (Hearing impaired 312-335-8882).

Many fear that Alzheimer's is genetic. Autopsies disclose that close to half of those who were thought to have that disease actually did not. This is one good reason to have an autopsy performed. See Chapter 31-b.

Chapter 27

Nursing Homes

On any given day, about one in twenty Americans over 65 will be cared for in a nursing home. Almost half of those turning 65 this year will be admitted to a nursing home at least once. Most stays will be fairly brief. However 20% of those admitted (or somewhat less than 10% of those over 65) will stay at least one year; one tenth stay over three years.

In the movies, there are never vegetarian dinosaurs and there are never attractive nursing homes. This is consistent with Hollywood's guiding adolescent fears: being eaten alive and growing old. Thanks to Hollywood, we have a very negative image of nursing homes—older folks slumped in wheelchairs staring at TV static.

It is clearly possible to live with dignity, with meaning, and with humor in a nursing home. There are new friends to be made, new hobbies to be tried, and new books to be read. And, if Woody Allen happens to be reading, yes, there is still sex. (By the way, the movie rights to this book are still available.)

In many ways, nursing home care is better than home care. While residents lose privacy and sense of home, nursing homes provide better medical treatment as they have nurses, and sometimes, physicians, on staff. Most provide extensive activities, such as exercise programs, craft classes, and field trips.

In some ways it's the same dilemma as to whether to put one's young child in child care: no matter how loving and energetic you are, hired folks offer expertise, activities, and friends.

Many people fear dying in a nursing home. This need not be a fear as it is always possible to return home at the time of one's last illness and receive hospice care. More of this in Chapter 30-b.

But the searing image remains—we don't want even to think about nursing homes. But let's just do it!

a. Financial Aspects

Nursing home costs can be staggering, with monthly charges of $2,000 to $6,000 or more. Medicare, even if supplemented with a Medigap policy, does *not* pay for traditional nursing home care, known as custodial care. Most insurance policies don't either. The costs must be paid by the individual or their family; these costs can bankrupt.

- Depending on your age, long-term care insurance is available. It is a relatively new form of insurance so there is still flux in the market. The National Association of Insurance Commissioners has a free booklet, *The Shoppers Guide to Long-Term Care Insurance.* Call 816-374-7259 to receive a copy.
- Medicaid (not Medicare) is a program for the poor. Medicaid does pay the costs of long-term care, but before one becomes eligible for Medicaid, one must *spend down* most of one's assets. There is a growing speciality in the law, Medicaid Planning, that helps individuals keep many of their assets and still be eligible for Medicaid. But these steps must be taken well before entry into a nursing home (usually at least three years before).
- Adult children are not liable for the bills incurred by their parents in nursing homes *unless* they have agreed to be. *Don't agree.* When signing the initial paperwork, nursing home officials will likely ask you to co-sign—refuse, even though it might put you in a "bad light." (Better in a bad light, than in a poor house!)

Chapter 8 is devoted to financing long-term care, either with insurance or with Medicaid.

b. The Need for Planning

Far too often individuals are put in nursing homes on a more or less emergency basis—when they are released from the hospital or suffer a stroke. Such decisions are not the best.

When it becomes clear that you (or a loved one) cannot continue to live at home much longer, begin planning.

The Department of Health and Human Resources has a wonderful booklet, *Guide to Choosing a Nursing Home* (Publication No. HCFA 02195). http://www.hcfa.gov/medicare/nurshm1.htm

It advises that a network be created to help decide if a nursing home is necessary and, if so, which one. The network might include friends and relatives, doctors and health care professionals, clergy and social workers.

One task is to decide what level of care is needed. Let's get some of the jargon out of the way:

Hospice care: This is end-of-life care, often at home, paid for by Medicare.

Skilled nursing home care: Skilled nursing home care usually follows hospitalization and is designed for the short term; it is expected that the patient will return home. Many of the costs of skilled nursing home care are picked up by Medicare.

Custodial care: This is long-term. It is expected that the patient will *not* return home *unless* it is to die at home. The costs of custodial care are not covered by Medicare.

And there are a host of alternatives to nursing homes, depending on the level of disability, including subsidized senior housing, Board and Care Homes, and Continuing Care Retirement Communities (CCRCs). For a discussion of these options, see Chapter 6-d and 6-e.

c. Selecting a Nursing Home

Some nursing homes are great; others, both figuratively and literally, stink. How to find a good one? Talk to knowledgeable folks, then visit at least two homes, and, always remember, "It's the location, location, location!"

Long-Term Care Ombudsman

There are over 500 local long term care ombudsman programs. Ombudsmen visit nursing homes, take complaints, and advocate for residents. They are a great source of information and advice. Although they cannot recommend particular homes, they can answer questions concerning:

- survey results
- number of complaints
- results of their investigations

Other good sources of information about nursing homes include:

- hospital discharge planners and social workers
- doctors and clergy
- volunteers who help the elderly

Visit

Visit at least two (to allow for comparison) and visit each several times, at different times of day. Things you might want to look at:

Staff. Does it seem adequate to give individual attention or does it seem overworked? How does the staff treat the residents?

Mealtimes. Do residents socialize? Residents needing help should be integrated with other residents rather than eating alone.

Resident rooms. Personalized or institutionalized?

Residents. Reasonably well groomed, clean, and dressed?

Restraints and bedsores. Too many residents physically or medically restrained and too many bedsores spell trouble.

Activities. Take a look at the schedule of activities and show up to observe some.

Location. The more the family can visit, the better. Not only are the visits good in and of themselves, but nurses will pay more attention to residents who do not appear to be abandoned. If you have questions concerning a family member's care, you have the right to inspect medical charts. The nursing home has 24 hours to make them available.

d. Patients' Rights

The federal Nursing Home Reform Act (NHRA) applies to any home that has Medicare or Medicaid patients (a majority of such homes). The NHRA requires that a patient Bill of Rights be given to residents and their families. The most important rights:

- the right to an individualized treatment plan,
- the right to see all of one's clinical and other records,
- the right to complain and be free of reprisal,
- the right to send and receive uncensored mail and to make private calls,
- the right to refuse treatment, and
- the right *not* to be physically or chemically restrained except to prevent physical harm, and then only upon instruction of a doctor.

We cannot stress the importance of the right not to be restrained except under very limited circumstances. In some nursing homes, patients are routinely tied to their chairs. By their arms.Think about it!

Chapter 28

The Legal Aspects of Mental Disability

> *"What I wanted was to maintain a sense of control. Even more than the dread of becoming a burden, helplessness triggers in us a manic terror that things are slipping from our grasp . . . "*

Nancy Mairs writes of her slide into the physical disability of multiple sclerosis. Her inspiring book is *Waist-High in the World.*

If a loved one starts slipping into disability, appreciate the psychological terrors.

a. Help Confront the "Manic Terror"

Like J. Alfred Prufrock, most of us "come and go, talking of Michelangelo." We are often reluctant to bring up unpleasant matters.

> *"You're looking good."*
> *"Are the nurses treating you right?"*
> *"How about them Bulls?"*

Who are we kidding? Our loved one knows what is going on, fears the future, but doesn't want to bring the matter up and worry *us.*

> *"Dad, we need to talk about the future. Decisions will have to be made. I want to help. Let's talk now, so I will know how to do the right thing."*

In our next chapter, we will discuss how you should go about making decisions for others. What are the dangers? Here, after a discussion of legal competence, we discuss the formal and informal procedures that will give you the power to decide for another.

We begin with philosophy. Where else?

b. The Concept of Legal Competence

> *The only purpose for which power can be rightfully exercised over any member of a civilized community, against his will, is to prevent harm to others. His own good, either physical or moral, is not sufficient warrant.*
>
> John Stuart Mill, *On Liberty*

The right to make our own decisions, even foolish ones, defines adulthood. It is premised, however, on our *capacity to make* responsible decisions. Obviously we need not actually make responsible decisions. Unfortunately, making bad decisions is part of adulthood too.

Legal capacity involves the ability to recognize *alternatives*, to *weigh* pros and cons, and to *project* into the future. We don't, for example, give much credence to a five-year-old's adamant:

> *"I'm running away and I'm taking Puppy with me, and this time I'm* really serious*!"*

Grown-ups make decisions for children because they do not have the capacity always to know their best interests, or what's best for their puppies.

A good way to check on someone's capacity is to engage them in a conversation concerning recognition of alternatives, judging pros and cons, and projecting into the future.

1. "What else might you do other than running away?"
2. "What's going to happen when you get there?"
3. "Why is running away better than locking yourself in the bathroom?"

Most elderly, even in old, old age, *retain* mental ability. Mental functions do not necessarily diminish. But some elderly do lose legal capacity. Accidents, strokes, disease, and acute depression happen. Then relatives or friends must step in.

c. Informal Intervention: Social Security Checks and Durable Powers of Attorney

It is possible to step in without going to court. If the disabled person's only source of income is Social Security (and other monthly checks), and their only expenses are monthly bills, consider a *representative payee account*. It can be created even *after* a person becomes legally incapable. (See Chapter 19-a.) Another possibility is a *convenience signer account* offered by many banks. Social Security can send the checks directly to the bank, and a relative, good friend, or neighbor can be added to the account to pay monthly bills.

These accounts are better than joint accounts because the convenience signer does not have an ownership interest in the account. His or her creditors cannot reach it. On the other hand, at time of death, the convenience signer cannot simply take what's left in the account. In other words, it cannot be used to pass money at the time of death.

If the disabled person's financial situation is more complicated—because of ownership of cars, houses, stocks, real property—then you should consider joint ownership or, more generally, a *Durable Financial Power of Attorney*. These choices are described in Chapter 19.

If the disabled person becomes unable to make medical decisions, a *Durable Health Care Power of Attorney* will be required. (See Chapter 18.) Documents creating joint ownership and Durable Powers of Attorney must be signed while the person is still competent. Once a loved one starts to slip, feel time's winged chariot hurrying near. If the needed documents are not signed, then you will have to seek something more formal.

d. Formal Intervention: Guardianship and Conservatorship

A majority of the elderly *never* need a guardianship because they *never* become incompetent. Even then, most guardianships are sought at the insistence of third parties:

1. *Financial institutions* may require appointment of a guardian or conservator to allow access to funds;

2. *Hospitals* may require appointment of a guardian for certain medical treatments; and
3. *Nursing homes* may require guardianship for admittance (under the laws of some states, formal guardianship is required).

Routine formal guardianships are quick and relatively inexpensive. A short court hearing will be held and usually the ward (the disabled person) will not be present. The person seeking the guardianship, his lawyer, and the lawyer for the ward (usually court appointed) will meet in an informal hearing to see if all is in order.

Contested guardianships are more like trials. When are guardianships contested?

1. When relatives seek to prevent an individual from squandering his money, and the individual wants to go on doing it. ("It sure doesn't feel like squandering to me!")
2. When relatives squabble as to who should be in charge of the ward's affairs.
   Note: Even after a guardianship has been granted, another relative or friend can petition the court to *remove* that guardian if the guardian is cheating the ward, or otherwise not doing a good job.
3. When family wants to discontinue life-sustaining treatment in the face of terminal illness where the individual has not left a Living Will indicating his preferences. (See Chapter 18-g; Chapter 30-d.)

e. What Will Happen in Court?

State laws govern guardianships and they vary a great deal. Here we will give an overview.

Petitions, Lawyers, and Costs

The Probate Court where the disabled person resides or is located has jurisdiction to grant a guardianship or conservatorship. A petition may be filed by almost anyone, including neighbors. In almost all cases, a lawyer will be needed by the petitioner and thus the costs may be substantial (in the neighborhood of $500 to $3,000). Pre-disability planning (Living Wills and Durable Powers of Attorney) *saves* these costs. (See Chapters 18 and 19.) If physicians testify, or if the matter is contested, the bills could be much higher. These charges will usually be paid by the ward's estate. All interested parties must be notified of the hearing, which they can attend.

What is required in the petition will vary by state. It will include allegations of why the guardianship is needed and often what plan the proposed guardian has for the ward. A listing of the ward's income, expenses, and assets may also be required. Some states require that the petitioner also explain why there is no *less restrictive alternative* to guardianship.

> *The legal concept of* least restrictive alternative *holds that, when the law is forced to interfere with a citizen's rights, it must accomplish its goal in the most narrow, and unobtrusive, possible way. For example, in the area of Free Speech, assume the mayor is concerned that a protest parade will disrupt traffic. She cannot simply bar the parade, but she can insist that it take a certain route. In the context of guardianships, there may be alternative steps that can be taken to protect the elderly person short of guardianship: trusts, durable powers of attorney, or simply sitting down and getting the person's consent to what you recommend.*

The Guardianship Hearing

The hearing comes quickly, usually in a few weeks (and emergency situations can make the system respond even more quickly). The alleged incompetent usually will not be present unless the matter is contested. Some judges will even go to the person's home to conduct the hearing. The individual has a right to an attorney (to resist the guardianship or to object to a particular person as guardian) and, in some states, if the individual cannot afford a lawyer, one will be appointed. In some states, before the hearing, the court will appoint a *Court Visitor*.

> *A* Court Visitor, *someone with a background in social work or medicine, may visit the ward before the hearing to make recommendations. Court visitors may also visit the ward thereafter to see how things are going.*

The Questions to be Decided

Has the individual lost legal capacity?
If so, what kind of guardian should be appointed?
Who should be the guardian?

If the judge (in some states, the jury if requested by the ward) finds the individual incompetent, the next question is what kind of guardian is needed.

Capacity is *not* an all-or-nothing proposition. Some may lack the capacity to manage their portfolio ("Sell pork bellies, buy soybeans!") but retain capacity to shop ("No soybeans tonight!") and pay routine bills. Others may lack financial capacity, yet retain capacity to decide where they wish to live and what medical treatments they do or do not want. Given this, the law recognizes three kinds of guardianships:

Financial guardians. These are also known as *Conservators* and provide for management of the ward's finances.
Personal guardians. Provide management of living arrangements and medical decisions.
Plenary Guardians. These have both powers and are appropriate only if the individual is incapacitated in both areas.

Guardianship is a sharp and broad sword. *The ward loses the legal capacity to act in the areas of the guardianship*. For example, if you are under guardianship, Smilin' Sam will *not* sell you the car because your promise to pay for it is not binding. ("But what if Smilin' Sam doesn't know about the guardianship?" Come to law school!)

Given the drastic nature of guardianships, some states allow for *limited guardianships* which allow the ward to make certain decisions. For example, if a ward cannot make medical decisions, a personal guardian can be given powers in that area while leaving the ward free to decide all other life decisions, such as where to live.

The final question the court will have to decide is "*Who* should be the guardian?" Usually it will be the petitioner, who is often a family member or close friend. However:

- In the case of large financial estates, it can be a bank or financial institution.
- If no family member can or wishes to serve, the guardian can be a *social service agency* or other institution which

will charge a fee. *Public Guardians/Public Fiduciaries* are available in some locales for individuals who cannot afford a fee or have no one else who is willing and qualified to act for them. If relatives are bitterly divided, a Public Guardian may be appointed as the default choice.

- Private care managers are also available. For information, you can contact the National Association of Professional Geriatric Care Managers, 1604 N. Country Club, Tucson, AZ 85716. Typically, family members serve without fee. Expenses (lawyers, accountants, travel) can be charged against the ward's estate. Institutional guardians charge for their services, usually on an hourly-fee basis or on a percentage of the estate assets.

f. Note: Disabled Parents in Distant Cities

If your parents live far away, you won't be there if they become disabled. Urge them to have Durable Financial Powers of Attorney and Durable Health Care Powers of Attorney. These will authorize old friends to act in the case of their disability. As to a personal guardian, one option might be a local social service agency or a private care manager. See above. If your parent lives out of state and you wish to be appointed guardian, you will have to go to that state to do so. Further, some states, but not most, require that the guardian reside in the same state as the ward.

g. Individuals Who Are a Danger to Themselves or Others

Guardianships are for mental incapacity, not for *insanity.* If an elder, or anyone for that matter, is suffering from mental illness that makes the person dangerous to themselves or others, then *civil commitment* should be considered. States have procedures that can be used to commit dangerously mentally ill people to state or local hospitals for treatment of their condition. Some states, but not all, allow for civil commitment of individuals who are in need of treatment—such as individuals who refuse to take needed medical treatment.

For further information about such care, contact a local mental health screening agency which you can locate by calling a nearby hospital or law enforcement agency.

Chapter 29

Deciding for Others

Don Quixote, Fighter of Dragons, Dreamer of Impossible Dreams, Reacher of Unreachable Stars, makes something of a fool of himself – off chasing Windmills when he should be at home, preserving his estate.

His niece is concerned, but only about him. True, he is wasting money she hopes to inherit and true, he is causing her great social embarrassment. But, to her credit, these factors don't even enter into her deliberations.

In *The Man from LaMancha* she sings:

In my body, it's well known
There is not one selfish bone . . .
I'm only thinking and worrying about him.

After much thought, she decides to have him locked up. It would be best for him!

* * *

It's tough deciding for others. You may have to—either informally in the give and take of family affairs, or formally, as a designated agent under a Durable Power of Attorney or as a Guardian appointed by a court. How should you make your decisions? How can you avoid conflicts of interest? We'll give you our best thinking.

a. How to Decide? The Standards

The law has struggled in defining the standard by which agents should make decisions for others. There are two possibilities:

1. Do what you think the other person would have done or wanted done; or
2. Do what you believe is in the "best interests" of the other person.

Lawyers love splitting hairs, but there is a real difference between the two. What if the person would want something done which was *not* in her "best interests"? Most recent law cases protect our right to be foolish by opting for the first standard (referred to as "substituted judgment"). It best protects personal freedom and choice.

Let's say you know that your mother would never consent to an amputation, even to save her life. As her medical decision-maker, you should refuse to consent to an amputation, even if you would consent if you were in that situation and even if you believe that it is in her best interests to consent and go on living.

Assume that you have no social conscience and would invest in any company, no matter what it did or how it did it. You know your father objects to polluters, cigarette pushers, or union busters. As his financial agent, don't invest his money in such companies, even if they pay above market.

If you don't know and can't find out what the other person would decide, only then are you to act in what you believe to be her "best interests" (not, by the way, necessarily what you would do if you were in her situation).

b. Coping with Conflicts of Interest

A man's interest far oftener distorts his judgment than it corrupts his heart.

A.V. Dicey, Legal Historian

Usually, it's money.

Say you are managing your parents' finances. As you or your children will inherit, you will want the estate to be as large as possible. This perfectly normal desire may distort your investment and health care decisions.

You will be tempted to invest in growth stocks rather than in stocks paying the highest income, when higher income may be in the best interests of your parents. You will be tempted to skimp on nursing home amenities which would improve your parents' lives.

Of course, things are never simple. Your parents have an interest not only in their own well being but also in making sure you receive a large inheritance. It might very well be that they would choose to have their money go to the college education of their grandchildren (or for a vacation for you) rather than a color TV set at the nursing home.

There are no easy answers. Perhaps the most important way to cope with the problem of self- interest is to admit that you have it. Repeat, after us:

"I have at least one selfish bone!"

Knowing temptation is the first step in resisting it. Philosophers have offered other solutions. Kant recommended that we universalize our decision as a way of factoring out our own interests.

"How would you have all guardians decide the issue you face?" In an interesting aside, note that the judicial doctrine of precedent operates in much the same way as does Kant's approach. As a judge's decision will become precedent and thus followed by future judges, the judge must think in terms of choosing the best rule of law for all similarly situated persons, not just the parties before him. It forces the judge to universalize.

Others recommend that when you are faced with a difficult decision, think of a wise person you know and ask, "How would he or she decide?" (At first blush, that struck us as not very helpful but, having tried it, there is more there than you might think.)

Of course, conversations are better than philosophy. Talk to the person affected, even if they don't seem "all there."

"What investment strategy do you want me to follow?" "If you move into a nursing home, should I go first class or keep an eye on the grandchildren's college education?"

If you are still in a quandary, realize that not to decide is often a decision and that quandaries don't self-correct. Robert Benchley once published a book entitled *My Ten Years in a Quandary*. Procrastinators take note. (It took imagination to work in the Benchley book. I just feel I owe it to him after all the pleasure his book gave me as a teen.)

Talk with other family members or with professionals, such as a stock broker or lawyer. If you think that someone might later challenge your decision, keep a record as to why you made it and with whom you talked concerning it.

If you are a court-appointed guardian, you can even go back to court and have the judge decide by filing a *Petition for Instructions*. Notice must be given to all interested persons – they have the right to have their opinions heard by the judge, but once the judge decides, they are bound by the decision.

c. Court-Appointed Guardians

State laws vary as to the specific powers and obligations of guardians, those individuals appointed by a court to make personal decisions for their ward. If you are appointed guardian, the judge will review your responsibilities and powers. Here's a likely list.

- You have the powers and responsibilities of a parent of a minor except that you do not have a support obligation. You are responsible for seeing that the ward's personal needs, such as food, clothing, and shelter are met. But you do not have to pay for these things from your own pocket. You do not need to live with the ward.
- You are responsible for the ward's medical decisions, often even over his or her protest. Generally you have the power to place the ward in a nursing home but not, without court approval, a mental health institution.
- You must take reasonable steps to protect the ward's personal effects.
- *Never, ever, not once, comingle funds*. It is simply too easy to forget that you put some of the ward's money in your checking account. People go to prison for things like this. Always have separate accounts.
- You are entitled to be paid a reasonable fee if the court approves.
- You cannot simply walk away from your responsibilities. You must go back to court to be relieved of them.
- You will be given an official court document to show to banks, doctors, and others.
- You will probably be asked to report back to the court yearly or even more frequently.
- *Never, ever, not once, comingle funds*. It is worth repeating. Or maybe you can write a book — "My Ten Years in State Prison."

d. Keep Records

Even if you are not court-appointed, records are a very good idea. Indicate what you spent, why, and, hopefully, the ward's involvement in the decision.

> *"After extended discussions with Uncle in the presence of his good friend Sancho, we used $4,000 to visit the windmill region of Spain. By the way, Uncle did reach the Unreachable Star. And, no matter what all of you may think, and despite your snickers, I'm next!"*

Chapter 30

Terminal Illness

The doctor tells you that your spouse has pancreatic cancer and only a very short time to live. Do you tell?

a. Disclosing a Terminal Diagnosis

Bad winds may blow your way. Now is the time to prepare. Start a discussion.

"Dear, I've been reading this book. Let me ask you something. If you had inoperable cancer and only a short time to live, would you want to know?"

Of course, your spouse has not given the matter very much thought. Expect something flip.

Spouse: *"You decide. I'm too busy with these tomatoes."*

Press the issue!

You: *"That's not fair. I want to know what you want me to do."*
Spouse: *"O.K., then don't tell me. Now I've got to get back to these tomatoes."*
You: *"Why wouldn't you want to know?"*

You want a discussion, not an answer. Discussion forces us to think long and hard, about death, about life. We may learn things about ourselves we didn't even know. This discussion can be part of the family conversation we recommend in Chapter 34. But what if, when and if the time comes, you still don't know your spouse's desires?

We believe that disclosure of terminal diagnosis is generally a very good idea. However, to force this knowledge on someone who doesn't want to know is as bad as keeping quiet when the person would want to know.

Sort out your emotions. You may not tell because you don't want to face the truth. Telling seems to make it more real. Telling will trigger an emotional crisis, a crisis you may not be prepared for. Or you may tell simply because you are too uncomfortable keeping the secret.

Try to put aside your fears. *Would my loved one want to know?* There are good reasons *not* to tell:

- Doctors have been wrong before.

A Native American at a Death and Dying Conference explained that, when an individual is hospitalized, family and friends get together and decide upon a spokesperson to deal with the doctors.

"If I have to give you a terminal diagnosis," a doctor from the audience asked him, "would you want me to tell your spokesperson or would you want me to talk to you?"

"Well, if you *could* give me a terminal diagnosis, you would be God. And I would love to talk to you."

- Hearing the diagnosis, your spouse may give up all hope.

In Oscar Wilde's *The Importance of Being Earnest,* the funniest play ever written, the main character makes up the existence of cousin Earnest. When he grows weary of the city, he visits Earnest. This works fine, but around the second act, Earnest becomes inconvenient. The solution: Earnest's death is announced, his death coming shortly after his doctor had given him only "a short time to live." Another character, hearing this, is quite impressed and remarks, "He seems to have had great confidence in the opinion of his physician."

Usually, however, the doctors have it right, and hope does not turn enough diseases around. There are good reasons to tell:

- Your loved one will probably find out accidentally, from a nurse or hospital technician.
- Your loved one probably already suspects the diagnosis, and fears bringing it up out of a desire not to burden you.
- If you believe that it is possible to die well, and we do, keeping the matter secret denies your spouse (and your family) the wonderful care of Hospice.

b. Hospice Care

What people fear most about death is not the pain; not even what comes next. What people fear most is dying alone.

Death in the hospital can be lonesome. And painful. We repeat the findings of a study we quoted earlier. The *Journal of the American Medical Association* studied five major hospitals and reports:

- 50% of terminal patients experience pain, moderate to severe, half the time.
- 38% of terminal patients spend ten or more days in a coma.
- 31% spend all, or most, of their family's savings during their final illness.

One expert concludes, "If you're in the hospital, get out; if you're not in the hospital, stay out." (Learned Hand, a famous judge, came to a similar conclusion about courtrooms—"If at all possible, never get involved in litigation.")

Only about 10% of people who could receive hospice care, do receive it. The figure should be 100%. It is marvelous.

Hospice care is home care—or care in a homelike setting. Death comes not among strangers, but with family and friends. Care is provided by a team, likely a doctor, a physical therapist, a nurse, a counselor, and a spiritual advisor. The goal of hospice care is *not* to lengthen life. Disease-fighting medications are *not* given. (Of course, if the patient desires it or if the patient goes into remission, hospice care can end.)

The three goals of Hospice are: pain elimination, education, and "dying well."

Pain elimination. Pain killers are freely given—the more pain, the more medication.

Education. What is the course of this disease? Of dying? How can the patient and the family make the most of the time remaining?

Dying well. More of this momentarily.

Hospice care is essentially free. Once the patient has been diagnosed as having six months or less to live, Medicare pays for up to two 90 day periods of hospice care. It will cover most of the costs—doctors' and nursing bills, drugs, health aides, homemaker services, and counseling. Long-term Care insurance may also pick up some of the expenses. (You can get a copy of *Medicare and Your Hospice Benefits* by calling 1-800-638-6833.)

c. "Dying Well"

> *"How would you like to die?"*
> *"Like my grandfather, peacefully, in his sleep. Not kicking and screaming, like his passengers."*

If we *only* hope for a death that doesn't involve a lot of pain, we are selling ourselves way short. We are selling our families way short. Those in the Hospice talk of dying as a growth experience.

> *"How can dying be a growth experience? At the end, we're dead."*

We think instrumentally. Nothing is good in its own right; it is good only to the extent it becomes an instrument used to achieve yet other goals. We study, but not because learning is challenging and fun; we study to get a better job. We exercise, not because it's great to feel exhausted, but because it will extend our lives and improve our looks. We read books, not to enjoy ourselves, but to improve ourselves and learn things (and—get this!—some of us even get mad when the author breaks our serious, joyless, march with some silly aside to *The Importance of Being Earnest*).

Dying well is our recognition of the riches we have, not of things we can buy; it is our recognition of who we are, not of who we can become.

The actor Anthony Perkins, dying of AIDS, said:

> *There are many who believe that this disease is God's vengeance, but I believe it was sent to teach people how to love and understand and have compassion for each other. I have learned more about love, selflessness and human understanding from people I have met in this great adventure in the world of AIDS than I ever did in the cut-throat, competitive world in which I spent my life.*

Dying well involves shutting down our roles, our fears, and our hopes. There are no more plans, no more failures, no more successes. We are just us. Of course, there will be pain. Viktor Frankl, who survived the Nazi death camps, wrote that people can survive pain, but they cannot survive the loss of meaning. What meaning, what purpose, can there be, lying in bed, drifting in and out of consciousness, with only days to live?

> *You can give your family and friends the opportunity to care for you.*

They can express their love and pay something back for all you have done for them. Caring for others is deeply human.

> *You can tell your stories.*

Children and grandchildren love to hear of times when everyone dressed up real funny.

> *You can drift towards greater understanding and peace.*

> *You can prepare yourself for what comes next.*

For two excellent books on this subject, see Ira Byock, M.D., *Dying Well: Peace and Possibilities at the End of Life,* and Elizabeth Kubler-Ross, *On Death and Dying.*

d. Ending Medical Treatment

At some point, knowing that death will result, you may have to consider ordering physicians to discontinue a loved one's treatment.

If the person has made his or her wishes plain in a Living Will or Durable Health Care Power of Attorney, your decision, while painful, will be relatively easy.

But what if no instructions were given? Without a patient's instructions and without the tacit agreement of physicians, you may very well have to get a court order terminating treatment. State law varies and is changing.

In 1990, the United States Supreme Court confirmed the right of a *competent* patient to order the removal of life-sustaining systems. For the patients who can no longer express their desires, the Court said that the guardians *can* order the removal of life-sustaining treatment, but before this can be done, a state can insist on proof that the patient, before becoming incompetent, expressed a desire that this be done. The state can require that this showing be made by *clear and convincing evidence.*

Most states have adopted this approach and hence our advice: *discuss the issue with the patient, while the patient is competent, in front of witnesses.* This can be early on, during a separate conversation or as part of the family conversation we recommend in Chapter 34.

Say your mother told you that if she had no prospect of recovery, she did not want to be kept alive by artificial means. Your testimony of this conversation, by itself, might not be enough to satisfy the clear and convincing standard. This is particularly true if you are paying her bills or stand to inherit from her. Far better proof is a series of statements, as specific as possible, to several non-interested witnesses on several different occasions.

Consider video taping the conversation.

One final, but essential, point in this regard: *it is far easier to keep feeding and hydration tubes out than it is to get them out.* If a loved one is in a nursing home, and the staff recommends such tubes, think long and hard before authorizing them. They have a financial interest in keeping the patient alive, no matter how dismal the prospects and no matter how painful the condition. Once the tubes are in, it may take a court order to get them out.

Of course you will want to know the current medical thinking of whether death by dehydration and starving is particularly painful. A 1994 study found that only 13% of terminal patients refusing to eat or drink were judged to have experienced discomfort during their dying period. Efforts were made to relieve dry mouth and thirst.

e. Euthanasia, Physician-assisted Suicide, Suicide

In March of 1998 an Oregon woman, dying of beast cancer, became the first person to use Oregon's Death with Dignity Law. She died peacefully in her sleep, at home, surrounded by her family. Her physician had given her medication; five minutes later she was asleep, thirty minutes later, dead.

Euthanasia is where a third party *helps* an individual end his life. It artificially *shortens* life. Euthanasia is *not* the same as removing life-sustaining help. Keeping tubes in artificially *prolongs* life; taking them out simply allows nature to run its course. As we have seen, the law protects your right to reject *life-prolonging* medical treatment. With a Living Will you can prohibit "heroic measures" from being taken; and, if you are competent at the time, you can reject them. If you are comatose, relatives may be able to have life-sustaining treatments ended.

On the other hand, you have no legal right to ask another's help in ending your own life. In all states euthanasia is criminal in the sense that it is not a defense to a homicide prosecution that the victim was a relative, had a terminal illness, was in great pain, and had begged to die. Recently the United States Supreme Court held that an individual does not have a constitutional right to ask for help in committing suicide, even when that help is from a physician. The court held that this issue should be left up to the states.

Physician-assisted suicide is legal in one state, Oregon. The law was passed in a general referendum. There is a very active debate whether other states should adopt similar laws.

The issues are extremely complicated. In support, there is the notion that freedom and, indeed, being human, entails the right to captain one's own destiny. Why shouldn't you have the right to seek medical help in ending your life? Why shouldn't you be allowed to avoid the great pain and expense generally associated with final illness?

There is another less obvious argument in favor of allowing for physician assisted suicide: it may actually reduce suicide. Many elderly, suffering from chronic illness, fear that it will eventually lead to unbearable suffering and that, when it does come, they will no longer have the ability to end it. In panic, they take their own lives. The mere promise that, if that time arrives, there will be someone there for them would stay their hand and immediately relieve their consuming fear. Once again they would be in control of their future. At peace, and finding that in fact their lives never do become unbearable, most would not commit suicide. Most people who have "saved up pills, just in case," never use them.

But there are strong philosophic and religious concerns against any form of euthanasia. No one should play God; the guiding principle of medicine is "first, do no harm;" and legal euthanasia, even if not widespread, will lead to a general cheapening of human life. There are practical concerns as well: if euthanasia is available, how can relatives be prevented from dumping expensive or inconvenient relatives? From trying to accelerate their inheritance?

There is also the real concern of the slippery slope. Although most proposals to legalize euthanasia, like the one in Oregon, are restricted to consenting adults who have a terminal illness (one which is likely to lead to death within six months), the fear is that these limits cannot hold. Why deny a consenting adult medical help in ending a life made unbearable by severe chronic fatal illness, such as Lou Gehrig's Disease, simply because that disease has not yet progressed to the "terminal stage"(although it will surely lead to death, it will not do so within the next six months). There is also the fear that voluntary euthanasia will slowly but surely lead to involuntary euthanasia. Once the law seems to acknowledge that some lives aren't worth living, the next step may be to put severely retarded or disabled individuals "out of their misery." Fanciful? One hears arguments that the elderly have a "duty" to step aside, and a group of severely disabled individuals, fiercely opposed to physician-assisted suicide, calls itself "Not Dead Yet."

One final point on the general topic of euthanasia. Pain relief which has the unintended result of causing death, is not euthanasia. For example, physicians will prescribe morphine for certain painful cancers; as the pain increases, so, too, the dosages. Increased dosages may lead to death. This is known as a treatment's "double effect." It is interesting to note that the Catholic Church, a vocal opponent of euthanasia, does not condemn the practice.

For a very interesting book on the history of the physician-assisted suicide debate, see Sue Woodman's fine book, *Last Rights: The Struggle over the Right to Die*.

Of course, there is always suicide. As to mechanics, there is a book, Derek Humphreys' *Final Exit,* which gives quite specific instructions on how to end one's life. The Hemlock Society offers counseling.

But if you are thinking of ending your own life, go slowly, ever so slowly. If you are considering suicide, two things are most likely true: you are very depressed and you fear the pain of your illness will eventually become unbearable. Consider:

- Depression can be treated and is transitory. "This too shall pass."
- Almost all pain can be alleviated by proper medication. The reason that many die painful deaths is not the inability of medicine to control pain but the lack of training of most doctors in dealing with terminal illness and their reluctance to prescribe high enough dosages. Hospice promises high enough dosages and hence a relatively pain free death. See Section "b" above.
- Suicide of a loved one is one of the hardest deaths to get over—guilt abounds ("Was this my fault?"). The message you send to relatives and family is of darkest human despair: "Some lives aren't worth living."

One thing for sure. Before you take any step toward suicide, talk to family, friends and spiritual advisers. If you don't, you do them a double wrong: your death and your cruel denial of their opportunity to reach out to comfort you.

f. Accelerated Benefits on Life Insurance (Viatical Settlements)

This smacks of "good news, bad news" jokes. Nonetheless, under many life insurance policies, the terminally ill patient, one who is expected to die within six months or a year, can receive a portion of his life insurance policy right now and *tax free* (better news) if certain conditions apply. These funds can be used for any purpose. They are not exempt from the claims of creditors (a definite "bad news").

Whether this is a good option depends in part on the discount rate (how much they charge you). Under many insurance policies all you lose is the interest on the amount withdrawn. Contrast this discount rate to those given by *Viatical companies*, which run between 20-40%. These companies have sprung up with the AIDS epidemic. "We'll buy your life insurance policy, paying you, say, $60,000 on the $100,000 policy. All you have to do for us is die." Once you get beyond the shock of this, realize the advantages:

- *Insurance doesn't pay for experimental medical treatments; money from these settlements can.*
- *The money can be used to provide home care.*
- *Finally, a lot can be said for one last trip.*

Spain?

Chapter 31

Death in the Family

When a loved one dies, it seems as if the world stops. Or that it should stop.

Stop all the clocks, cut off the telephone,
Prevent the dog from barking with a juicy bone,
Silence the pianos and with muffled drum
Bring out the coffin, let the mourners come.
......
The stars are not wanted now: put out every one;
Pack up the moon and dismantle the sun;
Pour away the ocean and sweep up the wood;
For nothing now can ever come to any good.

W. H. Auden

Thankfully there will be a lot of distracting details, a lot of running around to do, a lot of business to attend to. Burial decisions, short-term financial arrangements, insurance and Social Security survivor benefits, probate. These will get you through the first several months. Perhaps, after that, things again can come to good. Not like before, but still, to good. We begin with mourning.

a. The Myths of Mourning

On T.V. talk shows we hear that mourning is a process, with marked stages and with final goals. That has not been our experience. *Mourning is different for all of us.*

- Grieving is *not* a process that everyone needs to "work though" to get to some point where it is over, allowing you to "get on with your life."

If there is a goal to mourning, it is *not* to *get over* the death. It is to *relocate* the loved one—to create a different kind of relationship with the person:

> *"So that's what the President said. I wish I could call Dad and get his reaction. What would it be?"*

Mourning is *not* an interruption in life. Mourning will be part of the rest of your life. You won't be "OK" for a long time and memories will always rush back, unexpected.

– Depression and great distress are *not* inevitable during mourning.

Some grieve before the death and experience the actual death with relief. Expect complicated feelings—despair mixed with relief; dark, intense moments mixed with daily chores and gossip.

– Mourning is also self-mourning.

The poet Gerard Manley Hopkins got that right. He writes to a young girl, crying because a golden grove of trees is losing its leaves:

> *Margaret, are you grieving*
> *Over Goldengrove unleaving?*

She may think so, but she is really grieving her own mortality.

> *It is the blight man was born for,*
> *It is Margaret you mourn for.*

– Life is always in the present tense. You must figure out what to do tomorrow morning.

> *An elderly couple sits on the couch. The wife says,"If I die first, you should remarry. If you die first, I'll get a dog."*

With mourning, there are no rules, no stages, no end points. Just be with friends, neighbors, and relatives. Talk. Cry. Gossip.

Now, the distracting details.

b. The First Few Days: Funeral Homes and Burial

Funeral homes can be called at any hour. They will know what to do. In addition to funeral arrangements, they will take care of official notifications and will arrange for several copies of the official death certificate that you may need in notifying insurance companies, Social Security, retirement plans, and the like.

Often the individual, by Will or otherwise, has indicated a preference between cremation and burial and what kind of service they wish. If not, these decisions fall to the family.

Cremation is less expensive. There will be local regulations as to where ashes can be scattered. Permanent urns are also available. Some are quite beautiful and moving, either in their simplicity or in their religious and spiritual themes. Others strike us as more fanciful, such as the ones adorned with statuettes of golfers.

> *Query: In Heaven, do you* always *shoot a hole in one? Or is that in Hell?*

Funerals are expensive. Several years ago Jessica Mitford exposed funeral fraud in her book, *The American Way of Death*. Funeral Directors were portrayed as scum, sucking the blood of grieving families, selling them expensive coffins to "show their love for the dearly departed."

Hopefully, things have improved, but be wary. Funeral fraud continues in many areas. In 1984 the Federal Trade Commission promulgated the Funeral Industry Practices trade regulation rules. Funeral Directors must disclose the cost of all goods and services, even over the phone, and provide a *written list* when you inquire in person. You have the right to purchase individual funeral products and *need not buy* entire packages.

Consumer frauds to watch for:

a. Quoting one price on the phone and switching to a higher one in person.
b. Misrepresenting that state law requires embalming (some states do not).
c. Misrepresenting that state law requires caskets for cremation or outer burial containers for burial (some states do not).

It is a good time to remember your Bible. Over the long haul, no container, no plastic, can defeat life's cycle: "Dust to Dust."

You will be distraught. There will be strong psychological pressures to overspend. No one wants to appear "cheap" at a time like that. Everyone wants to show their loved one just how much they cared. We advise *extreme caution.*

On the first trip to the funeral home, you will be taken through the "Casket Room," complete with price listings and "warranties." (Warranties are a curious concept in this context; what does the "lifetime warranty" actually mean?) *Don't agree to anything that first visit. That's an order.* Go home and think about how else the family can use the money. Talk things over. As to showing the decedent you really cared, it is, alas, too late. (That's why we recommend a *Family Conversation.* See Chapter 34.)

As to being cheap, blame us: as lawyers it is our *job* to be cheap. On the other hand, don't assume that funeral directors are your enemy; they can provide a great deal of emotional support as well as practical advice.

Autopsies and Organ Donations

An autopsy is simply a post-death surgery designed to determine the cause of death and the presence of diseases and abnormalities. Although gruesome to envision, an autopsy might be quite helpful to the surviving family. For example, genetic diseases unknown to the family might be revealed so that family members can take steps to avoid them. Conversely, it might be discovered that Granddad wasn't suffering from the genetic disease his family feared. (For example, it is believed that Alzheimer's disease has a genetic component; family members have great anxiety as to their own futures. Autopsies reveal, however, that only about 50% of individuals believed to have that disease actually had it.)

A family can request that an autopsy be performed and can insist on a limited one, such as a brain autopsy looking for Alzheimer's or a heart autopsy looking for heart disease. If an autopsy is done, don't expect immediate answers. What with microscopic examinations of tissue, results typically take 30 days or longer.

The good news is that most hospitals throw in the autopsy for free. (Even with fierce competition for patients, hospitals seldom advertize this feature: "After your stay with us, enjoy a free autopsy.") Hospitals rely heavily on autopsies to assure that doctors are diagnosing and treating disease correctly. Frequently an autopsy will disclose that the cause of death was other than that which had been treated. Further, pathologists rely heavily on autopsies to better understand the causes and treatment of human diseases. That we live as healthy as we do today is in large part due to the autopsies of yesterday. In this light, agreeing to an autopsy can be viewed as a contribution to our grandchildren.

Under certain circumstances, the law requires that an autopsy be performed: if the cause of death is suspicious or unknown, and perhaps, depending on state law, if the individual died within a year of surgery or died without a physician present to certify the cause of death.

Organ donations can save lives and can help in medical research and training. If the decedent opposed making a donation, then that decision should and must be respected. However, even if the decedent (by Will, donation card, or driver-license designation), indicated a desire to donate, often doctors and hospitals may still seek the family's agreement (although, technically, their agreement is not required in the face of a valid directive of the decedent).

If the decedent left no instructions, the family can authorize an anatomical donation. State law lists, in priority order, who can make that decision: the surviving spouse, adult children, either parent, adult sibling, grandparent (in some states) and the person's guardian. Some families have religious and similar objections to donations. However, some object in the mistaken belief that they would delay the funeral. They generally don't.

Notifications

Family and friends should know as soon as possible. Phone trees work well. Obituaries in local papers can be arranged by the funeral home at a modest cost.

c. The First Few Weeks

Immediate Cash Needs and the Safety Box Ploy

Hopefully sufficient funds were kept in joint savings and checking accounts. The joint tenant can withdraw money. Similarly there should be no problem if the assets were in a Living Trust. Even if the decedent was the managing trustee, the trust will continue with notification to the back-up trustee.

Some advise keeping large amounts of cash in joint safety deposit boxes, the idea being that upon the death of one, the other can easily get to the cash and that the cash will not show up as part of the estate, thus cutting taxes. This probably isn't good advice. First, as to easy access, joint checking and savings accounts achieve the same goal. Second, as to avoiding taxes, it is against the law. And banks read the obituaries. They will seal joint safety deposit boxes, which can only then be opened in the presence of a state official. *Note to aging Flower Children:* Don't keep your stash in your safety box.

If the family's assets were kept in the decedent's name alone, there may be trouble reaching them. The quickest way is to immediately open a Probate Proceeding (we will tell you how momentarily) and have yourself appointed personal representative. You will then be issued papers by the Court which will allow you to access the decedent's accounts. Most states provide for a *Family Allowance* during probate (Chapter 32-c). It allows the family to draw needed money before and during the probate process, which can be lengthy.

Bills: Don't pay them!

It's a good idea to let things sort themselves out before you start paying any of the decedent's bills, such as hospital bills, doctors' bills, and nursing home bills. Why should you wait? If the estate is to be probated, the estate will pay the bills; if there is a Living Trust, the trustee will.

In any event, you may not be legally obligated to pay them. As a general rule, only the person (or his or her estate) who received the service is liable to pay the bill. Generally, family members (children and spouses) are *not* required to pay the bills out of their own pockets. (See Chapter 12.)

Finally, some of the bills sent to a decedent after his death may be *bogus*. Scam artists take advantage of a family's distress. (See Chapter 16.)

Send a letter to the creditors explaining that the individual has died, and that you will need time to sort out his affairs.

On the other hand, continue to pay *on-going* bills, such as rent, utilities, and, yes, the lawyer's fees for probate. If these bills are not paid, the services will stop.

The Search for Documents and Notifying Insurance and Social Security

The family should search papers and safety deposit boxes for Wills, insurance policies, and other important papers. If the decedent was working at the time, the employer should be asked if the company maintained life insurance on its employees. Many do.

If you are the co-owner of any of the decedent's property such as vehicles and real property (land and buildings), you should contact the appropriate governmental agency (Department of Motor Vehicles, Country Recorder's Office) as to how to have the title reissued in your name only.

To collect on life insurance policies, best to call the agent or company and see what procedure to follow.

Contact Social Security. Social Security acts as kind of a life insurance policy. The following people may be entitled to benefits:

Dependent children (including adoptive children, stepchildren, and in some cases grandchildren) may be entitled to monthly payments. The children must be under 18 or, if older, disabled or still in school. These benefits are available even if the decedent had not worked very long. The decedent had to be only *currently insured:* had six quarters of coverage in the last 13 preceding death (or was receiving disability benefits at the time of death). If there is such a child, then the decedent's spouse is also entitled to benefits even if he or she has not reached the age of 60.

Dependent parents in some cases.

Surviving spouse if

a. the decedent was fully insured (had 40 or more quarters into the program) *and*
b. the survivor is 60 or older (or 50 if disabled) *and*
c. the marriage lasted more than nine months.

Note: If you were both drawing Social Security at the time of your spouse's death, contact Social Security because it is likely that you may draw more in survivor benefits than you draw on your own account or as the spouse of an insured member. This is most likely true in the case of women.

If the couple was not married, the survivor may still get benefits if they had, or adopted, a child together.

Bottom line: If the decedent was working or had worked in jobs covered by Social Security (most jobs), call Social Security for current information on possible benefits.

There is also a *death benefit* of $255 which may be available and can help with funeral expenses.

To begin a chapter with the moving words of W. H. Auden and to end it discussing a $255 death benefit, seems to sin against art. But maybe, when all is said and done, life is not grand moments, but rather tiny details, those coming at us every moment.

I heard a Fly buzz—when I died—
The Stillness in the Room
Was like the Stillness in the Air—

Between the Heaves of a Storm—
The Eyes around—had wrung them dry—
And Breaths were gathering firm
For that last Onset—when the King
Be witnessed—in the Room—

I willed my Keepsakes—Signed away
What portions of me be
Assignable—and then it was
There interposed a Fly—

With Blue—uncertain stumbling Buzz—
Between the light—and me—
And then the Windows failed—and then
I could not see to see—

Emily Dickinson (1830-1886)

Chapter 32

Probate

Bleak House, Dicken's great novel, gave probate a bad name. The probate of a huge estate lasted for generations. The family went broke. The lawyers got rich.

Bleak House was biting social commentary. It sent law school applications soaring.

There are four reasons that might tempt you to read this chapter:

- A family member has died and you need to know if the estate should be probated. That's Section a.
- You have been cut out of someone's will (or got less than what you think you should). Do you have legal recourse? That's Section b.
- You are a family member and need support money, now. That's Section c.
- You are probating an estate and need to know what to expect. That's Section d.

Unlike other chapters of this book, this one contains very little knowledge that one needs to know in advance. *Skip it* until the need arises. (If we had had a choice, we wouldn't have even written it.)

a. When Is Probate Needed?

Often it isn't. If the person who died didn't have a Will, didn't have much property, and wasn't the only legal guardian of a minor child, probate probably won't be needed. The family can simply divide the personal property—furniture, heirlooms, jewelry, computers, pets, and so forth. *Personal property* is defined as all that stuff we own that does not have a "title" (an official piece of paper indicating who owns something).

But what of cars, houses, land, stock, bonds, and bank accounts? These items do have "title" and before the family can get ownership of them, the title must be rewritten to show the new owner.

Often these items do not present much of a problem either. If the title shows a co-owner, indicating the right of survivorship, it is easy for the co-owner to get the title reissued. They simply show the death certificate to the appropriate official, and a new title showing them as sole owner will be issued. With cars, the appropriate official is the DMV; with land and houses, the County Clerk; stocks and bonds, officials in those offices. As to bank accounts, a joint owner can simply withdraw all the money.

What if the title is *only* in the name of the person who died? Well then probate *will* be needed to get a court order changing ownership. However, if not much property is involved, almost all states allow for quick and inexpensive probate. Basically it involves taking the necessary papers to a Probate Clerk who will guide you through the process. Contact your Probate Court for specifics. Big time probate, *Bleak House* Probate, is reserved for the rich.

b. You May Already Be a Disgruntled Heir

A cartoon shows a Hot Dog standing by his mailbox. He has opened a letter which reads—"Congratulations! You may already be a Wiener!"

A disgruntled heir is someone who would get more under the law of intestacy than he or she would get under the Will. Not born yesterday, a disgruntled heir tries to get the Will thrown out and thus collect a larger share. This raucous group includes:

– *Surviving spouses*

If you are a surviving spouse and are not getting at least half of the estate, contact a lawyer. Sometimes "Dearly Beloved" tries to give away your stuff.

– *Forgotten children*

If you are a child of the decedent (natural, adopted or illegitimate) and are not named in the Will, then you may have claim. The argument will be that the person who died did not mean to cut you out, only forgot you. To be cut out of the will, you must be named in it: ("As to my son Sampson, who insisted on never cutting his hair, I give nothing.") If you were expressly cut out of the Will in this fashion, then your claim is that the decedent was of *unsound mind* or under the *undue influence* (arm-twisting) of someone. Delilah?

– *Children born and spouses married* after *the Will was written*

The claim is that the decedent didn't mean to cut them out.

– *Children of prior marriages*

If your mother or father remarried and died, leaving everything to your stepfather or stepmother, and when he or she died, you didn't get anything or very little of your parent's original estate, see a lawyer. Some couples upon remarriage agree to leave everything to the survivor with a promise that, when the survivor dies, the estate will be split between their respective children. Tempted by dark forces, the surviving spouse may renege and leave everything to his or her own children. We saw in Chapter 23-h that a Living Trust can solve this problem.

– *Heirs who suspect lack of capacity*

"Being of sound mind" is, of course, the stock opening in Wills. We prefer "It was the best of times, *now* it is the worst of times." No matter. If the testator had lost legal capacity before signing the Will, it is invalid.

– *Heirs who suspect undue influence*

Large gifts to nurses, neighbors, and TV evangelists are suspect. Was the person in a position to assert control over the testator by threats or by withholding care?

– *Heirs who suspect murder*

In most states, a murderer cannot inherit from the victim, even if named in the Will ("Someday, son, all of this will be yours."). There is a legal maxim—"You cannot profit from your own wrong." Given the nature of the world, however, this maxim is more inspirational than descriptive.

However, if Sis can prove Bro did in dear old Dad, he can't get a nickel. There's more for Sis. There is always someone willing to profit from wrong.

If you suspect *both* undue influence and murder, you've got yourself a novel. Throw in a few good trial scenes and a little sex, and you won't need to inherit.

– *Heirs who suspect lawyer incompetence*

If you did not receive what the decedent wanted you to because the lawyer who drafted his Will or created his Trust messed up, in many states you can sue the lawyer. The money comes out of the lawyer's pocket (or that of his malpractice insurer).

No matter your complaint, if you are a disgruntled heir, seek legal advice early, if possible, before the Will is submitted to probate.

c. Family Allowances

Most states have legislation which allows surviving spouses and minor or disabled children to draw living expenses from an estate while it is being probated. These laws also set aside for the surviving spouse certain property (usually the family house and its furnishings). These set-asides come off the top of the estate; that is, they must be satisfied before there are other distributions, even distributions pursuant to a valid Will.

d. The Probate Process

The steps are as follows:

- Establishing the existence of a valid Will. (If the Will isn't valid, the estate passes according to intestacy laws. Chapter 20-b).
- Appointing the personal representative.
- Gathering and protecting assets.
- Settling with creditors and paying taxes (income and estate).
- Wrapping up: distribution and accounting.

Let's go through each step.

Establishing the Will. Any interested party, usually the spouse or an adult child, can petition the Probate Court to take jurisdiction of a decedent's estate. In smaller estates, a relative can do this simply by going to the courthouse and filling out the correct papers. In larger estates, a lawyer should be retained. In any event, this should be done quickly as someone must be authorized to take possession of the individual's assets.

At the first hearing, there will be two orders of business: first establishing if the decedent had a valid Will and, second, appointing a *personal representative* to take charge.

To be valid, a Will must comport with the technicalities laid down by state legislatures in terms of witnesses and notaries (Holographic Wills, those written out by hand, need not meet these requirements. See Chapter 20-c). Even if a Will is found, be on the outlook for *codicils* (documents that modify the original Will) and *new* Wills (which have the effect of voiding all or part of prior Wills). Both codicils and new Wills must comport to the technical requirements of a Will.

Naming a Personal Representative. The personal representative (also called the *executor* or *administrator*) is the person or institution that takes charge of the estate and moves it though probate.

Usually the decedent has named a personal representative (and a backup) in his Will. If not, the court will appoint the personal representative. Usually it will be the person who filed the probate petition. Other relatives can, and should, intervene at this stage if they object to that person. State laws establish priorities as to who is appointed.

Usually the personal representative will have to *post a bond* so that, if he or she splits with the goodies, the heirs will be protected. Bonds cost money and that money will come from the estate. Traditionally people waive the bond if they nominate a family member or close friend.

Finding and Protecting Assets. The personal representative must search the decedent's papers, read the decedent's mail, and generally snoop around to find out what the decedent owned and owed. The personal representative will have access to safety deposit boxes and has the legal right to get information from stock brokers, bankers, and lawyers concerning the decedent's affairs. It is here you will learn that mild Aunt Mildred was, in fact, a CIA agent credited with, among other things, the fall of the Berlin Wall (accomplished by a series of poisoned, yet tasty, Peach Cobblers).

The personal representative must maintain the assets. This may involve such things as winding down the decedent's business and selling perishable assets. An inventory of assets must be prepared and filed with the court. Where appropriate, *insure the assets;* otherwise you might be liable for losses.

Notifying and Paying Creditors. The decedent's bills must be paid *but not just yet.* First discover the creditors and find out how much is owed. The personal representative notifies the known creditors and advises them to submit their claims. Usually ads must be placed in local newspapers advising unknown creditors to file their claims. If creditors do not present their claims on time, their debts are barred. However, if the personal representative knows about some and fails to list them, those creditors will not be barred.

The personal rep should not pay any bills until satisfied that they are legal. If the decedent had a good defense against a debt, the personal rep should decline to pay it, forcing the creditor to come to Probate Court. Further, *if there is any question about the estate's solvency,* the personal rep should not pay any bills before they *all* come in. Why?

Because, like Orwell's Pigs, some debts are more equal than others. Who gets to go to the trough first? State statutes list priorities, *usually* along these lines:

1. Expenses of administering estate
2. Funeral and burial expenses (a reasonable amount)
3. The expenses of last sickness (reasonable and necessary)
4. Family allowances
5. Debts and taxes given preference by federal and state laws
6. Judgments rendered against the decedent in his lifetime in order of date
7. All other claims

If a personal rep pays lower priority pigs, leaving higher ones unfed, the personal rep may have to *personally* make up the difference.

Making support payments to immediate family. Most state statutes provide for a *family allowance* to help the family make ends meet. The personal rep should get further information concerning the scope and operation of this allowance. Most courts have pamphlets explaining it.

Paying taxes. The personal rep will be responsible for having prepared and filed the last state and federal income tax returns of the decedent as well as paying any federal and state estate taxes out of the estate.

Wrapping Up. Locating assets and paying the bills should take at least four months (creditors are given at least this amount of time to make their claims). Probate often runs much longer, but finally there comes a day to distribute the goodies.

After distribution, the personal rep will have to file a *Final Accounting* with the Court. Again, the disgruntled can object.

How to distribute the property? If there is no Will, this will be done according to the intestacy laws (but you know that already). If there is a Will, well, then, you need to know just a little more. There are three kinds of bequests:

Specific bequests (objects): To my only daughter, my family home.

General bequests (money): To my only son, $75,000.
Residuary bequest (remainder): To my then living grandchildren, divided equally, the remainder of my estate.

Well and good. But what happens if there is not enough in the estate to make good on all the bequests? Say the home was sold prior to Dad's death? Does the daughter get nothing? What if there is a house but no $75,000? Does the son get nothing?

This gets complicated and you'll need legal advice.

Part Six

Getting (and Giving) Help

Chapter 33

Getting Professional Help

A noted cancer researcher once remarked that, if you know the basic principles, the details can take care of themselves.

Having worked with this book you now know the basic principles. But you'll need a little help with the details.

Lawyers are less expensive and more helpful than they look. A basic Will Package (including a simple Will, a Living Will, and a Durable Power of Attorney) prepared by a lawyer to reflect your individual needs should cost between $300 and $500.

Don't try to draft these documents yourself. Don't use self-help books and store-bought forms. A lawyer-drafted-document will conform to recent changes in the law and will reflect your individual wishes. What you are really purchasing, bottom line, is peace of mind. If things go wrong, you want a lawyer to stand by you or your family. (Or, if they go very wrong, you'll want someone to sue.)

If you have a large estate, your lawyer will save you vastly more than she will charge. There are, after all, taxes to be avoided. You may need help finding and dealing with a good lawyer. We'll cover:

- How to find a lawyer
- Getting ready for your first interview
- Fees
- Ways to save money
- What to expect
- What to do if there are problems

Although we focus on lawyers, what we have to say will help you deal with other professionals: accountants, financial planners, stock brokers, insurance agents, and even doctors.

a. How to Find the Right Lawyer (and Other Professionals)

If you suffer insomnia, you've heard the late night ads:

> *If you've been seriously injured, somewhat injured, almost injured, or if you have an occasional bad dream, come on down. We'll find someone for you to sue.*

The United States Supreme Court has ruled that Bar Associations cannot prohibit lawyer advertising; such bans, in the Court's opinion, deny lawyers free speech. The Supreme Court has made worse mistakes. Before you hire a lawyer, *interview at least two*. We see by contrasts. Interviewing a second lawyer will tell you a lot about what you liked and didn't like about the first. While there are objective ways to evaluate lawyers (experience, fees) probably the most important things are subjective and intangible. Will you be able to openly discuss difficult and personal matters with this lawyer? Will you like working with this person? How to get the names of two good prospects:

Direct Referral

Friends, neighbors, and relatives can give you recommendations, as can bankers, stock brokers, and doctors (although, for some reason, doctors don't seem to like lawyers).

Speech or Seminar

Lawyers often make presentations at church groups, service organizations, clubs, or seminars sponsored by a bank or brokerage firm. You can get a good sense of the person by attending.

Lawyer Referral

In most larger communities, the local bar association maintains a lawyer referral service. This program maintains a list of qualified lawyers who have indicated a willingness to accept cases in certain areas of law. Initial interviews are usually free or at a reduced rate.

Yellow Pages

Generally not the best place to find a lawyer. Be leery of lawyers who list, as their areas of speciality, just about everything. Also be leery of the big layouts—they cost a lot of money and thus the lawyer must do a lot of business. Mass production isn't what you need. Specialists will be listed separately and are a good, albeit expensive, choice.

TV Advertising

Generally these firms do only personal injury work (with some expanding into bad dreams). Many make their money by volume—taking many cases and settling them quickly. The argument against this kind of practice is that individual clients may have their cases neglected or not pursued with sufficient vigor.

b. Getting Ready for the First Interview

Read the chapter in this book that deals with the problem you want to discuss with the lawyer. This will allow the interview to go faster and will allow you to get a sense of whether the lawyer is competent in the area of concern.

Ask yourself: *"Do I have any papers or documents the lawyer should look at?"* If you have a consumer problem, take a copy of the contract; if you want a new Will, take copies of prior Wills; if you want a new spouse, take a wish list.

When you call to arrange your initial appointment, explain your problem or needs in general terms and ask if you will be charged for the initial conference. Initial interviews are usually free and short, around thirty minutes. Don't expect many answers or services in that amount of time.

During the initial interview, briefly explain the type of services you need. For example, if you want a Will, do not tell the lawyer all of the reasons you wish to cut out Uncle Charlie. If you want a Power of Attorney, do not explain all of the reasons you object to certain types of investments. Simply advise the lawyer in general terms of what you want.

Think of the initial interview as a two-way street: the lawyer learns something of your case *and* you learn something of the lawyer. Consider the following questions:

- How long have you been practicing law?
- Do you regularly practice in this area of law? Do you have any special training?
- How many cases like mine have you handled, and what results have you gotten?
- What professional organizations do you belong to?
- Are there or have there been any lawsuits or professional disciplinary proceedings against you?
- What have been the outcomes?

Even good lawyers get sued and have complaints filed against them. They are helpless to prevent the frivolous suit or complaint. The fact that the lawyer may have been sued for malpractice or settled a malpractice lawsuit is not a reason for failing to hire the lawyer *unless* the lawyer fails to give you an adequate explanation. However, if the lawyer has been *disciplined* by the State Bar, get the details.

- Will I get copies of everything about my case?
- How quickly do you return all phone calls?

The lawyer should be willing to fully and freely answer these questions, each of which is important to help you make your decision.

c. What to Look for in a Lawyer

You will be looking for three basic things:

Someone who has the needed competence.
Someone who listens and has time to handle your case.
Someone who has no conflicts of interest with you.

Competence

This usually equates with experience. There is an old saying that the wise person wants "an old lawyer and a young doctor." However, there may be a trade-off in terms of fees—you may be paying for expertise that you don't really need. A young lawyer, eager to learn a new field, may be quite adequate for your needs.

Some states recognize legal specialities. These lawyers must have experience in the area and must take additional education and training.

Likely they were recommended by judges and other lawyers and may be required to pass a special test.

Someone Who Listens and Is Accessible

> *A criminal defendant asked the judge for a new lawyer. "What's wrong with the one you've got?" asked the judge.*
>
> *"He never pays any attention to me ."*
>
> *Turning to the lawyer, the judge asked"What do you say to that, counselor?"*
>
> *"Excuse me, Your Honor," the lawyer responded, "but I wasn't paying any attention."*

Some lawyers take on too many clients and cannot devote enough time to any. If you get the sense that the lawyer is hurried (keeps looking at the clock) watch out.

Conflicts of Interest

Lawyers may not have this problem; other professionals do. Bank financial officers will steer you to investments managed by the bank, stock brokers will wax poetically about stocks, and insurance agents will deliver you into their own company's "good hands."

It is generally best to hire professionals who are not associated with any institution and who are paid by the hour rather than by commissions.

A similar problem arises with physicians who work for an HMO. They may be discouraged by their employer from ordering costly tests or procedures that you might need. In choosing an HMO, ask about its policies concerning their physicians' authority to order treatments and make referrals.

Lawyers can fall into the trap of divided loyalty. Billing by the hour, they may think you need a lot more work than you do. This is known, affectionately, as *churning the file*. This usually occurs in litigation where lawyers on both sides make work for each other by engaging in pointless discovery and by filing near pointless motions.

Insist at the beginning of the relationship on some estimate as to the total hours that will be needed. Obviously, it will be rough and subject to change, but it is important to get some ballpark commitment. And, during representation, insist on explanations as to why certain expenses were necessary. Why was it necessary to file that motion? Why did you orally depose that witness rather than use written (and much cheaper) interrogatories? Why did you question the butler?

Lawyers face conflict problems if they try to represent two people whose interests might conflict. Couples occasionally ask a lawyer to write a prenuptial for them or handle their "friendly divorce." A lawyer really cannot do that because the interests of the parties are likely to conflict. Two lawyers must be retained—if the first lawyer learned too much before the conflict became apparent, that lawyer will have to drop out altogether.

d. Fees

Fees seem outrageous. Fees in excess of one hundred dollars an hour can make grown men cry and curse the day they didn't go to law school. But that's not take-home. It is costly to run a law office: support staff (receptionists, secretaries, paralegals), rent, supplies, equipment (computers, libraries, continuing education), phones, malpractice insurance, and a whole lot more. All told, overhead can come to 75% to 80%, which takes a big bite out of the $100. All lawyers have to sell is their time. Lawyers' fees are usually set in three basic ways:

A *flat fee* with a set charge for a specific task.
An *hourly rate.*
A *contingent fee* where the lawyer is paid an agreed-upon percentage of the recovery on behalf of the client. These are used only in personal injury work.

You will also be asked to pay costs, such as those associated with discovery or expert testimony. They can be very high. Ask for an estimate. For most work you will be charged either a flat fee or an hourly rate.

You should get a *written retainer agreement* that spells out the fee arrangement and what other costs you will have to pay. If the lawyer doesn't give *written* fee agreements and leaves the matter to handshakes, seriously consider going elsewhere. It should cover:

1. Fees and billing periods.

2. Scope of representation (what the lawyer will do and will *not* do).

Flat fee. Ask the lawyer to indicate specifically which items are included and which are not. If you have decided that you need a Will, a Durable Financial Power of Attorney, a Living Will, and a Durable Health Care Power of Attorney, confirm that all are included in the set fee.

Hourly rate. Ask for an *estimate* of the total bill. If the lawyer can't give you one, be sure you understand why. Ask the lawyer to *bill you monthly* so that you can keep track of the charges. The bill should reflect who has been working on your case, how far along the work is, and the rates you are being charged.

Check the bill over. *Mistakes can be made* in adding hours and figures. Make sure you understand what the lawyer will do and what the charges will be. Make sure you understand what the representation *doesn't cover* as well as what it does. For example, if there is to be a trial, what will be the charge if it is settled before trial? Does the amount agreed upon cover appeals?

Most lawyers charge in addition to their fees for *out-of-pocket expenses* such as long-distance phone charges, copying, and postage. Some lawyers add on charges for the computer time used in preparing your documents, secretarial time, outside charges of law clerks or paralegals, or other expenses. Know in advance. This should be set forth in the retainer agreement.

e. Ways to Save Money

The lawyer will set the fee, whether a fixed fee or an hourly fee, based in large part upon the amount of time spent or expected to be spent. The main way you save money on legal fees is to reduce the amount of time your work will take.

Know what you want by doing your homework.

Come to the lawyer's office with an understanding of the kind of work you want done. This book will have given you a clear idea of the kinds of documents you will need and the answers to most of the questions the lawyer will ask. Hours will be saved. You will have fewer questions. You will have already made your decisions on most issues.

Bring your documents.

Is there any document that the lawyer will need to read to help me? Ask this question and eliminate one office visit—err on the side of bringing too many documents.

Encourage the use of legal assistants.

Many law firms employ legal assistants (often called "paralegals"), to prepare documents, draft pleadings, do investigations, inventory assets, deal directly with clients' phone calls and questions, and get the coffee. Legal assistants are not lawyers and may not give legal advice. Their involvement can, however, greatly reduce your total legal fee. Their hourly rates are far less than those of the lawyers they work with. The lawyer will, of course, be responsible for all of the work performed in his or her office.

Limit your contacts.

Try to keep your visits and your phone calls to the lawyer brief and to a minimum. Each time you call, you are likely to be charged for the time involved. Visits will be charged for as well. Speak to the secretary or legal assistant when possible.

Allow time for your work to be done.

If you place unreasonable time requirements upon your lawyer, the fee is likely to be higher. Ask at your initial meeting when you can expect to hear from the lawyer or receive drafts of documents.

Listen carefully.

Listen carefully to what you are asked to do, what decisions you will need to make, and what additional documents you may need to provide. Take notes during the meeting or ask the lawyer to make a list.

f. What to Expect from Your Lawyer

Some lawyers love to lean across the desk, give a conspiratorial wink, and whisper, "Everything you tell me is in confidence," which leads many clients to think, "This guy must think I'm a serial killer."

Lawyers are covered by the *attorney-client privilege*. Basically this means that nothing you tell your lawyer and nothing your lawyer learns while representing you can be disclosed without your permission. This is true even if the lawyer is called in a trial and put on the stand and asked. This privilege kicks in during your first interview *even if* you end up not hiring, or later firing, the lawyer. Thc privilege does not apply, however, if a third party is in the room, nor does it apply to a client's declaration that she or he will commit a future crime or fraud. Confessions of past crimes are covered.

Besides confidentiality, you are entitled to *information* and *explanations*. The lawyer should advise you in advance of what will be done for you. You should be kept posted about what is being done, both through *copies* of correspondence or documents and through a monthly bill that itemizes the work done.

Before you are asked to sign a document or agree to an action being taken on your behalf, the work should be thoroughly explained to you. While you do not necessarily need to understand every word or phrase, you should expect to have the effect of everything explained to you.

Accessibility. You should be able to reach someone at the law office with questions, whether that person is the lawyer, the secretary, the legal assistant, or the bookkeeper. This does not mean that the person need always be there, but it does mean that phone calls should be promptly returned.

g. What to Do If There Are Problems

In most states you have an absolute right to fire your lawyer, at *any* time, for *any* reason. If you do, you must pay for work they have already put in, but they must *return* any unearned portion of your retainer. They must give you or your new lawyer all of your papers.

However, before dropping the Big One, talk to the lawyer. As the chain-gang guard said in *Cool Hand Luke*, "What we have here is a failure to communicate." The lawyer or the lawyer's staff may not be aware of your unhappiness.

Complain to the Bar Association.

All lawyers are licensed by their states to practice law, and every state has some sort of disciplinary procedure regarding lawyers. If you think that something the lawyer has done is unethical or illegal, you should notify the bar association in your state and give them full details. Complaints include your lawyer ignoring your case, giving you incorrect information, taking actions without your consent, missing a deadline, failing to disclose a possible or actual conflict of interest involving your case and, of course, running off with your money.

Note: Many state bar associations have funds to compensate victims of lawyer fraud.

If you have a *fee dispute* with your lawyer, most Bar Associations have arbitration procedures.

Consider a Lawsuit.

If you have been damaged financially or your position compromised because of the lawyer's action or failure to act, you may have a malpractice claim against the lawyer. This will require another lawyer's examinations of all of the facts, but it may be well worth your while to consider such action.

Most legal malpractice claims involve lawyers who have drafted documents that failed their purpose, such as Wills that were later thrown out, or have failed to file a claim within the Statute of Limitations.

Chapter 34

A Family Conversation

A tribe, somewhere, long ago, made important decisions differently than you and I. First, they would meet formally and, after a careful review of pros and cons, decide. Nothing surprising there. The next night, they would garner festive clothes and break out brew and music. In the wee hours, they would revisit their decision. If it still made sense, fine. But if it couldn't survive the bright and flashing insights of drunken analysis, they scrapped it and, the following morning, began anew.

We confuse *significant* and *meaningful* with *somber* and *mournful.*

A graduate student was about to turn in his term paper. Another asked,

"How is it?"

"Well, I don't know how good it is, but it's real funny."

"Funny? You made your paper funny?"

"Yes, don't you remember? Professor said, 'Never forget, humor is the enemy of death.'"

"He didn't say that. He said, 'Never forget, humor is the enemy of depth!'"

Get the family together to talk about the issues it must someday face—property distribution, disability, terminal illness, funeral arrangements.

No doubt our college professor friend would place everyone around the dining room table, turn on Mozart's *Requiem,* and begin with his checklist:

"Topic One: Anatomical Donations."

Forget the long face. Loosen up. Have fun. Sherry might help, and, if you want music, how about the Beatles?

Will you still need me?
Will you still feed me?
When I'm Sixty-Four?

Remember when you first heard that song? "Me? Sixty-four? No way!"

Getting the conversation started may be hard. One way may be to describe your own estate plans or burial desires. Or:

"I've been reading this book, and the authors recommend we have a family conversation concerning such things as death and dying. I think it is a stupid idea too, but let's try it."

Or you might want to sneak up:

"Neither Richard Nixon nor Jackie Kennedy was placed on life support. I wonder if they had Living Wills?"

"A what?"

a. Why Have a Family Conversation?

It will help your family get through the hard times.

Death and disability will cause great emotional strain. Difficult decisions, in unfamiliar areas, are coming. Without knowing everyone's wishes, your family will struggle and, often, disagree. Family feuds in these times can split families forever.

It will save suffering and money.

If you are hospitalized with a painful terminal illness, no one will want to appear heartless and cheap by shouting *"Enough!"* Families will most likely opt for the continuation of aggressive yet futile life-sustaining treatment, increasing your suffering and decreasing your estate. Even if you have executed the proper documents, only a family conversation will make *sure* everyone understands and approves your choices. If they don't approve or understand your choices, talk them out.

At your death, if you haven't had a family conversation, dollars to donuts, your family will spend too much on funeral arrangements.

It will make your family closer.

Many of us will die in emotional isolation. We will know we are dying and our family will know it too, but no one will talk about it. Instead, we'll get smile faces, false bravado, and weather updates.

In our practice of Elder Law, we hear way too often the lament of survivors:

"I never told Mom I loved her."

"I always regret not telling Dad how much he meant to me."

Once the topic of death is opened ("Who gets the Grandfather Clock?"), it's okay to talk about things that matter. *The denial of death is the denial of life.* By not talking about death, families may remain isolated, not saying the things that need to be said, not celebrating the events that need to be celebrated. After the initial discomfort, expect the celebration of the humor and the joy of life.

"Do you remember the trip to the farm? When Dad fell off the horse?"

"What about prom night when I lost the keys?"

b. Some Topics to Consider

In elementary school, a friend read the last page of the comic book first. Unless you are of his ilk, you have read at least some of this book. You probably have some things you would like to discuss with your family. (*"If your doctor tells me you are dying, should I tell you?")*

As the conversation will deal with disability and death, reread Chapter 25: *On Training for Ill, Pumping Iron, and Sending Dylan Thomas to Bed*. It is short.

Here are some recommendations as to topics:

- Pushing the necessary documents
- Property distribution
- Possible disability
- Last illness
- Funeral arrangements

Pushing the Necessary Documents

We never know when the fat lady will sing. A family conversation is a good opportunity to make sure *everyone* has put their legal house in order.

We recommend, for *everyone* over 18:

A Health Care Power of Attorney (Chapter 18)

This allows you to appoint a trusted friend or relative to make necessary medical decisions for you.

A Living Will (Chapter 18)

This allows you to direct doctors and hospital personnel as to the kind of treatment you want (and don't want) during terminal illness.

We cannot stress the importance of these two documents too much. Of course, we are all too busy. Mo Udall was. Mo was a lawyer who served in the House of Representatives for three decades, running for President in the 1960s and even writing of his experiences, *Too Funny to Be President*. Alas, not only was he too funny, he was too busy. Working on the nation's business, he didn't take time to take care of his own—he died without a Living Will. He suffered for it. He had Parkinson's Disease which is physically devastating but which usually does not attack mental facilities. In 1991, he had a fall and head injury; he never spoke again. Seven years later he died. Lying all those years, with tubes in his stomach, what thoughts did he have? What did he want to tell his family?.

Mo's nephew, Dr. Don Udall, of Newport Beach, California, has created a foundation, CARE, Concerned Americans for a Responsible/dignified Exit, the sole goal of which is to promote Living Wills.

In addition to Health Care Documents, for the middle-aged, we also recommend:

A Will or Will Substitute—such as a Trust. (Chapters 20, 21, and 22.)

These are not as important during the early years as in the later years. However, young parents can use a Will to nominate guardians for their children.

Get everyone to agree to collect their important papers, such as insurance policies, deeds, auto title, Wills. They should be stored where they can be found, such as a particular desk drawer.

Property Distribution

Well, who does get the Grandfather Clock?

"Letting the kids figure things out later" is not helpful. It usually causes fights or (best case) hurt feelings. Go through the family heirlooms, decide who gets what and then, just to play it safe, write down the decisions. Memories tend to fade. A *Holographic Will* might help. (See Chapter 20-c.)

Key provisions of Wills should be discussed, particularly if they are likely to cause hurt feelings or trigger family fights.

- How come Sis is getting the house? How come Brother is getting more cash? Why is Cousin Mary appointed Executor? Why is Uncle Bob defamed?
- Going over Wills allows family members to express their wishes. Often estate fights are triggered by "insignificant" items (Mom's ring or Dad's old watch).
- *Blended families*—remarriage with children from previous marriages—present problems. Suspicion between stepchildren is likely. Sit everyone down and explain who is to get what and why. Best to have everyone there at the same time to avoid "Well, that's not what they told me!"

Possible Disability

Disability is far from certain but your family should discuss the possibility.

Who is to say "Mom, it's time to stop driving"? Who is to say "Dad, I don't think you should go on living alone"? A discussion now will help later:

"Now Mom, you agreed! If I thought your driving was unsafe, you would quit."

If a family member becomes senile or too ill to act:

- Who should manage the financial affairs?
- Who should make health care and living decisions?

What of nursing homes? Should top dollar be spent for care or should money be saved for heirs?

Durable Powers of Attorney can address these possibilities. If they have been executed, they should be discussed, to get feedback and support. Even if they have not been executed, discussions can help.

Many folks open joint bank accounts with children or grandchildren, either as a method of passing on the money at their death or allowing it to be used for them if they become incapacitated. To avoid misunderstandings, other family members should know of these arrangements.

Last Illness

If you have executed a Living Will (indicating what treatments you want and don't want during your final illness), it is *very important* that you discuss its terms with your family. If the time comes, doctors may not honor it if your family has strong objections.

The problem with most conversations is that they are just *too general* to be helpful when actual decisions must be made:

> "I don't want a lot of pain."
>
> "I don't want to be hooked up to a lot of machines."

Best to focus on the specifics. We refer you to our grim checklist at Chapter 20-f.

Funeral and Burial Arrangements

Time for another glass of sherry.

Death calls on your family to make many unpleasant decisions, at the worse possible time. The more guidance, the better.

- Have provisions, such as joint bank accounts, been taken to deal with short-term money problems?
- What about organ donation? (Even if it's "Yes" on a driver's license or in a Will, a family can likely upset that choice by refusing its permission.)
- Cremation or burial?
- How much money do you want spent on arrangements? ("Not much" isn't too helpful for bereaved family members. Give a dollar range "No more than $3000.")

One of our dogs, Shadow, has a Living Will which provides "In no event spend over $50."

Finally, Tombstones.

On the whole, I would rather be with W.C. Fields

Not a bad exit line.

* * *

Finally we have come to this place. We've told you what we know and we have exhausted our best advice. If that were all, we could tell a quick joke and call it a day. But looking back, we realize that this book, for us, is about more than factual tidbits, about more than clever legal moves. For us, at bottom, it is about love. A joke won't do.

Better yet, some thoughts about our futures, yours and ours. Let's agree, here and now, not to be glum. Aging offers new opportunities—for travel, for time with the family, for new interests, and, indeed, for sowing oats. Let's, with T.S. Eliot, wear our trousers rolled, eat a peach, and dare to disturb the universe (or perhaps, less grandly, at least our neighbors). As would the poet Jenny Joseph, let's go out in the rain with our slippers on, take flowers from other people's gardens and "learn to spit."

That said, the time will come when we slow down. That won't be so bad either.

> *The old grief, by a great mystery of human life, gradually passes into quiet, tender joy; instead of young, ebullient blood comes a mild, serene old age; I bless the sun's rising each day and my heart sings as before, but now I love the setting even more, its long slanting rays, and with them, mild, tender memories, dear images for the whole of a long and blessed life.*
>
> The Elder Zosima
> *Dostoyevsky, The Brothers Karamazov*

Thanks for being with us.

Index

Acknowledgments

A lot of people have helped: Barbara Atwood, Scott Bronnimann, Sherina and Michael Cadnum, Martha Fenn, George Gross, Sally Hart, Kathy Kay, Kay Kavanagh, Norma Kelly, Dave Metz, Laura Mckinney, Barbara Sattler, Irv Sattler, Kristen Strange, Carolyn Scott and Beth Smith. The scores of law students who struggled through earlier drafts of this work helped us clarify our language and thoughts.

And then there's Mel Roach, who refused to believe in this book when we did.

Kenney Hegland has always been blessed with a forgiving and supportive audience, from Larry Durbin, and his enthusiasm for an early Latin translation of "Long Tall Sally," to his dear late colleague, Tom Hall, who advised him "Never change your style, even if it would mean getting published." There have been a lot of others: Bill Boyd, Robert Glennon, Larry Hamlin, Terry Holpert, Sylvia Lane, Paul Marcus, Toni Massaro, Jamie Ratner, Mike Sacken, Starr Sanders, Sallie Saltzman, Andy Silverman, Joel Seligman, Jimmy Stiggall, Tom Sullivan, and David Wexler.

I also thank James E. Rogers who has shown me that, while it is always tempting to sit back and relax, it is not nearly as satisfying as pushing harder, making the best our talents to help others make the best of theirs.

When it comes to family, no one can ever thank them enough as many of their gifts are buried so deep that they are part of us. That said, I thank my sister, Sherina, and my late parents, Sheridan and Edwina, for a terrific childhood (well, not always), and finally my boys, Robert, Alex, Caleb and Ben, and my wife, Barbara, for a terrific adulthood (well, almost always).

Allan Bogutz thanks all of those who have contributed so much to the establishment of Elder Law in the United States. Nancy Coleman, director of the American Bar Association's Commission on the Legal Problems of the Elderly, truly helped recognize the special legal needs of older persons as has John Pickering of Wilmer, Cutler and Pickering in Washington, D.C., long time chairman of the Commission and a seemingly tireless advocate of the elderly. The late Arthur Flemming, former Commissioner of Social Security, was truly a crusader for the older population of our country and brilliant in able to see the global legal issues of aging. Laury Adsit, executive director of the National Academy of Elder Law Attorneys has, through her leadership and focus, helped make Elder Law a recognized specialty area of practice and led the leaders of the profession in creating high ethical and professional standards. These persons have all been my friends and mentors and have all helped to provide the information contained in our book. Marion Lupu, director of the Pima Council on Aging in Tucson, Arizona, and I have worked together for twenty-five years to provide services of all types to the aging - her energy and her sense of right have truly been an inspiration in keeping my focus on the issues of aging. My law firm partners, Craig Gordon and Brian Bjorndahl, have provided support and encouragement in all of my professional endeavors and have no doubt worked harder to permit me the time to work on this project. My wife Chary has not only been a fine editor but has been an outstanding example of a caring person, gentle and loving, and full of compassion for the needs of my clients.

Finally we would both like to thank the thousands of students and clients we have worked with over the years. To them, it may have felt like teaching but, to us, it felt like learning.